KU-029-309

HUME'S
PHILOSOPHY
OF MIND

for Hodgie

JOHN BRICKE

———

HUME'S
PHILOSOPHY
OF MIND

EDINBURGH

AT THE UNIVERSITY PRESS

© John Bricke 1980

EDINBURGH UNIVERSITY PRESS

22 George Square

ISBN 0 85224 322 7

Set in Monotype Barbou by
Speedspools, Edinburgh
and printed in Great Britain by
Clark Constable Ltd
Edinburgh

Contents

Acknowledgments

Páll S. Árdal and George E. Davie, supervisors of the PhD dissertation on Hume's theory of action that I submitted to the University of Edinburgh in 1968, have assisted my study of Hume from the first. Their enthusiasm for Hume's philosophy has spurred my own interest, and their exemplary standards of philosophical scholarship have provided a model that I have tried to emulate. I deeply appreciate their generous attention to my own work on Hume and, in particular, their incisive criticisms of earlier versions of the first five chapters.

I have benefited greatly from discussions with Professor W. H. Walsh. But I am especially conscious of my debt to him for his early and continuing encouragement to get my thoughts on Hume into publishable form. Were it not for that my book would have been much longer in the making than it has been.

I am indebted to Donald Brownstein, Anthony Genova, Peter Jones, Rex Martin, Arthur Skidmore, J. Michael Young, and especially Richard Cole. I have tested my view of Hume in conversation with each, and each has read some portion of the book in typescript. The friendly if searching criticism of these colleagues and friends prompted closer argument than I would otherwise have devised.

James Noxon has read the whole of the book in its penultimate form and has made many valuable suggestions. His contention that the argument of chapters 6 and 7 needed clarification was especially helpful, even if painful to acknowledge. My readers and I owe a particular debt to George P. Morice, who has been the ideal editor. His close scrutiny has eliminated countless infelicities, obscurities and needless diversions, as well as egregious grammatical mistakes; and with sound philosophical judgment he has suggested a great many improvements in the conduct of the argument itself.

Professor William Beattie, Director of Edinburgh University's Institute for Advanced Studies in the Humanities, and Margaret Swift, secretary to the Institute, helped provide the happiest of environments in which to begin work on my book in 1975 – 6.

Constance Ducey, Phillip Miller and Aurora Ripley have given me the ablest assistance in preparing the typescript for publication, often in the most trying of circumstances.

From my wife, Hodgie, I have had constant support and encouragement. My son Ian, whose birth coincided with the beginning of the book, has, in his winning and diverting way, lightened the burden of composition.

The University of Kansas has generously supported my research by awarding me several grants from the General Research Fund, and by granting me sabbatical leave for the academic year 1975 –6. The Department of Philosophy of the University of Kansas has provided extensive secretarial and other help. The American Council of Learned Societies provided a Grant-in-Aid during my sabbatical leave. And I am grateful to the University of Edinburgh for electing me a Visiting Research Fellow of its Institute for Advanced Studies for the same period.

Edinburgh University Press is grateful for permission to reproduce extracts from various works detailed in the bibliography.

Introduction

———

H U M E makes very good philosophical company: he is sophisticated, inventive, surprisingly systematic, profound. He is extraordinarily stimulating, if also a source of very great perplexity. He is all of these things in his thinking about mind. I propose, in his also agreeable company, to explore some of the central issues in the philosophy of mind.

I have three aims. I wish to ascertain Hume's own views about mind; to determine the adequacy of these views, and the reasons for thinking them adequate or inadequate, in whole or in part; and to make some advance on the philosophical issues themselves.

My first aim is to provide an accurate, detailed, well-articulated reading of that philosophical theory of mind that Hume presents in his *Treatise of Human Nature* and, to a lesser extent, in his *Enquiry Concerning Human Understanding*. I wish to discover what are the principal, and what the peripheral, elements in that theory, how these elements fit together, and what are the theory's more interesting implications. I am particularly concerned to give an accurate rendering: hence the amount of space devoted to close scrutiny of the texts, and of any arguments Hume presents. Those familiar with work on Hume's philosophy of mind will readily see points at which my account departs markedly from received interpretations. But I make little effort to map my interpretation on to those of others or to draw explicit attention to significant differences. A satisfactory interpretative theory must meet the test of detail, and I believe that mine does. It is also, I believe, in the crucial sense coherent: it makes sense of much that is otherwise baffling in what Hume says of the mind. In the relevant way my account saves the textual appearances.

I shall make a sustained critical assessment of the theory of mind that I ascribe to Hume. Lest confusions arise, however, I would be as plain as possible about my mode of proceeding. In two words, I propose to be thoroughgoing yet sympathetic. The upshot of my argument will be that many of the foundational elements in Hume's considered theory of mind must be scrapped: his theory of introspective awareness, much of his theory of thinking, his epistemological idealism, his reification of perceptions and his scepticism with regard to the senses. One must also recognize his inability to provide, in his own way and on his own premises, an empiricist explication of the very idea of mind. Many other elements in his theory require drastic revision. Although a number of central elements (some of them quite surprising ones) in a Humean theory of mind will survive this scrutiny many of Hume's most characteristic doctrines will not. Still, I insist, I shall be sympathetic in criticism.

My meaning can best be made clear by a description of the manner in which I shall proceed. I shall attempt to provide a perspicuous account both of the problems Hume proposes to solve and of the solutions he proposes. Often, this alone will have the effect of making the defects in Hume's stated position all too apparent. Should it prove possible to turn the first line of objections by emending the stated position in ways consonant with the main lines of Hume's philosophy, however, I shall make the needed emendations, and shall take the emended theory to be the interesting object of critical assessment. Although Hume's actual linking of resemblance and personal identity is, once understood, easily refuted, his account, if suitably emended, deserves serious attention. It seems to me proper to make these emendations and to accord it that attention.

There are places at which a perspicuous rendering of Hume's theory reveals defects that no tinkering changes can repair. If we read him sympathetically, however, there may be opportunity even at such places for profitable advance. For one may ask whether, with more than minimal emendations, made perhaps at Hume's own prompting, a more satisfactory, if less straightforwardly Humean, position can be devised. To be sure, there are places where it is merely the clear recognition of remediless defects that will promote advance on the philosophical questions. But at each point I propose to ask how far we can go with Hume while retaining clearly traceable ties to doctrines to which he subscribes. Although it will often be useful to take him strictly at his word I shall at every point ask whether damage done by criticism can be repaired in a more-or-less Humean way.

Being sympathetic in this manner has nothing to do with kindness, loyalty or *parti pris*. The extent to which I shall criticize Hume will demonstrate this. It is, rather, a matter of getting as much help as we can from Hume on the demanding issues that he addresses. I am trying to use Hume to the maximum philosophical advantage, hence must not too quickly discard his theory when an initial survey displays grave defects.

I shall be a sympathetic critic in another sense as well. I shall restrict my objections to ones that can be constructed from Hume's own premises; that arise in the light of Hume's own construals of his philosophical problems and the constraints that must be met by satisfactory solutions. Such internal criticism has several advantages over criticism done from some external philosophical standpoint, from a Kantian standpoint, say, or a Wittgensteinian one, or from that of ordinary language. For one thing, one may be more confident that one's criticism actually holds against Hume. For another, the effort required to criticize Hume this way makes it more likely that one will interpret him aright.

And there may well be serendipitous benefits as well. One may in this way unearth problems, assumptions, not-quite-formed ideas, reflection on which may serve to advance one's understanding of mind. To render such unanticipated side effects likely one must scrutinize in a painstaking way what Hume says on a philosophically central topic even when that topic is not at the focus of his attention. We shall in fact get such results when examining what Hume says of judgment and predication, the possibility of mishap at the level of perceptions, causality and personal identity, and several other matters.

My account of Hume's philosophy of mind does not purport to be comprehensive. I say little about reasoning and memory, almost nothing about emotion, volition and action, and nothing at all about sympathy. But there are certain general topics that receive extended treatment over several chapters: the assemblage of issues tied to Hume's reification of perceptions; his claims about the observability of inner states; the roles he assigns to causality and to the body in his account of the workings of mind. I provide an extended treatment of Hume's views on the central metaphysical and epistemological questions concerning the nature of the self, the conditions for personal identity, and the relations of mind and body. And I conduct a detailed examination of his analysis of such basic mental items (to use a neutral term) as concepts, judgments, including introspective judgments, and perceptions. My investigations of Hume's views on judgment and perceptions bear quite directly, I should say, on the interpretation and assessment of his theories of memory, emotion and volition. The spelling out of these connections must, however, await some other occasion.

CHAPTER ONE

Scepticism, Perception and Physical Objects

———

1. My concern is Hume's philosophy of mind. But I begin by examining, in a fairly sketchy fashion, the character of his 'scepticism with regard to the senses' (*T* 187).[1] There are several reasons for this.

Unless one understands how to take Hume's scepticism one will find oneself at a loss to determine how, or how seriously, to take the many positive contributions that Hume apparently intends to make to our understanding of certain phenomena. Does his scepticism bar him from consistently advancing any positive theory of mind, of body, or of their interrelation? Does he intend that it serve as a bar? Since I shall ascribe a quite elaborate constructive theory of mind to Hume I must consider how such theory construction fits with his scepticism.

Hume constructs sceptical arguments on many matters. Given my own concerns, however, it is his scepticism concerning physical objects that is especially important. I shall credit Hume with formed views about the multiple relations in which minds stand to bodies, where bodies are construed as items distinct from minds, neither reducible to mental phenomena, nor reducible, with minds, to some neutral stuff. On occasion I shall argue that, although he does not do so, Hume both can and should invoke features of bodies to help solve his puzzles about minds. Thus I shall focus explicitly on the roles that Hume assigns, or can and should assign, to bodies in a study of mind when I argue, in chapter 2, that he is a dualist interactionist and, in chapter 3, that he is at times a realist about mental dispositions. To some degree in chapter 4, and quite centrally in chapter 5, I shall make purportedly Humean suggestions about the links between bodies, selves and personal identity. In chapters 6 and 7 bodily considerations will move from centre stage but will nonetheless continue to play a part. Given the kind of view about mind that I shall ascribe to Hume I clearly must deal with his scepticism with regard to the senses.

An examination of his sceptical arguments regarding physical objects will also provide an opportunity to secure some initial purchase on Hume's notion of what he calls 'perceptions', the constituents of minds. We shall be concerned with the analysis and characterization of perceptions throughout this study: in chapter 2, when examining Hume's dualism; in chapters 4 and 5, when considering the relative merits of the so-called substrate theory and Hume's bundle theory of mind; and in chapters 6 and 7 when we examine in detail Hume's account of conception, of judgment, of sensation, and of introspective awareness.

What he says of perceptions in the course of his sceptical arguments has a direct bearing on each of these questions.

So an examination of his scepticism with regard to physical objects must serve as a prolegomenon to our examination of his philosophy of mind. I shall concentrate on Hume's actual arguments; to do otherwise would be philosophically pointless. But I shall not here attempt a critical assessment of those arguments. My purpose, at this stage, is simply to use an understanding of his scepticism to facilitate our understanding of what he says of mind. In any case, once the arguments have been properly articulated their weaknesses are all too apparent. And later, in a somewhat incidental way, I shall have opportunity to reject the most important assumptions on which these sceptical arguments rest.

Hume's examination of belief in physical objects has a constructive as well as a sceptical side. He purports to offer an explanation of our coming to have the beliefs we do have about such objects. I shall have a great deal to say about this in chapter 5 when we consider his empiricist programme. For the sake of understanding his scepticism concerning physical objects, however, I must here say a few preliminary things about this constructive explanation of our ordinary beliefs.

My discussion in this chapter has, then, three parts. I begin by drawing attention to Hume's characterization of ordinary belief about physical objects and to certain significant features of his explanation of such belief. Then I distinguish three stages in Hume's sceptical argument concerning the physical world. I shall try to show that there *are* three distinct stages in Hume's argument and that distinguishing these is a prerequisite to settling some of the more vexing questions that arise about his scepticism. Lastly, I consider what Hume takes to be the upshot of his sceptical arguments, and the character of the position about perception and physical objects that, in the last analysis and in practice, he marks out as his own.

2.   Although Hume nowhere gives an extended account of the matter one may gather, from his general discussion of the topic, what he takes to be the principal ingredients in one's ordinary, unreflective, conception of physical objects. Such objects, as one conceives them, are things, often quite complicated things, that have an existence independent of one's occasional awareness of them (Hume speaks of distinct or independent existence), and that continue to exist when one ceases to notice them (Hume speaks of continued existence). They are susceptible, in varying degrees, of a variety of changes while remaining the same physical objects. Although physical objects may come and go (a different matter from the coming and going of one's awareness of them), they have, while they exist, a continuous existence. Characteristically they have such properties as colour, smell, taste, temperature, shape, size, weight and solidity. They can not only be noticed at different times, but can also be perceived by different senses and by different observers.

Some physical objects, namely, the bodies of persons, have a special role to play in the experience of the persons who have them, and a person can be aware of his own body in a way in which he cannot be aware of those of others. Physical objects have a fundamentally spatial and temporal character: they exist in a four-dimensional space-time framework. In terms of this framework one thinks of physical objects as existing at the same or at different times (or as partially overlapping temporally), as being near to or distant from one another, as excluding co-temporary objects from some spatial location, and as capable of being, at some time, at a place at which some other object has been or will be.

3. Without going into the details of Hume's explanation of one's acquiring this conception of physical objects (for this see chapter 5) there are certain general features of that account to which I draw attention.

Hume assumes that one's ordinary conception of physical objects involves a naively realistic view of the things one perceives. That is to say, the ordinary man takes it that he directly perceives physical objects: that some of the very things he perceives are the things that have an independent and continued existence. '[T]he vulgar confound perceptions and objects, and attribute a distinct continu'd existence to the very things they feel or see' (*T* 193). 'Those very sensations', Hume says, 'which enter by the eye or ear, are with them the true objects, nor can they readily conceive that this pen or paper, which is immediately perceiv'd, represents another, which is different from, but resembling it' (*T* 202). Again: ''Tis certain, that almost all mankind, and even philosophers themselves, for the greatest part of their lives, take their perceptions to be their only objects, and suppose, that the very being, which is intimately present to the mind, is the real body or material existence' (*T* 206). The same is said in the first *Enquiry*:

> [W]hen men follow this blind and powerful instinct of nature, they always suppose the very images, presented by the senses, to be the external objects, and never entertain any suspicion, that the one are nothing but representations of the other. This very table, which we see white, and which we feel hard, is believed to exist, independent of our perception, and to be something external to our mind, which perceives it. (*E* 151–2)

Hume's explanation, then, must accommodate this naive realism of the plain man.

Hume also holds that there are no *logical* objections to the plain man's naive realism. Without considering his arguments[2] we may note their conclusion. '[T]here is no absurdity', he says, 'in separating any particular perception from the mind; that is, in breaking off all its relations, with that connected mass of perceptions, which constitute a thinking being' (*T* 207). In the same vein he says:

The same continu'd and uninterrupted Being may ... be sometimes present to the mind, and sometimes absent from it, without any real or essential change in the Being itself. An interrupted appearance to the senses implies not necessarily an interruption in the existence. The supposition of the continu'd existence of sensible objects or perceptions involves no contradiction. (*T* 207–8)

The plain man's naive realism may well be false; indeed Hume will argue that it is false. But it is not, he claims, absurd.

'The plain man takes the very things he perceives to be physical objects.' This is a comment about the plain man's formed beliefs, and it must not cause us to overlook the crucial fact that, for Hume, there is a sense in which the very things the plain man perceives (his perceptions) are, as perceived, neutral. There is a level of analysis at which it cannot be true that the plain man takes his perceptions to be physical objects. (Nor, at that level, could he take them to be perceptions in the sense of mental items of some kind.) For the point of Hume's empiricist programme must be to explain the formation of one's conception of a world of bodies (and of minds), and thus the acquisition of the concepts in terms of which one comes to distinguish perceptions from physical objects. To assume one's possession of these concepts would render the explanation Hume offers otiose. Although the passages are not unambiguous, I suggest that Hume indicates this neutrality of perceptions when he writes that 'every impression, external and internal, passions, affections, sensations, pains and pleasures, are originally on the same footing' (*T* 190) and that 'as far as the senses are judges, all perceptions are the same in the manner of their existence' (*T* 193).

As we shall see, Hume holds that the very things we perceive are perceptions, in the sense of specifically mental items, and not physical objects. He is thus committed to the claim that the neutral data on which the plain man bases his conception of a world of physical objects (and of minds) are likewise mental items. But it is important to realize that this is not something Hume assumes, and that this view plays no role in his causal explanation of belief in physical objects. Once again Hume's language is not unambiguous, but he does say: 'I shall at first suppose; that there is only a single existence, which I shall call indifferently *object* or *perception*, according as it shall seem best to suit my purpose, understanding by both of them what any common man means by a hat, or shoe, or stone, or any other impression, convey'd to him by his senses' (*T* 202). And it is not until his explanation of the plain man's belief has been completed that Hume goes on to *argue* that the things one perceives are not physical objects but merely perceptions. The argument for this point constitutes the first stage in Hume's critique of the ordinary belief in physical objects. It must be admitted that Hume often writes in ways that anticipate this later conclusion. And the fact that he uses the mentalistic term 'perceptions' throughout the discussion is bound to mislead. These infelicities of presentation do not, however, affect the essentials of Hume's account.

Hume purports to give a causal explanation of one's ordinary conception of a world of physical objects but denies that this conception is a product of causal inference. He begins by asking 'whether it be the *senses*, *reason*, or the *imagination*, that produces the opinion of a *continu'd* or of a *distinct* existence' (*T* 188), and argues that neither the senses nor reason provide the requisite explanation. His point about the senses is that the very things one perceives do not come ready-marked, as it were, as independent or continuing existents. With respect to reason he claims that as a matter of fact we do not go through any explicit process of causal inference, and that, given the character of the belief to be explained, we could not do so. By exclusion, then, it must be some more or less automatic, unreflective, activity of the imagination that produces the belief in question. Two variables must be distinguished in the causal explanation Hume actually provides: the imaginative construction of the physical world is a joint product of certain features of some of the perceptions one has and certain characteristics of one's imagination. Hume writes: 'Since all impressions are internal and perishing existences, and appear as such, the notion of their distinct and continu'd existence must arise from a concurrence of some of their qualities with the qualities of the imagination; and since this notion does not extend to all of them, it must arise from certain qualities peculiar to some impressions' (*T* 194).[3] These all-important qualities of some perceptions are the relational features that Hume designates 'constancy' and 'coherence', and that Price helpfully calls 'gap indifference'.[4] Given one's awareness of constancy and coherence one fills in the gaps in one's perceptions by imagining that some of the very things one perceives continue to exist when not perceived. There are many important questions of detail here, but this brief account must do for my present purposes.

In thus explaining the acquisition of one's conception of a physical world Hume does not go back on his claim that this conception is not a product of causal inference. 'But tho' this conclusion from the coherence of appearances may seem to be of the same nature with our reasonings concerning causes and effects; as being deriv'd from custom, and regulated by past experience; we shall find upon examination, that they are at the bottom considerably different from each other, and that this inference arises from the understanding, and from custom in an indirect and oblique manner' (*T* 197). Causality is a matter of constant conjunction whereas in the 'inference' involved in one's imaginative construction of the physical world one invents a regularity greater than that actually encountered in experience: we 'bestow on the objects a greater regularity than what is observ'd in our mere perceptions' (*T* 197).

It is worth noticing, finally, what Hume says about the connection between the notions of independent and continued existence. He premises that an object has the one property if and only if it has the other: 'For if the objects of our senses continue to exist, even when they are not perceiv'd, their existence is of course independent of and distinct from the perception; and *vice versa*, if their existence be independent of the perception and distinct from it, they must continue to exist, even tho' they be not perceiv'd' (*T* 188).[5] The weaker thesis that the independence of an object is a necessary condition for its continued existence (or that its continued existence is a sufficient condition for its independent existence) is crucial to Hume's overall strategy concerning belief in the physical world. For his constructive account amounts to a causal explanation of the specific belief that one's perceptions *continue* to exist when unperceived. Having given this explanation he offers a causal argument to show that one's perceptions are not *distinct* or *independent*. Thus a conflict is displayed between equally natural activities of the imagination. At the point in *Treatise* I iv 2 where positive explanation gives way to sceptical objections Hume writes:

> I have already observ'd, that there is an intimate connexion betwixt those two principles, of a *continu'd* and of a *distinct* or *independent* existence, and that we no sooner establish the one than the other follows, as a necessary consequence. 'Tis the opinion of a continu'd existence, which first takes place, and without much study or reflection draws the other along with it, wherever the mind follows its first and most natural tendency. But when we compare experiments, and reason a little upon them, we quickly perceive, that the doctrine of the independent existence of our sensible perceptions is contrary to the plainest experience. This leads us backward upon our footsteps to perceive our error in attributing a continu'd existence to our perceptions. (*T* 210)

We shall see more of this conflict within the imagination.

4.　To grasp the character and extent of Hume's scepticism with regard to the senses three general points must be kept firmly in mind. First, his overriding objective here is to show that an unavoidable antinomy results from equally natural activities of the imagination in dealing with the physical world. On the one hand, we are led by a natural activity of the imagination to hold certain beliefs about the existence and character of physical objects. On the other, specifically causal inference is an equally natural activity of the imagination, but when as philosophers we engage in this activity we are led, ineluctably, to the conclusion that there are no such objects. Hume puts his point forcefully in the concluding chapter to Book I of the *Treatise*:

> No wonder a principle [i.e. imagination] so inconstant and fallacious shou'd lead us into errors, when implicitly follow'd (as it must be) in all its variations. 'Tis this principle, which makes us reason from causes and effects; and 'tis the same principle, which convinces us of the continu'd existence of external objects, when absent from the senses. But tho' these two operations be equally natural and necessary in the human mind, yet in some circumstances

they are directly contrary, nor is it possible for us to reason justly and regularly from causes and effects, and at the same time believe the continu'd existence of matter. How then shall we adjust those principles together? Which of them shall we prefer? Or in case we prefer neither of them, but successively assent to both, as is usual among philosophers, with what confidence can we afterwards usurp that glorious title, when we thus knowingly embrace a manifest contradiction? (*T* 265–6)

Indications that Hume's particular sceptical arguments about the senses are designed to serve the further purpose of displaying this antinomy can also be found in section 12, part 1, of the first *Enquiry*.[6]

The second point to be kept in mind is this. Both in the *Treatise* and in the first *Enquiry* Hume distinguishes three sceptical arguments concerning the physical world, with importantly different targets and conclusions. The first target is the naive realism of common sense: the view that some of the very things one perceives are physical objects, having independent and continued existence. This view can be shown to be 'contrary to reason' (*E* 155) by a causal argument. The second target is a philosophical theory: the representative theory of perception. According to this theory the very things one perceives are perceptions, never physical objects, but some of one's perceptions are caused by physical objects. This theory can be shown by philosophical reflection to carry 'no rational evidence with it, to convince an impartial enquirer' (*E* 155). The third target may be described in either of two ways: as the representative theory, in so far as it makes the claim that at least some of the qualities of some perceptions resemble qualities of physical objects; or as the fundamental claim, common to naive realism and the representative theory, that there is a physical world. However this target be described, Hume holds that it can be shown, by philosophical reflection including causal argument, to be 'contrary to reason' (*E* 155).

That Hume is presenting three different arguments, with correspondingly different targets and conclusions, is plain enough from the paragraph in section 12, part 1, of the first *Enquiry*, where he summarizes his discussion of scepticism with regard to the senses:

Thus the first philosophical objection to the evidence of sense or to the opinion of external existence consists in this, that such an opinion, if rested on natural instinct, is contrary to reason, and if referred to reason, is contrary to natural instinct, and at the same time carries no rational evidence with it, to convince an impartial enquirer. The second objection goes farther, and represents this opinion as contrary to reason: at least, if it be a principle of reason, that all sensible qualities are in the mind, not in the object. Bereave matter of all its intelligible qualities, both primary and secondary, you in a manner annihilate it, and leave only a certain unknown, inexplicable *something*, as the cause of our perceptions; a notion so imperfect, that no sceptic will think it worth while to contend against it. (*E* 155)

The alternatives distinguished under 'the first philosophical objection' are the first two arguments distinguished above. The 'second objection' is the third of the three arguments.

Things are not set out quite so explicitly in the *Treatise*, but it is clear that the three arguments are distinguished there as well. The first two are contained in *Treatise* I iv 2 ('Of scepticism with regard to the senses'). One first comes upon the attack on the naive realism of common sense: Hume claims that 'a very little reflection and philosophy is sufficient to make us perceive the fallacy of that opinion', that is, the opinion that ascribes 'a continu'd existence to those sensible objects or perceptions' (*T* 210). Then Hume turns to the representative theory and argues that ''Tis impossible . . . that from the existence or any of the qualities of the former [that is, perceptions], we can ever form any conclusion concerning the existence of the latter [that is, physical objects], or ever satisfy our reason in this particular' (*T* 212). As we shall see, the arguments for these two conclusions in the *Treatise* parallel, in large measure, those for the same conclusions in the *Enquiry*. The third argument in the *Enquiry* rests on an examination of the distinction between primary and secondary qualities. Its parallel is to be found not in *Treatise* I iv 2 but in *Treatise* I iv 4 ('Of the modern philosophy') where Hume concludes:

> Thus there is a direct and total opposition betwixt our reason and our senses; or more properly speaking, betwixt those conclusions we form from cause and effect, and those that persuade us of the continu'd and independent existence of body. When we reason from cause and effect, we conclude, that neither colour, sound, taste, nor smell have a continu'd and independent existence. When we exclude these sensible qualities there remains nothing in the universe, which has such an existence. (*T* 231)

It is especially important to distinguish Hume's third argument from the other two. Their conclusions are the relatively weak, not especially surprising, ones that the naive realism of the plain man is false and that the representative theory cannot be justified by causal reasoning. Its conclusion is the extraordinary one that the very belief in physical objects can be shown, by causal reasoning, to be false. Striking confirmation of the need to distinguish his third from his other arguments is provided by Hume himself. In the conclusion to Book I of the *Treatise* Hume refers, in summary fashion, to the sceptical arguments he has deployed on a variety of topics (reason, the senses, causality). He expresses the upshot of his sceptical discussion of physical objects in this way: 'nor is it possible for us to reason justly and regularly from causes and effects, and at the same time believe the continu'd existence of matter' (*T* 266). He then indicates, by providing a footnote cross-reference, just where in the *Treatise* this has been argued. It is significant that this footnote refers not, as one might expect, to *Treatise* I iv 2 ('Of scepticism with regard to the senses') but to *Treatise* 1 iv 4 ('Of the modern philosophy'). On my interpretation this comes as no surprise. For Hume does not carry his sceptical attack to its conclusion in *Treatise* 1 iv 2; his targets there (naive realism and the representative theory) are relatively limited. His attack concludes only when he has examined the distinction between primary and secondary qualities at *Treatise* 1 iv 4. And there his target is the very belief in physical objects.

The third point to be kept in mind is that Hume's discussion concerns, specifically, the existence of *physical* objects. Although much of his discussion focuses on the properties of independent and continued existence, and although these are taken to be essential characteristics of physical objects, Hume is well aware that a specifically physical object must have certain other properties as well. What other properties Hume takes to be essential we shall see.

Let us turn to a detailed examination of Hume's three arguments. This will provide further support for the claim that there are indeed three.

5. According to Hume, the ordinary man holds the naively realistic view that some of the very things he perceives are physical objects: that it is these very things that are independent of our perception of them and that continue to exist though unperceived. His first sceptical argument is designed to show that this, at any rate, is a 'fallacy' or an 'error' (*T* 210); is 'contrary to reason' (*E* 155). In the *Treatise*, Hume's argument against naive realism runs as follows:

'Twill first be proper to observe a few of those experiments, which convince us, that our perceptions are not possest of any independent existence. When we press one eye with a finger, we immediately perceive all the objects to become double, and one half of them to be remov'd from their common and natural position. But as we do not attribute a continu'd existence to both these perceptions, and as they are both of the same nature, we clearly perceive, that all our perceptions are dependent on our organs, and the disposition of our nerves and animal spirits. This opinion is confirm'd by the seeming encrease and diminution of objects, according to their distance; by the apparent alterations in their figure; by the changes in their colour and other qualities from our sickness and distempers; and by an infinite number of other experiments of the same kind; from all which we learn, that our sensible perceptions are not possest of any distinct or independent existence. (*T* 210–11)

In the *Enquiry* the corresponding argument mentions only one of the 'experiments':

But this universal and primary opinion of all men [naive realism] is soon destroyed by the slightest philosophy, which teaches us, that nothing can ever be present to the mind but an image or perception, and that the senses are only the inlets, through which these images

are conveyed, without being able to produce any immediate intercourse between the mind and the object. The table, which we see,
seems to diminish, as we remove farther from it: but the real table,
which exists independent of us, suffers no alteration: it was, therefore, nothing but its image, which was present to the mind. (*E* 152)

If we are to be clear about the character of this argument several
things must be noted. First, the argument is designed to show that perceptions, the very things we perceive, are not *independent* of perception;
that they do not have *continued* existence would follow given the premise,
mentioned earlier, that the former property is a necessary condition for
the latter. (Here we can see the first step in Hume's development of the
antinomy indicated above: by equally natural activities of the imagination we are led to the incompatible beliefs that some of the very things
we perceive have a continued existence and that these same things do
not have an independent existence.) But what precisely does it mean to
say that perceptions do not have independent existence? In the view of
the ordinary man a perception has independent existence in the sense
that 'our presence bestows not being on it: our absence does not
annihilate it', it 'preserves its existence uniform and entire, independent
of the situation of intelligent beings, who perceive or contemplate it'
(*E* 152). As Hume's argument makes fairly clear, the point might be
better put in this way: if the very thing we perceive is independent of
perception then its existence and qualities are not dependent on the
conditions of its being perceived, including, especially, the bodily states
of the perceiver. It is assumed that there *is* something that we directly
perceive in the circumstances envisaged, something possessing such
characteristics as colour, shape and size; it is this that the ordinary man
takes to be a physical object such as a table or chair. It seems further to
be assumed that if these items we perceive are not physical objects they
must be mental ones. These assumptions lead directly to the reification[7]
of perceptions, viewed as specifically mental particulars, when Hume's
argument is done. Throughout the argument it is also assumed that one
has a great deal of knowledge about physical objects, including one's
body. In particular it is assumed that physical objects do not change
in ways relevantly correlated with changes in the very things one
perceives.

Within this framework Hume produces a series of 'experiments', a
series of causal investigations, that purport to show that none of the
very things one perceives are independent of the conditions of their
being perceived, and thus that none are physical objects. The pressing
of the perceiver's eyeball causes him to see two chairs though there is in
fact only one. Variations in the distance between the perceiver's body
and a chair cause variations in the size of the chair he sees. What he
actually sees, then, can not be a chair. So too with the other 'experiments'. It may be suggested that some, though not all, of the very things
we perceive are physical objects. Thus, in the case of double-vision it

may be said that one of the chairs one sees is an actual chair. But to this Hume replies that 'they are both of the same nature', that is, that the purportedly differing chairs one sees are, to the senses, no different from one another. A similar move would block the suggestion that at *one* of the distances from the chair one actually sees the chair.

Hume formulates the conclusion to his argument in a variety of ways, the differences between which deserve to be noticed. In its weakest form it reads: 'all our perceptions are dependent on our organs, and the disposition of our nerves and animal spirits' (T 211), 'our perceptions are not possest of any independent existence' (T 210), and 'our sensible perceptions are not possest of any distinct or independent existence' (T 211). In short, perceptions are not physical objects. On the very next page, however, he says, as if making the same point, that 'no beings are ever present to the mind but perceptions' (T 212), suggesting that perceptions, the very things we perceive, are themselves reified mental items. Earlier, in a similar vein, he had said: 'philosophy informs us, that every thing, which appears to the mind, is nothing but a perception, and is interrupted, and dependent on the mind' (T 193). The specifically mental status of reified perceptions is if anything clearer in the *Enquiry*: 'nothing can ever be present to the mind but an image or perception, and . . . the senses are only the inlets, through which these images are conveyed, without being able to produce any immediate intercourse between the mind and the object' (E 152); 'the existences, which we consider, when we say, *this house* and *that tree*, are nothing but perceptions in the mind, and fleeting copies or representations of other existences, which remain uniform and independent' (E 152). Leaving aside the suggestion, in the two *Enquiry* passages, of a representative theory of perception, Hume's conclusion is that, in sensation, the things we directly encounter, with which we have 'immediate intercourse', have the status of mental particulars. The mentalistic connotations of Hume's term 'perception' may now be taken at face value.

6. Although sometimes, as in the *Enquiry* passages just quoted, he writes as if the proof of the mental status of perceptions displays the truth of a representative theory of perception, Hume's considered view is very different from this. The representative theory, he claims, is a concoction of philosophers who, faced with the falsity of naive realism, attempt to patch up the situation by distinguishing perceptions (as mental representatives or images) and objects (the physical objects represented or imaged), and holding that the former are caused by the latter. Whatever the genesis of the theory, however, Hume is clear that there is something seriously wrong with it. The difficulty is that 'philosophy finds herself extremely embarrassed, when she would justify this new system, and obviate the cavils and objections of the sceptics' (E 152). '[T]o justify this pretended philosophical system, by a chain of clear and convincing argument', he says, 'or even any appearance of

argument, exceeds the power of all human capacity' (*E* 152). We must be clear about the character of Hume's claim. Hume does not, as he did in the case of naive realism, here claim that the representative theory is 'false', an 'error', or 'contrary to reason'. Hume's second argument purports only to show that the representative theory 'carries no rational evidence with it, to convince an impartial enquirer' (*E* 155). The theory, that is to say, is incapable of rational justification or of justification by causal argument.

Hume's principal objection appears in both the *Treatise* and the *Enquiry*. Briefly, if it is granted that perceptions (in the sense, now, of specifically mental particulars) are alone perceived, then one cannot support the causal judgment, essential to the representative theory, that physical objects cause one's perceptions. For causal judgments must be based on experience of the conjunction of cause and effect and this, by hypothesis, is ruled out. The point is clearly made in the *Treatise*:

> The only conclusion we can draw from the existence of one thing to that of another, is by means of the relation of cause and effect, which shews, that there is a connexion betwixt them, and that the existence of one is dependent on that of the other. The idea of this relation is deriv'd from past experience, by which we find, that two beings are constantly conjoin'd together, and are always present at once to the mind. But as no beings are ever present to the mind but perceptions; it follows that we may observe a conjunction or a relation of cause and effect between different perceptions, but can never observe it between perceptions and objects. 'Tis impossible, therefore, that from the existence or any of the qualities of the former, we can ever form any conclusion concerning the existence of the latter, or ever satisfy our reason in this particular. (*T* 212)

The same point is made, rather more succinctly, in the *Enquiry*:

> It is a question of fact, whether the perceptions of the senses be produced by external objects, resembling them: how shall this question be determined? By experience surely; as all other questions of a like nature. But here experience is, and must be entirely silent. The mind has never anything present to it but the perceptions, and cannot possibly reach any experience of their connexion with objects. The supposition of such a connexion is, therefore, without any foundation in reasoning. (*E* 153)

There can, in short, be no 'convincing argument from experience to prove, that the perceptions are connected with any external objects' (*E* 154).

Another objection to the representative theory appears in the *Enquiry* but not in the *Treatise*. Its point seems to be that there are no rational grounds for choosing between the numerous candidates that might be proposed as non-perceptual causes of one's perceptions. Even if one were to admit that some of one's perceptions have items other than perceptions as their causes why must these causes be physical ones?

By what argument can it be proved, that the perceptions of the mind must be caused by external objects, entirely different from them, though resembling them (if that be possible) and could not arise either from the energy of the mind itself, or from the suggestion of some invisible and unknown spirit, or from some other cause still more unknown to us? (*E* 152–3)

If Hume's second sceptical argument is sound it is in principle impossible to confirm the representative or any other causal theory of perception. Apparently, however, Hume thinks that his second argument leaves open the question whether the representative theory, although unverifiable, is nonetheless true. Only if one recognizes a gap between these two claims can one make sense of his going on to show, by a further argument, that the representative theory, in particular the constituent belief that there is a physical world, is in fact false. Surprisingly, he seems not to assume here that a purportedly empirical proposition that is unverifiable in principle is meaningless. Nor does this assumption play any role in his third and concluding sceptical argument, to which I now turn.

7.   This third argument rests on a consideration of the relation between primary and secondary qualities. Accordingly, in the *Treatise* it appears in the section 'Of the modern philosophy', not in 'Of scepticism with regard to the senses'. Its target is the belief, common to the naive realism of common sense and the representative theory of perception, that there are objects that are independent of perception, that continue to exist when unperceived, and that possess such additional properties (for example, colour, shape, size and solidity) as entitle one to think of them as physical objects. Although there are some suggestions to the contrary, the third argument is not designed to show that there is no independent and continued cause of perceptions. It is specifically physical causes that are to be rejected.

When the argument is viewed in this way, the conclusion stated at one place in the *Treatise* is too strong:

When we reason from cause and effect, we conclude, that neither colour, sound, taste, nor smell have a continu'd and independent existence. When we exclude these sensible qualities there remains *nothing* in the universe, which has such an existence. (*T* 231, my italics)

Later, Hume expresses himself with greater care: 'nor is it possible for us to reason justly and regularly from causes and effects, and at the same time believe the continu'd existence of *matter*' (*T* 266, my italics). Similar care is displayed in the *Enquiry*: 'Bereave matter of all its intelligible qualities, both primary and secondary, you in a manner annihilate it, and leave only a certain unknown, inexplicable *something*, as the cause of our perceptions' (*E* 155). Again: 'the opinion of *external* existence . . . [is] contrary to reason' (*E* 155, my italics). The expression 'contrary to reason', which is used also of naive realism and which contrasts with the weaker 'carries no rational evidence with it', indicates that, in Hume's view, the belief in physical objects has been shown to be false. From its falsity he does not, it seems, infer that the belief makes no sense.

Clearly Hume does not think that the falsity of the belief in physical objects follows either from the fact that the mind has 'immediate intercourse' only with perceptions or from the fact that the representative theory cannot be justified by causal reasoning. What more is needed then if Hume is to make out his extraordinary conclusion? What he must show is that the properties (other than independence and continuance) that we take to designate specifically physical objects are, as a matter of fact, properties only of perceptions: that only perceptions have colour, smell, shape, size, solidity, and so forth. Although there are many defects in his expression of the argument it is obvious that this is what Hume does try to show.

There is, however, a feature of Hume's language that can mislead the reader as it may, at times, have misled Hume. To put it very roughly, his language has a tendency to mask the necessary distinction between a property of a perception and that, namely the perception, which has the property. Thus, instead of saying that secondary qualities are properties only of perceptions he tends to say that they are (only) perceptions. To cite but one instance: 'all the *sensible qualities* of objects, such as hard, soft, hot, cold, white, black, etc. are merely secondary, and exist not in the objects themselves, but *are perceptions of the mind*' (*E* 154, my italics). This feature of Hume's language may lead one to overlook the critical gap between claiming that only perceptions are directly perceived and claiming that only perceptions have those properties, other than independence and continuance, that are taken to characterize physical objects. Without this gap, however, there is no work for Hume's third argument to do. Let us now look at the argument itself.

The *Enquiry* statement of the argument makes up in clarity of overall structure for its relative lack of detail:

> It is universally allowed by modern enquirers, that all the sensible qualities of objects, such as hard, soft, hot, cold, white, black, etc. are merely secondary, and exist not in the objects themselves, but are perceptions of the mind, without any external archetype or model, which they represent. If this be allowed, with regard to secondary qualities, it must also follow, with regard to the supposed primary qualities of extension and solidity; nor can the latter be any more entitled to that denomination than the former. The idea of extension is entirely acquired from the senses of sight and feeling; and if all the qualities, perceived by the senses, be in the mind, not in the object, the same conclusion must reach the idea of extension, which is wholly dependent on the sensible ideas or the ideas of secondary qualities. (*E* 154)

The argument is glossed by the statement that 'an extension, that is neither tangible nor visible, cannot possibly be conceived: and a tangible or visible extension, which is neither hard nor soft, black nor white, is equally beyond the reach of human conception' (*E* 154–5). The argument takes the following form: secondary qualities are properties only of perceptions; but the relation between primary and secondary qualities is such that if the latter are properties only of perceptions then so are the former; therefore both primary and secondary qualities are properties only of perceptions. Given what we have seen to be the target of the argument, we must add the premise that if there are no objects other than perceptions that have either the primary or the secondary qualities then there are no specifically physical objects. This enables one to draw the conclusion that there are no physical objects.

In the passage quoted from the *Enquiry* Hume does not say, in so many words, that secondary qualities are properties only of perceptions. Moreover he does not offer any support for this premise: he simply remarks that it is 'universally allowed by modern enquirers'. In the *Treatise*, however, he produces an argument that he claims to 'find . . . satisfactory' (*T* 226) for the conclusion that 'colours, sounds, tastes, smells, heat and cold . . . [are] nothing but impressions in the mind, deriv'd from the operation of external objects, and without any resemblance to the qualities of the objects' (*T* 226). This conclusion is 'deriv'd from the variations of those impressions, even while the external object, to all appearance, continues the same' (*T* 226). He assumes that 'the same [physical] object cannot, at the same time, be endow'd with different qualities of the same sense' (*T* 227) and that 'the same quality cannot resemble impressions entirely different' (*T* 227). But there are 'variations' of impressions, depending 'upon several circumstances' (*T* 226). Thus:

> Upon the different situations of our health: A man in a malady feels a disagreeable taste in meats, which before pleas'd him the most. Upon the different complexions and constitutions of men: That seems bitter to one, which is sweet to another. Upon the difference of their external situation and position: Colours reflected from the clouds change according to the distance of the clouds, and according to the angle they make with the eye and luminous body. Fire also communicates the sensation of pleasure at one distance, and that of pain at another. (*T* 226)

Given his assumptions, plus the variations cited, 'it evidently follows, that many of our impressions have no external model or archetype' (*T* 227). The point is then generalized to all instances of secondary qualities:

> Many of the impressions of colour, sound, etc. are confest to be nothing but internal existences, and to arise from causes, which no ways resemble them. These impressions are in appearance nothing different from the other impressions of colour, sound, etc. We con-

clude, therefore, that they are, all of them, deriv'd from a like origin. (*T* 227)

That is to say, no secondary qualities of any perceptions represent qualities of physical objects; they are qualities only of perceptions.[8]

The crux, of course, is to show that the same is true of primary qualities. To make this point Hume does not, as one might expect, invoke variations in the shape, size, and other primary qualities of perceptions. Of the 'many objections [that] might be made to this system [i.e., the view that primary qualities are also qualities of physical objects]', he confines himself to one that is, in his opinion, 'very decisive' (*T* 227). Applying the doctrine of space developed in book I, part ii, of the *Treatise*, he contends that one can form no idea of the primary qualities of objects 'without having recourse to the secondary and sensible qualities' (*T* 230); ideas of the former qualities are 'wholly dependent on the sensible ideas or the ideas of the secondary qualities' (*E* 154). From this he infers that since secondary qualities are properties only of perceptions, the same must be true of primary qualities: 'If colours, sounds, tastes, and smells be merely perceptions, nothing we can conceive is possest of a real, continu'd, and independent existence; not even motion, extension and solidity, which are the primary qualities chiefly insisted on' (*T* 228). There are, then, no specifically physical objects that are independent of our perceptions and that continue to exist when unperceived.

By this route Hume reaches the final stage in the development of the antinomy described earlier. Concluding *Treatise* I iv 4, in which the argument just recounted appears, he says:

> Thus there is a direct and total opposition betwixt our reason and our senses; or more properly speaking, betwixt those conclusions we form from cause and effect, and those that persuade us of the continu'd and independent existence of body. When we reason from cause and effect, we conclude, that neither colour, sound, taste, nor smell have a continu'd and independent existence. When we exclude these sensible qualities there remains nothing in the universe, which has such an existence. (*T* 231)[9]

8.   I have taken pains to show that Hume has three importantly different sceptical arguments concerning physical objects and what the relations among these three arguments are. I have taken particular pains to isolate Hume's astonishing third argument from the others. This seems to me important if for no other reason than that, so far as I can ascertain, the character and function of this third argument have gone unnoticed. Typically, commentators take the sceptical argument concerning the senses to be completed by the end of *Treatise* I iv 2 with the claim that one can provide no rational justification for belief in physical objects. But Hume's sceptical tale is very far from told at that point, and it has a very strange ending indeed.

This is not merely a matter of correcting an oversight of the commentators; for I am inclined to think that one cannot properly grasp Hume's scepticism unless one sees the strange goings-on at *Treatise* I iv 4 as the most important part of the tale. Hume's is not merely the milk-and-water scepticism that claims to display the inadequacy of the grounds on which we rest our beliefs about physical objects. He claims to provide an irrefutable argument to the conclusion that there are no such objects. Just how is one to take this? What does this reveal of his scepticism? We must begin from the fact that his scepticism is far more radical than the received wisdom has it.

Underscoring the radical character of Hume's third argument may seem an unlikely route to one of my stated objectives. For I propose to give an account of Hume's philosophy of mind that places maximum allowable stress on the roles that Hume assigns, or can and should assign, to a person's body. It is one thing to claim that in his own theoretical work (and, presumably, in his more mundane activities) Hume employs a belief that, if his argument is sound, can have no rational justification. It seems quite another matter to have him using a belief that he claims can be shown to be false by irrefutable argument. If the second reading is correct should not one convict him of the most flagrant inconsistency? In any case, it is an odd starting-point for an interpretation that emphasizes the body.

Of course, Hume believes there are bodies: he is not like Descartes' madmen, who believe themselves to be pumpkins or to be made of glass. And he begins the section 'Of scepticism with regard to the senses' with the statement: '[']T]is in vain to ask, *Whether there be body or not?* That is a point, which we must take for granted in all our reasonings' (*T* 187). His own sceptical arguments, as we have seen, plainly rest on the assumption that there are such objects. Indeed he seems, at times, to hold some form of a representative theory of perception. As we shall see there is ample evidence that, in Hume's view, one's sensations are caused by the action of physical objects. As we have already seen, he tends to reify perceptions, including sensations, and to assign to these reified perceptions the characteristically physical qualities of colour, shape, size, and so forth. This commits him to the view that some perceptions are caused by physical objects that they to some extent resemble. And there are numerous passages, including some that occur while he is developing his sceptical arguments, in which he writes in the idioms of the representative theory. To cite only two instances, if fairly striking ones:

> [T]he slightest philosophy . . . teaches us, that nothing can ever be present to the mind but an image or perception, and that the senses are only the inlets, through which these images are convey'd, without being able to produce any immediate intercourse between the mind and the object. The table, which we see, seems to diminish, as we remove farther from it: but the real table, which exists in-

dependent of us, suffers no alteration: it was, therefore, nothing but its image, which was present to the mind. These are the obvious dictates of reason; and no man, who reflects, ever doubted, that the existences, which we consider, when we say, *this house* and *that tree*, are nothing but perceptions in the mind, and fleeting copies or representations of other existences, which remain uniform and independent. (*E* 152)

Again:

> We may observe, that 'tis universally allow'd by philosophers, and is besides pretty obvious of itself, that nothing is ever really present with the mind but its perceptions or impressions and ideas, and that external objects become known to us only by those perceptions they occasion. (*T* 67. Compare *E* 151, *T* 191–3, 210–11, 216, 230, 237, 239)

Of course he is well aware of the defects of representative realism as he construes it; we have already seen his objections. Nonetheless he seems at times to take it up himself.

What are we to make of all this? Can we find some way to accommodate his seemingly radical scepticism, his flirtations with representative realism, his plain man's approach to bodies, and his adoption (we have yet to see that he does adopt it) of a dualist interactionism? Shall we say that the sceptical arguments are not intended to have the argumentative force I have attributed to them? But Hume uniformly assesses his several arguments as satisfactory, as very decisive, and as leading with certainty to their conclusions. Having developed his sceptical arguments in the youthful *Treatise* he repeats them, with no substantive changes, in the later *Enquiry*. Shall we simply shrug our shoulders and mutter about his lack of seriousness? Until we have examined the alternatives such a response would itself be frivolous. Shall we say that his sceptical arguments are intended (though Hume gives no hint that this is so) as an elaborate *reductio ad absurdum* argument to show that one must begin and end with naive realism? There is something to this, but it fails to explain Hume's at least occasional representative realism. I should like to suggest a different reading, one that makes it intelligible that Hume would adopt a representative theory of perception while at the same time being serious both about his claim to discover a fundamental and ineradicable antinomy in the imagination and about his assessment of his three sceptical arguments. This reading should also help us to understand his attitude towards the construction of theories about mind.

Hume says of Berkeley:

> That all his *arguments*, though otherwise intended, are, in reality, merely sceptical, appears from this, *that they admit of no answer and produce no conviction*. Their only effect is to cause that momentary amazement and irresolution and confusion, which is the result of scepticism. (*E* 155n, my italics for 'arguments')

Later he says that 'a Pyrrhonian may throw himself or others into a momentary amazement and confusion by his profound reasonings' (*E* 160). While he 'keep[s] within his proper sphere, and display[s] those *philosophical* objections, which arise from more profound re-searches . . . he seems to have ample matter of triumph' (*E* 159). Yet he is unable to 'produce a conviction, which will remain constant and durable' (*E* 160), his philosophy cannot 'have any constant influence on the mind' (*E* 160). 'Nature', Hume says, 'is always too strong for principle' (*E* 160), and even the sceptic 'must assent to the principle concerning the existence of body' (*T* 187). In the last analysis the sceptic's objections 'can have no other tendency than to show the whimsical condition of mankind, who must act and reason and believe; though they are not able, by their most diligent enquiry, to satisfy them-selves concerning the foundation of these operations, or to remove the objections, which may be raised against them' (*E* 160). In short, the sceptic's argument cannot be refuted but, thanks to nature, its conclusion literally cannot be believed.

A distinction between believing an argument to be irrefutable and believing that argument's conclusion is, it seems to me, essential to an understanding of the position Hume finally takes with respect to per-ception and physical objects. He takes each of his three sceptical argu-ments (against the naive realism of commonsense, against the repre-sentative theory of perception, and against the very belief in physical objects) to be irrefutable. But what of the conclusions to these argu-ments? Here a further distinction must be made. Hume certainly holds that the conclusion of his third argument, that there are no physical objects, cannot be believed. He says as much at several places. There is another thing that Hume thinks we cannot do: we cannot conceive of an object that has only the primary and none of the secondary qualities. However, he nowhere claims that we cannot believe the conclusions to his first and second sceptical arguments. He holds, of course, that in our ordinary way of thinking we do not believe that what we perceive are perceptions, that is, mental entities rather than physical objects. It would follow from this that, in our ordinary way of thinking, we do not believe that the perceptions we perceive are caused by physical objects resembling them. But I can find no evidence that, in Hume's view, we cannot, *at least when doing philosophy or science*, hold both of these beliefs. Again the proviso must be entered: whether in our ordinary thinking or when doing philosophy we cannot conceive of physical objects ex-clusively in terms of primary qualities.

There are, it should be noted, several places at which Hume indicates a difference between two perspectives: that of the ordinary man and that of the philosopher or scientist. Philosophers 'immediately upon leaving their closets, mingle with the rest of mankind in those exploded opinions, that our perceptions are our only objects, and continue identically and uninterruptedly the same in all their interrupted appearances' (*T* 216). Earlier he had said that 'the persons, who entertain this opinion concerning the identity of our resembling perceptions, are in general all the unthinking and unphilosophical part of mankind (that is, all of us, at one time or other), and consequently such as suppose their perceptions to be their only objects, and never think of a double existence internal and external, representing and represented' (*T* 205). Significantly, in both passages the contrast is not merely that between plain man and philosopher but that between plain man and representative theorist.

But even if, when doing philosophy, one can believe a representative theory to be true, why *should* one believe it to be true when doing philosophy? Why not stop with the naive realism of the plain man? A further question arises. Even if one should hold a causal theory of perception, why should one hold that the causes of one's perceptions are physical objects? Why not say, with Berkeley, that God is their cause? Why not adopt some other causal hypothesis?

To find some reasonable answer to these questions several things must be kept in mind. First, Hume appears to have some, admittedly rather obscure, notion of *degrees* of scepticism (not to be confused with *kinds* of scepticism). As he writes in the *Treatise*:

'Tis impossible upon any system to defend either our understanding or senses; and we but expose them farther when we endeavour to justify them in that manner. As the sceptical doubt arises naturally from a profound and intense reflection on those subjects, *it always encreases, the farther we carry our reflections*, whether in opposition or conformity to it. (*T* 218, my italics)

Perhaps he thinks that, in stepping back from the unbelievable conclusion one reaches when one proceeds through his three sceptical arguments, one should stop at the point that concedes as much as possible to the irrefutable sceptical arguments but does not yet deny the existence of physical objects. That point, from Hume's perspective, would be the representative theory.

In any case, Hume claims to have shown that the naive realism of common sense, although believable, is false. The situation of the representative theory is quite different. If his third sceptical argument is put to one side, Hume claims only that the theory cannot be justified by causal reasoning. Moreover, he raises no doubts about its intelligibility, appears to grant that it can be believed, and takes as true the constituent claim that the only things directly perceived are perceptions.

As we have seen, Hume holds that there are no logically compelling grounds for choosing *physical* objects as the cause of one's perceptions. As against Berkeleyan or other such causal hypotheses, however, the representative theory has the virtue of being relatively natural. This is the positive side of Hume's contention that the representative theory 'acquires all its influence on the imagination from the vulgar one' (*T* 213). To put the point in a different way, the existence of physical objects is, while the existence of God or of other possible causes of our perceptions is not, 'a point, which we must take for granted in all our reasonings' (*T* 187).

To be sure, Hume refers to the representative theory as a 'monstrous offspring' (*T* 215) of the claims of nature and reason, a product of the inextinguishable belief in physical objects and the recognized falsity of the plain man's unreflective view about the very things he perceives. In the light of the considerations I have mentioned, however, we can make some sense of Hume's adopting this 'monstrous offspring' as his own.

Clearly enough, Hume's radical scepticism is not designed to advance the thesis that there are no physical objects. I suggest that its object is, rather, to put a rein on radical departures from the plain man's metaphysics. This it purports to do by displaying the irremediably antinomic character of the human imagination when its subject is the physical world. Given this feature of the imagination, with what confidence can one engage in the construction of extraordinary metaphysical systems ? Even if they are constructible how can they be believed if they conflict with the ineluctable demands of common sense ? (Recall what Hume says of Berkeley.) For putting such a rein on our extraordinary metaphysical pretensions, Hume says, 'nothing can be more serviceable, than to be once thoroughly convinced of the force of the Pyrrhonian doubt, and of the impossibility, that anything, but the strong power of natural instinct, could free us from it' (*E* 162).

Despite his own sceptical arguments, then, Hume contends that one must be a plain man and believe in bodies that have distinct and continued existence. But he seems also to think that, with a tincture of experimental science, one may hold, when in a scientific frame of mind, that more sophisticated combination of beliefs that is the representative theory of perception. In the ordinary run of things the plain man's beliefs are unavoidable. Perhaps those of the enlightened man of common sense are, in a suitable setting, nearly so: 'the philosophical system [representative realism] is found by experience to take hold of many minds, and in particular of all those, who reflect ever so little on this subject' (*T* 213). In any case, adoption of such a view departs in a relatively limited way from the viewpoint of the plain man, correcting that viewpoint on one central point; which should remind us that, in Hume's view, the upshot of sound philosophizing should be 'the reflections of common life, methodized and corrected' (*E* 162). Here, it seems, as elsewhere, 'the true philosophy approaches nearer to the sentiments of the vulgar, than to those of a mistaken knowledge' (*T* 222–3).

I suggest that Hume's scepticism presents no bar, and is intended to present no bar, to his holding a theory of mind that keeps suitably in touch with the plain man's views. This, for Hume, means a theory that countenances connections between a person's (mind-independent) body and his mind.

CHAPTER TWO

Mind and Body

1. The picture that emerges from our examination of Hume's views about perception is that of a mind-body dualist who admits some degree of mind-body interaction. To many readers, however, the suggestion that Hume countenances both bodies and minds, that he takes them to be distinct yet allows causal transactions between them, will seem preposterous. To some it is plain that Hume reduces matter to mind, that he adopts a radical subjective idealism without benefit of Berkeley's God or Berkeleyan minds. In the view of others he reduces both minds and bodies to some neutral stuff, anticipating the neutral monism of James and Russell. Some recent writers see Hume as flirting with a reduction of mind to matter in the manner of behaviourism or, more plausibly, so-called identity theories. Some think that, as a consistent sceptic, he has no constructive view about the matter of mind and matter at all. That such utterly different interpretations claim the field should make us wary of the contention that some other claimant is plainly preposterous. So let us address the question whether Hume is a dualist interactionist directly.

To keep our heads here, and to be seen to avoid begging the question, we must proceed by slow steps. I shall begin by showing that Hume insists on the logical possibility of psychophysical causation. I shall then display the wealth of textual evidence for the view that Hume admits psychophysical causation to be a fact. I shall then conduct a thought experiment, the formulation of a Generalized Humean Theory (GHT) of psychophysical interaction, constructed from Hume's explicit interactionist claims and a set of premises taken from his analysis of causality, in order to see whether a fundamentally Humean theory can make any contribution to more recent discussions of the mind-body problem.

The case made for Hume's interactionism I shall then turn to his dualism. (It should be obvious that one can be an interactionist without being a dualist: Armstrong and Davidson, both physicalists, allow psychophysical causation in both directions.[1]) For the most part my argument will take the form of a critique of attempts to show that Hume is a reductionist, whether of a physicalist, idealist or neutral monist variety. Having argued that he is a dualist I shall in the last section examine, briefly and inconclusively, Hume's characterization of the differences between the mental and the physical.

I shall not of course argue that Hume is a *Cartesian* dualist. A Humean self is very different from anything Descartes would recognize as a self.

But there is no reason to suppose that a dualist cannot think in terms of causal transactions between bodily events and the perceptions that constitute a mind. A *bundle* dualist may be an interactionist.

2.   At the end of *Treatise* I iv 5 ('Of the immateriality of the soul') Hume argues that there is no *logical* objection to psychophysical causality. Philosophers have presented an argument designed to show that it is 'impossible, that thought can ever be caus'd by matter' (T 247)[2]. 'Few', he says, 'have been able to withstand the seeming evidence of this argument; and yet nothing in the world is more easy than to refute it' (T 247). This easily refuted argument runs, in Hume's words, as follows:

> Matter and motion . . . however vary'd, are still matter and motion, and produce only a difference in the position and situation of objects. Divide a body as often as you please, 'tis still body. Place it in any figure, nothing ever results but figure, or the relation of parts. Move it in any manner, you still find motion or a change of relation. 'Tis absurd to imagine, that motion in a circle, for instance, shou'd be nothing but merely motion in a circle; while motion in another direction, as in an ellipse, shou'd also be a passion or moral reflexion: That the shocking of two globular particles shou'd become a sensation of pain, and that the meeting of two triangular ones shou'd afford a pleasure. Now as these different shocks, and variations, and mixtures are the only changes, of which matter is susceptible, and as these never afford us any idea of thought or perception, 'tis concluded to be impossible, that thought can ever be caus'd by matter.
> (T 246–7)

Hume takes the main point to be the claim that 'there appear[s] no manner of connexion betwixt motion or thought' (T 247). This assumes that in genuine cases one finds an apparent connection between cause and effect. The argument involves two further assumptions: that one must be able to understand why a purported connection obtains if one is to be entitled to claim that it does obtain; and that causes and effects must be items of the same basic kind. The first of these underpins the argument's suggestion that one cannot understand why a physical event of a given kind is the cause of a psychological event of one kind rather than another (why is the shocking of two globular particles the cause of pain and not of pleasure?), or why some physical events have psychological effects while others do not (why does elliptical motion cause a passion or a moral reflexion, whereas circular motion has no psychological effects?). The second assumption is not readily seen in the argument as stated but is presupposed by Hume's reply.

In his reply Hume rejects the several assumptions on which the argument rests:

> We need only reflect on what has been prov'd at large, that we are never sensible of any connexion betwixt causes and effects, and that

'tis only by our experience of their constant conjunction, we can arrive at any knowledge of this relation. Now as all objects, which are not contrary, are susceptible of a constant conjunction, and as no real objects are contrary; I have inferr'd from these principles, that to consider the matter *a priori*, any thing may produce any thing, and that we shall never discover a reason, why any object may or may not be the cause of any other, however great, or however little the resemblance may be betwixt them. (*T* 247)

The question of the possibility of psychophysical causation reduces to that of the possibility of constant conjunction between psychological and physical events. But since "'tis possible we may . . . perceive a constant conjunction of thought and motion; you reason too hastily, when from the mere consideration of the ideas, you conclude that 'tis impossible motion can ever produce thought, or a different position of parts give rise to a different passion or reflexion' (*T* 247–8).

The direction of the alleged psychophysical causation is immaterial. And though Hume here mentions only the possibility of physical causation of psychological events he elsewhere makes good his omission. In the first *Enquiry* he poses a rhetorical question to which his own answer is obvious: 'Is it more difficult to conceive that motion may arise from impulse than that it may arise from volition?' (*E* 73). Earlier, in the *Treatise*, he writes: 'Any thing may produce any thing. Creation, annihilation, motion, reason, volition; all these may arise from one another, or from any other object we can imagine' (*T* 173). It is possible that matter should act on mind, and that mind should act on matter.

Interestingly, there is one rejoinder Hume does not make. He does not grant the third assumption, for the sake of argument, and then reject the claim that mind and matter are very different sorts of things. Instead he stresses the point that psychophysical causality is possible 'however great, or however little the resemblance may be betwixt' purported cause and effect (*T* 247) and asserts that 'we find by the comparing their ideas, that thought and motion are different from each other' (*T* 248). Were he thinking along monistic lines he could have conceded this third assumption and still hoped to block the conclusion that the notion of psychophysical causation is objectionable.

3. Granted that psychophysical causality is a logical possibility, does Hume believe that mind-body interaction in fact takes place? If he does, what is his view about the character and extent of such interaction? Let us begin with the physical causation of psychological events.

I am inclined to think that, for Hume, all psychological occurrences (in his terminology all 'perceptions') have physical causes. It is certain, he says, that we experience 'a constant conjunction of thought and motion' (*T* 247). Not only is it not 'impossible motion can ever produce thought, or a different position of parts give rise to a different passion or reflexion' (*T* 248); it is 'certain' that we have experience of just such transactions: 'every one may perceive, that the different dispositions of his body change his thoughts and sentiments' (T 248). We 'find by experience' that 'thought and motion' are 'constantly united', and thus 'may certainly conclude, that motion . . . actually is, the cause of thought and perception' (T 248). The context of these remarks (recall 'the shocking of two globular particles') suggests that Hume is thinking primarily in physiological terms. Be that as it may, there is no question that these claims are seriously intended: they occur just after his defence of the logical possibility of psychophysical causality.[3] To allay misgivings, however, let us look for other evidence of Hume's views. And let us take each of Hume's three sub-classes of perceptions in turn: impressions of sensation (sensations), impressions of reflection (passions) and ideas.

Hume holds that all sensations have physical causes. Indeed, he appears to hold that all sensations have physical causes falling into each of three groups: causes in the physical world outside one's own body, causes in one's body as normally observable, for example, the condition of one's sense organs, and causes in one's brain and central nervous system as well as other inner physical causes. Let us call these, respectively, 'external', 'bodily' and 'physiological' causes. Here, as in the case of other perceptions, I shall be especially concerned to display Hume's views about physiological causation.

'Original impressions or impressions of sensation are such as without any antecedent perception arise in the soul, from the constitution of the body, from the animal spirits, or from the application of objects to the external organs' (T 275). Each kind of physical causality is invoked for tactile sensation: 'An object, that presses upon any of our members, meets with resistance; and that resistance, by the motion it gives to the nerves and animal spirits, conveys a certain sensation to the mind' (T 230). Hume says explicitly that all sensations have both bodily and physiological causes: 'all our perceptions [sensations] are dependent on our organs, and the disposition of our nerves and animal spirits' (T 211). Sensations of smell and taste confirm the general claim: 'The nerves of the nose and palate are so dispos'd, as in certain circumstances to convey such peculiar sensations to the mind' (T 287). He makes frequent reference to the external and bodily causation of sensations. He mentions 'the pains and pleasures, that arise from the application of objects to our bodies, as by the cutting of our flesh with steel, and such like' (T 192). Again: 'Let a man heat one hand and cool the other; the same water will at the same time, seem both hot and cold, according to the disposition of the different organs' (T 372).

At one point Hume states, misleadingly, that sensations 'arise . . . in the soul originally, from unknown causes' (T 7). Significantly, however, he goes on to say that 'the examination of our sensations belongs more to anatomists and natural philosophers than to moral' (T 8). He makes his point more clearly later: 'Original impressions or impressions of sensation are such as *without any antecedent perception* arise in the soul' (*T* 275, my italics). That is to say, they have no psychological causes. But they do have physical, including physiological, causes. That is why their proper study requires the physical sciences: 'as these depend upon natural and physical causes, the examination of them wou'd lead me too far from my present subject, into the sciences of anatomy and natural philosophy' (*T* 275–6).

Notice that if sensations do not have psychological causes, they must, on Hume's own premises, have physical ones; for, as a determinist, he holds that every event has a cause. And there is no evidence in the text of events other than physical and psychological ones.

What is to be said of Hume's two other sub-classes of perceptions? There is no direct textual evidence in addition to the general statements, quoted earlier, that Hume holds to the physiological causation of the passions. But there is some evidence for the case of ideas. Hume writes of the imagination being disordered by 'any extraordinary ferment of the blood and spirits', and of 'chimera[s] of the brain' (*T* 123). More importantly, he offers a 'specious and plausible' hypothesis designed to explain, in physiological terms, the association of ideas: "Twou'd have been easy to have made an imaginary dissection of the brain, and have shewn, why upon our conception of any idea, the animal spirits run into all the contiguous traces, and rouze up the other ideas, that are related to it' (*T* 60). Continuing, he gives an 'account' of the mistakes generated by the association of ideas:

> [A]s the mind is endow'd with a power of exciting any idea it pleases; whenever it dispatches the spirits into that region of the brain, in which the idea is plac'd; these spirits always excite the idea, when they run precisely into the proper traces, and rummage that cell, which belongs to the idea. But as their motion is seldom direct, and naturally turns a little to the one side or the other; for this reason the animal spirits, falling into the contiguous traces, present other related ideas in lieu of that, which the mind desir'd at first to survey. (*T* 60–1)

There are problematic aspects of this excursion into antique physiology.[4] The crucial point, however, is clear. Hume assumes that there is a physiological basis for the regularities captured by his psychological laws of the association of ideas. Since these laws are alleged to explain the occurrence of most ideas, however, it must follow that, for Hume, most ideas have physiological causes.

Several simplifying extensions suggest themselves. If Hume's theory admits physiological causes for most ideas it is simplified if extended to all. In any case he must assume that any ideas not explainable by the principles of association have *some* cause. What candidates, other than physiological ones, could present themselves to Hume?[5] If he admits a physiological basis for the association of ideas, his overall associationist theory is simplified if a similar basis is assigned for the associationist laws governing the passions. This would not entail that all passions have a physiological explanation, for the 'primary' passions[6] are not, according to Hume, governed by the laws of association. But, once again, if most passions have physiological causes, simplification is achieved if one assumes that all do. And surely some of these 'primary' passions, for example hunger and lust, are thought to be physiologically caused. These simplifying extensions are countenanced by the general thesis, noted at the start, 'that motion . . . actually is, the cause of thought and perception' (*T* 248).

I have focused on the direct and physiological causation of passions and ideas. Obviously, if one broadens the framework to include indirect causation, there is further evidence of Hume's belief in the physical causation of passions and ideas. It is more illuminating, however, to notice two wider considerations which must lead Hume to the view that the occurrence of many passions and ideas is physiologically caused. I discuss each of these extensively elsewhere, so I shall, here, be brief.[7]

The first consideration is this. Hume claims that the mind is a system of causally related perceptions. He also holds that a mind is a discontinuous entity in that there are periods during its existence when it is unconscious, when it has no perceptions. In addition he holds that a cause and its effect are temporally contiguous; if a purported cause and its effect are not temporally contiguous they must, if causally connected, be linked by a continuous series of contiguous causes and effects. Putting these points together we can see Hume's need to admit physical, presumably physiological, causal links between the perceptions occurring before and after any gap in consciousness. There must be such links on the assumptions that there is no substantial self distinct from its perceptions, and that the relevant class of possible linking events includes only psychological and physiological ones. Obviously it would not follow that every occurrence of a passion or idea is physiologically caused, but it would follow that some are.

The second consideration concerns the use Hume makes of dispositional properties in his account of mind. Crucially, these include traits of character, the possession of concepts, the ability to use language, the knowledge of causal connections and, in general, the retention of what one has learned or experienced. Hume tends to offer a reductionist analysis of such properties. As I shall argue later, however, he must, and in fact does, take a non-reductionist line when he employs these properties in his causal explanation of what goes on in the mind. To put the point too crudely he must and does treat dispositional properties as causes. But it is clear that he cannot, and does not, construe these causal properties as perceptions. Adopting a fairly weak assumption about his ontology we can see that the possession of dispositional properties must involve the possession of relatively long-term physical, specifically physiological, properties. These long-term physiological properties are needed to explain such things as recollection, expectation, sense perception (so far as it involves more than mere sensation), the employment of abstract ideas, desires, intentions and volitions. And this is to say they are required for the causal explanation of many occurrences of passions and ideas.

So much for the action of body on mind. Let us turn to the question of psychophysical causality running from mind to body. The clear case is that of volitions involved in bodily actions. According to Hume, volitions are involved in any intentional action we perform, whether the action be a bodily or a purely mental one.[8] '[B]y the *will*, I mean nothing but *the internal impression we feel and are conscious of, when we knowingly give rise to any new motion of our body, or new perception of our mind*' (T 399).[9] In the case of a bodily action there is, Hume says, a causal connection between 'an act of volition, and a motion of the body' (T 632). In the first *Enquiry* he spells out the specifically physiological effects of volitions:

> We learn from anatomy, that the immediate object of power in voluntary motion, is not the member itself which is moved, but certain muscles, and nerves, and animal spirits, and, perhaps, something still more minute and more unknown, through which the motion is successively propagated, ere it reach the member itself whose motion is the immediate object of volition . . . Here the mind wills a certain event: Immediately another event, unknown to ourselves, and totally different from the one intended, is produced: This event produces another, equally unknown: Till at last, through a long succession, the desired event is produced. (E 66)

Of course there are limitations: 'the will [has] an influence over the tongue and fingers, not over the heart or liver' (E 65).

There is not much direct textual evidence that, in Hume's view, perceptions other than the volitions that give rise to bodily movements have direct physiological effects. The physiological basis of the association of ideas does, of course, commit Hume to claiming that those ideas that cause other ideas via association also have physiological effects. And he says as much: 'upon our conception of any idea, the animal spirits run into all the contiguous traces'; 'the mind is endow'd with a power of exciting any idea it pleases . . . it dispatches the spirits into that region of the brain, in which the idea is plac'd' (T 60–1). At one or two places he *seems* to say that some passions have physiological effects: he mentions the 'emotion [which] the poetical enthusiasm may give to the spirits' (T 630), and says that a passion experienced in an aesthetic context 'has no other than the agreeable effect of exciting the spirits, and rouzing the attention' (T 631).

Despite the dearth of compelling textual evidence we may legitimately make use of extensions and wider considerations similar to those employed earlier. If the association of ideas involves mental causation of physiological events it is likely that the same is true of the associations that give rise to the passions. If perceptions immediately before and after gaps in consciousness are to be causally linked, there must be physiological effects of the former as well as physiological causes of the latter. When dispositional properties are acquired then, given Hume's general conception of things, one's relevant past perceptions must have the physiological effect of leaving traces in the brain and central nervous system. This would hold for the acquisition of traits of character, for the retention of what one has learned or experienced in the past, and for the specific ability to recall one's past experiences, whether one's sensations, one's passions, or one's ideas. But if some perceptions from each of Hume's three sub-classes have physiological effects, his theory of the mind achieves a much simpler form if he assumes that all do. Similar remarks apply to the volitions involved in purely mental actions.

Once again, if one broadens the frame of reference to include indirect causation there is ample further textual evidence for the view that mind acts on body.

To sum up this for the most part textual investigation, there is no serious question that Hume is an interactionist. It is a sufficient condition of his being an interactionist that a philosopher holds that *some* psychological events have physical causes and that *some* have physical effects. (It is not necessary to hold that any psychological events have physical events as both cause and effect.) On this, admittedly weak, criterion the evidence from the cases of sensation and volition confirms my interpretation. Can we go further than this? There is strong textual evidence that, in Hume's view, *all* perceptions have physiological *causes*. It is not, on the other hand, clear that he is committed to the position that *all* perceptions have physiological *effects*. To be sure he *could* hold this view: there is nothing in his general philosophy to prevent his doing so. But we have so far been concerned to determine only what Hume actually thinks on the question.

4. Having discovered what Hume actually thinks let us now move to the construction of a Generalized Humean Theory (GHT) of mind-body interaction. GHT is a generalized theory in two ways: it provides a comprehensive articulated interactionist theory, and it takes every perception to have both physiological causes and physiological effects. GHT is minimally Humean in that it is compatible with the main elements of Hume's general philosophy. That it *is* Humean in this minimal sense is itself a salutary thing to notice. But GHT is Humean in a somewhat stronger sense as well. It is not obviously Hume's own way of viewing the relation of mind to body: he does not pursue questions of mind-body interaction far enough to be forced to take a stand on such a theory as GHT. But GHT is constructible from a basis for the most part provided by what Hume says about psychophysical interaction and about the analysis of causality. This is so only for the most part. At several points I shall introduce further assumptions or read Hume's claims about inter-action in a way clearly stronger than he intends. I shall indicate where

this occurs. The point of this constructive exercise is not to reproduce Hume's views but to conduct a philosophically useful thought experiment along lines that Hume marks out.

Hume is, I have argued, committed to the proposition:

(1) All perceptions have physiological causes.

The considerations I have advanced suggest, although they do not require, that he also subscribes to the proposition:

(2) All perceptions have physiological effects.

Let us assume that he does subscribe to (2). In addition, however, he holds:

(3) Some perceptions have psychological causes;

and

(4) Some perceptions have psychological effects.

His five laws of association are designed to specify the psychological causes of many perceptions, that is, most ideas and most passions, and this implies, of course, that some perceptions have psychological effects. He does not think that all perceptions have psychological causes: witness what we have already seen about sensations. It is likely that he thinks that some perceptions do not have psychological effects; that some have no *direct* psychological effects is a consequence of his belief about gaps in consciousness. Let us assume that the causal relations in (1) to (4) are direct, that is to say, do not require intervening causal links. For (1) and (2) this is reasonable since physiological, not merely bodily or external, causes and effects are in question. For (3) and (4) it is the most reasonable rendering of what Hume says about associative connections.

We have already noted Hume's claim that cause and effect are temporally contiguous. Two further assumptions about his analysis of causality, at least for ideal scientific contexts, appear to be legitimate. First, he holds a nomological theory of causality: if a singular causal statement is true it follows that a causal law is true.[10] Second, Hume holds that a causal law states the necessary and sufficient conditions for the occurrence of an event of a given kind. Thus, he gives as the fourth of his 'rules by which to judge of causes and effects':

> The same cause always produces the same effect, and the same effect never arises but from the same cause. This principle we derive from experience, and is the source of most of our philosophical reasonings. For when by any clear experiment we have discover'd the causes or effects of any phaenomenon, we immediately extend our observation to every phaenomenon of the same kind, without waiting for that constant repetition, from which the first idea of this relation is deriv'd. (*T* 173–4)

These assumptions may be taken as interpretations of Hume's remarks about constant conjunction.

Given these assumptions about Hume's analysis of causality, together with propositions (1) to (4) as we have construed them, two consequences follow. First, every perception that is causally related to another perception must be governed by causal laws, biconditional in form, and of three distinct kinds: exclusively psychological, psychophysiological, and doubly psychophysiological. Consider a perception that falls under the scope of proposition (3). Such a perception must be governed by an exclusively psychological law stating that a necessary and sufficient condition for the occurrence of a perception of its kind is the prior occurrence of another perception of a certain kind. It must also be governed by a psychophysiological law stating that a necessary and sufficient condition for the occurrence of a perception of its kind is the prior occurrence of a physiological event of a certain kind. It follows that the perception must also be governed by a doubly psychophysiological law, that is, a law giving as a necessary and sufficient condition for the occurrence of a perception of the kind in question the prior occurrence of both a perception of a certain kind and a physiological event of a certain kind. If explanation is, as Hume seems to think, a matter of showing that an event falls under a causal law, we have three alternative laws with which to explain the perception in question. In such a case we may say that the perception has a psychological cause, that it has a physiological cause, and that it has a psychological-cum-physiological cause. Similar results can be derived for the case of perceptions that cause other perceptions, as well as for perceptions that both are caused by, and cause, other perceptions.

The second consequence is this. Any perception that is either cause or effect of another perception must be correlated by a psychophysiological law with a co-temporary physiological event of a certain kind (of that kind, namely, that is mentioned in the relevant psychophysiological causal law). Such a correspondence law will state that the occurrence of a perception of its kind is a necessary and sufficient condition for the co-temporary occurrence of a physiological event of a certain kind. Such correspondence laws are to be construed as logically contingent in character. Given Hume's rule that a cause must precede its effect, these correspondence laws, though logically contingent, are not causal laws. Corresponding perceptions and physiological events are to be viewed as joint causes (effects) of the immediately succeeding (prior) items, whether perceptions or physiological events or conjunctions of these, to which they are linked by specifically causal laws.

We may now add three propositions to our Humean list:

(5) Some perceptions (all those covered by (3)) have psychophysiological causes.

(6) Some perceptions (all those covered by (4)) have psychophysiological effects;
and

(7) Some perceptions (all those covered by either (3) or (4)) stand in one-to-one correlations with co-temporary physiological events.

Let us go two steps further. First, let us replace (7) by the stronger:

(7′) All perceptions stand in one-to-one correlations with co-temporary physiological events.

This merely extends the notion of one-to-one correlation, or of psycho-physiological correspondence laws, to those perceptions, if there are any, that are neither causes of, nor caused by, other perceptions (and that thus fall under no exclusively psychological causal laws). (7′) does not follow from what has gone before but its introduction renders the overall interactionist theory a simpler one.

To complete the construction of GHT let us add:

(8) Some, but not all, physiological events stand in one-to-one correlations with co-temporary perceptions.

Given Hume's admission of gaps in consciousness, (8) is merely a consequence of what has gone before.

Implicit in this construction of GHT is a reading of propositions (1) to (4) that is much stronger than Hume intends. I have taken (1) to (4) to be interpretable in terms of the stringent demands imposed by the analysis of causality that Hume endorses for ideal scientific contexts. Specifically, I have taken the causes referred to (whether physiological or psychological) to be both necessary and sufficient conditions for their effects. Even at his most scientific, however, as when he proposes his own associationist laws, Hume cannot think he has met such very stringent demands. But although Hume *may* not subscribe to propositions (1) to (4) thus stringently construed there is nothing in his general philosophy that implies that he *must* not.

Or is there? It may seem that Hume rules out the possibility of conjoining, say, (1), (3) and (5), that is, of allowing that a perception may be governed by alternative causal laws. For he gives as his fifth 'rule by which to judge of causes and effects': 'where several different objects produce the same effect, it must be by means of some quality, which we discover to be common amongst them' (*T* 174). But one must distinguish the claim made by the conjunction of (1), (3) and (5) from the claim that a perception is sometimes caused by another perception, sometimes by a physiological event, and sometimes by a psychological-cum-physiological event. It is only the latter claim, involving multiplicity of causes, that falls foul of Hume's rule.

Can Hume allow logically contingent non-causal laws of the kind I am calling correspondence laws? He says: 'of those three relations [identity, situation in time or place, causation] which depend not upon the mere ideas, the only one, that can be trac'd beyond our senses, and informs us of existences and objects, which we do not see or feel, is *causation*' (*T* 74). On some reasonable assumptions, this implies that, for Hume, all empirical laws are causal ones. So far as the *Treatise* goes the objection must be granted. But its force can be blunted by noting that his apparent rejection of non-causal empirical laws stems from a remediable defect in his initial account of empirical relations, and that his principal doctrines concerning empirical laws are clearly compatible with the notion of non-causal ones. Hume's neglect of these seems to be an oversight, not a fundamental matter of doctrine. He sees things more clearly in the first *Enquiry*:

> If we anatomize all the other reasonings of this nature [reasonings concerning matter of fact], we shall find that they are founded on the relation of cause and effect, and that this relation is either near or remote, direct or collateral. Heat and light are collateral effects of fire, and the one effect may justly be inferred from the other. (*E* 27)

5. The fact that Hume can adopt GHT stands him in good stead. For one thing, it allows him to admit the possibility of what may be called 'the completeness of physiology'. Keith Campbell claims that, given recent advances in brain physiology, it is very likely that 'for explaining events in the brain, physiology is, in principle, complete'.[11] He envisages the possibility of explaining every brain happening by purely physical laws, that is, laws referring only to physical events and states. Given a complete physiology every brain event would 'follow recognized physical laws'[12] and no brain event would involve a 'departure from physical law'.[13] It is clear that GHT can satisfy this requirement: although it denies that all physiological events are governed exclusively by physical laws it asserts that all physiological events are governed by exclusively physical laws.

While it is scientifically plausible in this sense, GHT is an interactionist theory admitting the action of mind on body and of body on mind. For it maintains that all perceptions have physiological causes (thus far agreeing with epiphenomenalism) and that all perceptions have physiological effects (thus departing from epiphenomenalism). It hence accords with common sense.

GHT nonetheless permits the formulation of exclusively psychological laws. Although it denies that psychological events are governed exclusively by psychological laws it holds that many are governed by exclusively psychological laws. On GHT it is a matter of choice whether, in a given situation and assuming the requisite knowledge, one explains a psychological event by a psychological law, a physiological law, or even a doubly psychophysiological one. Given Hume's objectives in the *Treatise* this is a very useful feature of GHT; for he compartmentalizes the sciences and for the most part restricts his attention to formulation of the exclusively psychological laws of association – a perfectly legitimate methodological restriction.

GHT will further enable Hume to dissipate a certain bafflement that a man of 'enlightened common sense' (to use Broad's expression) might feel in this area. For GHT permits one to speak with the Humean psychologist and with the physiologist, as well as with the plain man. To say that the pain caused me to move my hand from the stove, or that the desire for revenge caused me to decide as I did, is to say nothing that need embarrass the physiologist.

G H T will assist Hume in the formulation of the determinist position he defends in both the *Treatise* and the first *Enquiry*. It will also enable him to deal with problems generated by admitted gaps in consciousness, by the causal role assigned to dispositional properties, and by the inexplicability (from the side of Humean psychology) of sensations.

One can recognize the advantages that accrue to Hume if he adopts G H T without having to assume that he is a dualist. So far as G H T goes he could be a physicalist. Indeed the correspondence laws that G H T requires are precisely those whose possibility is often assumed by contemporary physicalists. Since I have yet to argue that Hume *is* a dualist it is well to recognize this fact.

G H T is not, however, without significant difficulties. Some would object that the purported psychophysical laws may not, properly speaking, be called laws. Psychophysical laws, unlike physical ones, purport to correlate phenomena of relative simplicity (psychological events) with phenomena of staggering complexity (brain events). The purported laws cannot be derivative for they are not capable of revealing any causal mechanism; they cannot be fundamental for they are incapable of mathematical formulation. If admitted they would be 'nomological danglers': laws falling outside the otherwise inclusive and unitary body of physical science. Hume's reply to such objections is contained in his defence of the logical possibility of psychophysical causation. To adapt his maxim to the present case: 'A priori, instances of any kind of thing may be lawfully correlated with instances of any other kind of thing'. Whether there are lawful correlations of mental and physical events depends simply on whether there are appropriate constant conjunctions. Additionally, he might argue that some of the conditions imposed beg the question by requiring laws to have properties that only exclusively physical laws could have.[14]

Others attack the notion of psychophysical laws in other ways. Putnam argues that, if psychological predicates are understood in a properly functionalist way, there are no prospects for securing the kind of psychological/physiological correlations required for psychophysical laws. Functionally identical mental states may be realized in various physiological as well as non-physiological ways.[15] Donald Davidson argues[16] from the holistic character of the mental, and especially the fact that 'the attribution of mental phenomena must be responsible to the background of reasons, beliefs, and intentions of the individual',[17] to the conclusion that psychophysical laws are in principle impossible to secure. Hume might attempt to meet *these* objections by rejecting the highly controversial premises on which they rest, namely functionalism and holism, as incompatible with his own radically empiricist account of perceptions. The adequacy of such a defence of G H T could, of course, be no greater than that of Hume's characterization of psychological occurrences. This last is a question for chapters 6 and 7.[18]

6. It is time to make out my case for Hume's being a mind-body dualist. I shall do this by examining the arguments which might be offered in support of various non-dualist interpretations. There are four principal ones. On three of these Hume adopts a monistic position, reducing mind to matter, or matter to mind, or both matter and mind to some neutral stuff. On the remaining alternative Hume's scepticism proscribes any constructive position about mind, body and their inter-relation. If these accounts are found wanting we shall have compelling reason to take at face value the dualism to which Hume subscribes in both the *Treatise* and the first *Enquiry*.

There is no question of Hume's not reducing mind to matter in a be-haviourist way. Having noted some difficulties in using an introspective method in psychology, he does say in the 'Introduction' to the *Treatise*: 'We must glean up our experiments in this science from a cautious observation of human life, and take them as they appear in the common course of the world, by men's behaviour in company, in affairs, and in their pleasures' (*T* xxiii). But this has a merely methodological, not a metaphysical, force. More plausible is the suggestion that Hume inclines towards the view of modern identity theorists who hold that all per-ceptions (to use Hume's term) are identical with states or occurrences in the brain or central nervous system.

One can find apparent textual support for this reading. When offering his conjecture about the physiological basis of the association of ideas Hume writes of the mind's 'dispatch[ing] the spirits into that region of the brain, in which the idea is plac'd' (*T* 60–1). Discussing the logical possibility of psychophysical causation he maintains that it is *not* 'absurd to imagine, that motion in a circle . . . shou'd be nothing but merely motion in a circle; while motion in another direction, as in an ellipse, shou'd also be a passion or moral reflexion' (*T* 246). Elsewhere he is led to say: 'Bodily pains and pleasures . . . arise originally in the soul, or in the body, whichever you please to call it' (*T* 276). He also argues explicitly for the anti-Cartesian thesis that 'there are impressions and ideas really extended' (*T* 240), and extension, for Hume, implies spatial location. And if he *were* to adopt G H T it might prove very tempting to think along materialist lines in the contemporary manner.

I am not persuaded by these considerations; for the textual evidence is very far from compelling. As we shall see, the obscure remark about bodily pains and pleasures can take a dualist reading. The remarks about absurdity are especially misleading. Their context is an argument to the logical possibility of psychophysical *causality*; and causality, for Hume, requires logically independent, non-identical, items as cause and effect. His point is that there is no absurdity in the suggestion that elliptical motion *causes* a passion or moral reflexion. In its context what seems to be the language of identity ought to be understood as one understands the causal statement 'To pull that plug is to sink the boat'.

The other texts may seem more intractable, for the first suggests that ideas are located in the brain, and the other allows ideas to be extended, hence locatable. Properly interpreted, however, they provide no grounds for a physicalist reading. For Hume insists that some 'perceptions, so far from requiring any particular place, are absolutely incompatible with it' (*T* 236); that many ideas may, indeed must, '*exist, and yet be no where*' (*T* 235). *Such* ideas, within a Humean framework, cannot be in the brain. In any case the extension and spatial location that Hume allows to some ideas is the extension and location of what is imaged. When he says that 'the idea of extension . . . is extended' (*T* 240) he means, for example, that if one is imaging a cathedral one's idea has the shape of a cathedral; the location in question is the imaged location of the cathedral. For the passage to support location in the brain Hume would need rather to think of ideas as having the shape and location of the postulated animal spirits or of some other physiological entities, and this he does not do. He urges caution on the matter of location, and claims that we sometimes assign spatial location to items that, taken strictly, cannot possess it. Interestingly, we make such secondary ascriptions in virtue of the spatial location of the causes of the naturally but illegitimately located items (*T* 237). Perhaps Hume indulges this natural propensity in his own remarks about the location of ideas in the brain. Perhaps by 'that region of the brain, in which the idea is plac'd' he means merely that region the excitation of which is causally responsible for the occurrence of the idea in question.

In chapter 5 we shall consider Hume's views about identity, but we may anticipate that discussion to notice two points of special interest in the present connection. Hume takes all identity statements to be contingent. To this extent the prospect of a materialist interpretation along modern lines is promising. But Hume also takes all identity statements to be serial: the terms of the identity relation must exist at different times. He is clearly mistaken in this. Be that as it may, he can not consistently allow the identity of co-temporary perceptions and physiological states. Given seriality, he must eschew mind-brain identity.

Is Hume a subjective idealist, one who thinks matter can be reduced to mind? Though the passage is not unambiguous Ayer appears to read him in this way: 'Hume, who saw no grounds for holding that anything existed but sensory impressions and the ideas which copied them, may . . . be regarded . . . as having tried to effect the reduction of body to mind'.[19] As a rigorously empiricist successor to Berkeley, it may be said, Hume can admit in his ontology only what is left over when God and minds are excised from Berkeley's catalogue of things, namely, perceptions. That, it may be said, is just the point of the sceptical argument at *Treatise* 1 iv 2. Certainly one premise of Hume's sceptical argument is that one has direct access only to one's own perceptions. Also,

Hume rejects the notion of substrates in the case of both bodies and minds. And he does claim that "tis impossible for us so much as to conceive or form an idea of any thing specifically different from ideas and impressions' (*T* 67).

This account of the matter is riddled with confusions and rests on a foundation of quite unwarranted assumptions. One must not confuse epistemological idealism, the doctrine that the only things one directly perceives are mental, with the metaphysical doctrine, which I call subjective idealism, that only mental things exist. Hume is an epistemological idealist. But it does not follow that he adopts an idealist metaphysics. As we saw in chapter 1, he purports to give an irrefutable argument to the conclusion that there are no physical objects in the plain man's sense. But we also saw that, in his view, one simply cannot accept that conclusion. His arguments are, as he says, like those of *Berkeley*: *'they admit of no answer and produce no conviction'* (*E* 155n). What one cannot believe are the specifically idealist elements in Berkeley's metaphysics.

But does not Hume claim that belief in independent physical objects is unintelligible? Not at all. As we have seen, his sceptical argument takes the belief to be intelligible even if provably false. And the point of the passage cited above is not that items other than perceptions are unintelligible but that one can make no sense of objects that do not possess properties of the kind that perceptions are observed to possess, such as colour, shape and smell. That is the point of Hume's stress on *specific* difference. Thinking, presumably, of Locke Hume says: 'The farthest we can go towards a conception of external objects, when suppos'd *specifically* different from our perceptions, is to form a relative idea of them, without pretending to comprehend the related objects' (*T* 68, *Hume's* italics). Going on to characterize the plain man's view he says: 'Generally speaking we do not suppose them specifically different; but only attribute to them different relations, connexions and durations' (*T* 68). Hume, of course, rejects the notion of material *substrates* as unintelligible, but it does not follow from this, nor is there any reason to think Hume believes it to follow, that there are no independent physical objects or that the idea of such objects makes no sense.

The evidence for his interactionism is also evidence against an idealist reading of Hume. This is not to say that an interactionist theory cannot be accommodated within an idealist metaphysics. I am thinking, rather, of the specific causal claims Hume makes, where the intended causes are clearly not perceptions: the non-psychological causes of sensations, for example, the causation that underpins one's identity through gaps in consciousness, and the causation involved in the possession of dispositional properties. Again and again Hume refers to causes of which one is not conscious. And he does not have Berkeley's God to take up the slack.

If he is not a subjective idealist is Hume perhaps a neutral monist in the manner of James or of Russell? Does he reduce both mind and matter to a common neutral stuff? James illustrates his thesis by saying of what he calls the 'pure experience' of a room:

> [T]he experience is a member of diverse processes that can be followed away from it along entirely different lines. The one self-identical thing has so many relations to the rest of experience that you can take it in disparate systems of association, and treat it as belonging with opposite contexts. In one of these contexts it is your 'field of consciousness'; in another it is 'the room in which you sit,' and it enters both contexts in its wholeness, giving no pretext for being said to attach itself to consciousness by one of its parts or aspects, and to outer reality by another. What are the two processes, now, into which the room-experience simultaneously enters in this way?

> One of them is the reader's personal biography, the other is the history of the house of which the room is part. The presentation, the experience, the *that* in short (for until we have decided *what* it is it must be a mere *that*) is the last term of a train of sensations, emotions, decisions, movements, classifications, expectations, etc., ending in the present, and the first term of a series of similar 'inner' operations extending into the future, on the reader's part. On the other hand, the very same *that* is the *terminus ad quem* of a lot of previous physical operations, carpentering, papering, furnishing, warming, etc., and the *terminus a quo* of a lot of future ones, in which it will be concerned when undergoing the destiny of a physical room.[20]

In his essay 'On Propositions: What They Are and How They Mean' Russell amends James's 'view that the mental and the physical are not distinguished by the stuff of which they are made, but only by their causal laws',[21] in effect adopting a qualified neutral monism. According to Russell:

> [W]hen we come to consider the stuff of the two sciences [psychology and physics], it would seem that there are some particulars which obey only physical laws (namely, unperceived material things), some which obey only psychological laws (namely, images, at least), and some which obey both (namely, sensations). Thus sensations will be both physical and mental, while images will be purely mental.[22]

Given what we have earlier seen Hume could not readily accept what Russell says of the various laws governing the several kinds of items distinguished. But does he hold *some such* view as that of James or Russell? In particular, does he hold the view that some so-called perceptions are neutral in character, being construable either as mental or as physical depending on the context of description and explanation? Commenting on a passage from the *Treatise* H. H. Price says that Hume 'here takes the current view that impressions of sense are mental events',[23] but goes on immediately to say that 'according to his developed theory of the self they are neither mental nor physical, but are the neutral elements out of which both selves and bodies are constructed'.[24]

There are three considerations that may support this reading of Hume. First, it may be suggested that Hume's bundle theory of the self entails neutral monism.[25] Second, neutral monism may be thought to follow from the fact that, in pursuance of a thoroughgoing empiricist programme to explain the acquisition of mental and physical concepts, Hume must postulate an original situation in which one is neutral regarding the items one encounters in experience.[26] It should be apparent that neutral monism follows from neither of these theses. Minds may be merely bundles of perceptions. But it does not follow that the constituents of such mental bundles are not numerically distinct from, and perhaps quite different from, bodies or the constituents of bodies. And the neutrality of the empiricist programme's starting point is not metaphysical but conceptual; its question is not whether one can derive a conception of minds and bodies from encounters with objects that are neither mental nor physical, but whether one can explain the acquisition of such a conception starting from a position in which one *takes* what one encounters neither as mental nor as physical because, by hypothesis, one does not yet possess the necessary concepts.

Still, there is one passage in the *Treatise* that may seem to commit Hume to some version of neutral monism. Its importance requires that it be given in full:

> [W]hat we call a *mind*, is nothing but a heap or collection of different perceptions, united together by certain relations, and suppos'd, tho' falsely, to be endow'd with a perfect simplicity and identity. Now as every perception is distinguishable from another, and may be consider'd as separately existent; it evidently follows, that there is no absurdity in separating any particular perception from the mind; that is, in breaking off all its relations, with that connected mass of perceptions, which constitute a thinking being . . . If the name of *perception* renders not this separation from a mind absurd and contradictory, the name of *object*, standing for the very same thing, can never render their conjunction impossible. External objects are seen, and felt, and become present to the mind; that is, they acquire such a relation to a connected heap of perceptions, as to influence them very considerably in augmenting their number by present reflexions and passions, and in storing the memory with ideas. The same continu'd and uninterrupted Being may, therefore, be sometimes present to the mind, and sometimes absent from it, without any real or essential change in the Being itself. An interrupted appearance to the senses implies not necessarily an interruption in the existence. The supposition of the continu'd existence of sensible objects or perceptions involves no contradiction. We

may easily indulge our inclination to that supposition. When the exact resemblance of our perceptions makes us ascribe to them an identity, we may remove the seeming interruption by feigning a continu'd being, which may fill those intervals, and preserve a perfect and entire identity to our perceptions. (*T* 207–8)

If this passage bears upon neutral monism at all, it amounts to no more than an admission of its logical possibility. In its context the point of the passage is to argue that the plain man's perceptual beliefs are not absurd. The plain man believes that some of the very things he perceives are physical objects whose existence does not depend on their being perceived. In Hume's view the very things the plain man perceives are perceptions: elements constitutive of minds. According to his bundle theory, however, these perceptions are logically capable of independent existence.[27] Thus Hume argues that the plain man's belief is not absurd; for it is indeed logically possible that the very things he perceives exist unperceived. Now this argument appears to commit Hume to the view that a given sensation could be a physical object, at least in the sense that it could exist unperceived. But it is, when perceived, a mental item. So the sort of thing that James and Russell say could, logically speaking, be true.

Admitting the logical possibility of neutral monism does not, however, commit Hume to endorsing the theory. In fact, he quickly goes on to argue in a way that commits him to its falsity. As we saw in chapter 1, he argues that perceptions do not in fact exist unperceived. So although sensations *could have been* independent they *are* not. The same goes for such other perceptions as passions and ideas, which in any case are unlikely candidates for construal on neutral monist lines.

The remaining non-dualist alternative is that Hume's scepticism bars him from holding *any* constructive views about mind, body and their relation. If my opening account of his scepticism is correct, however, this is simply not so. Rather, one must say that his scepticism bars Hume from holding any constructive views that are literally extra-ordinary. His brand of scepticism commits him to the plain man's metaphysics, or possibly to the metaphysics of enlightened common sense, which is that of the plain man with a tincture of experimental science. These metaphysical views are ineluctable or nearly so. So there is little or no question that they will in fact be held. Idealism, physicalism and neutral monism, by contrast, are extraordinary philo-sophical doctrines. Arguments in their support are necessarily suspect, and in competition with the metaphysics of the plain man they *must* quit the field. The metaphysics of the plain man or of enlightened common sense is, in Hume's view, a dualist metaphysics. It is also an inter-actionist one. Hume encounters grave difficulties in the detailed articula-tion of this common-sense metaphysics. But it is the metaphysics on which he settles. In his words:

[W]e find by the comparing their ideas, that thought and motion are

> different from each other, and by experience, that they are con-
> stantly united; which being all the circumstances, that enter into
> the idea of cause and effect . . . we may certainly conclude, that
> motion may be, and actually is, the cause of thought and per-
> ception. (*T* 248)

(Hume here omits mention of psychophysical causation from mind to body.)

7. Although Hume is a mind-body dualist one looks in vain to him for a developed philosophical account of the differences between the mental and the physical; between perceptions and the features of physical objects.

In the course of the elaborately paradoxical argument of *Treatise* I iv 5 ('Of the immateriality of the soul') he explicitly rejects one traditional criterion for the distinction, namely, that which takes the material to be essentially extended and the mental to be neither extended nor spatially locatable. In Hume's view, the distinction between the extended and the non-extended cuts across that between the material and the mental. Some perceptions, such as the passions, are neither extended nor locatable; but others, including visual and tactile sensations, are both. 'All our perceptions are not susceptible of a local union, either with what is extended or unextended; there being some of them of the one kind, and some of the other' (*T* 250). And some features of physical objects, their smells and tastes, for example, are like the passions in being neither extended nor locatable. To be sure, there are radical confusions in the arguments by which Hume reaches his conclusions: he quite mis-construes the relation between location and extension, and he commits himself to the absurd view that properties such as colour and shape may be univocally ascribed to both physical objects and perceptions. What-ever the defects in his arguments, however, he embraces their anti-Cartesian upshot.

Apart from these negative remarks Hume says little about the dualist distinction. He signals it by several reiterated pairs of expressions: 'moral philosophy' and 'natural philosophy' (*T* 175; compare *T* xix, 8, 275–6); 'moral phenomena' and 'natural phenomena' (*T* 136); the 'intellectual world' and the 'natural world' (*T* 232, 263). But each of these distinctions is made to rest on the prior distinction between per-ceptions and physical events, hence does nothing to advance the analysis. Hume's preferred contrast is that between the 'internal' and the 'external' (*T* 36, 108, 160, 240; *E* 47, 62, 63, 66, 74). This amounts to contrasting the modes of access one has to one's own perceptions, on the one hand, and to bodies and the perceptions of others, on the other. There is some suggestion, also, of an allied contrast in the epistemo-logical status of the respective beliefs. This is hardly surprising since the linked notions of privacy, privileged access and incorrigibility are well entrenched in this area. Hume's preferred criterion is not readily elaborated, however, since, as we shall see in chapter 7, there are grave difficulties both in the interpretation of his views on introspective awareness and in the views themselves.

At numerous places in the *Treatise* Hume insists on the limits to what can be known about mind. 'What is known concerning it [the intellectual world], agrees with itself; and what is unknown, we must be contented to leave so' (*T* 232). Again: '[T]he essence of the mind . . . [is] equally unknown to us with that of external bodies' (*T* xxi). Such remarks have an anti-rationalist point; they are designed to press the exclusive claims of 'experience and observation' (*T* xx). Clearly the desired demarcation of mind and body must meet this empiricist requirement. Equally clearly, the reader's desire for a Humean account of the demarcation goes largely unsatisfied.

CHAPTER THREE

Mental Dispositions

———

1.   I turn now to examine Hume's views about what I shall call 'mental dispositions', that is to say, the various capacities, abilities, powers, skills, qualities of intellect, habits, traits of character, tendencies and dispositions (in the ordinary sense) that we ascribe only to beings with minds. This investigation should shed further light on two topics discussed in the preceding chapter: the explanation of psychological phenomena, and the range and character of mind-body interaction. It will also prove useful in our subsequent discussion of other central topics in Hume's philosophy of mind.

I do not propose a full-dress examination of Hume's views on mental dispositions. In particular, characteristics of specific mental dispositions must be left to emerge in subsequent chapters. Here I want to concentrate on the fact that Hume endorses two inconsistent views of mental dispositions, a reductionist view, and a realist one. I shall begin by defending the ascription of each of these views to Hume, then canvass some of Hume's reasons for holding each view, and show that his reasons for being a reductionist are not compelling ones.

By 'reductionism' I mean the view that any apparently categorical sentence used to ascribe a mental disposition, for example, 'He is conscientious' or 'He knows how to speak French', can be exhaustively analysed into another sentence which is hypothetical in form. As I am using the term, a realist, while admitting that hypotheticals form part of the analysis of categorical sentences used to ascribe mental dispositions, would insist that an unanalysable categorical element must also appear in the analysis. I shall further explain the distinction as we proceed. Given recent associations between behaviourism and reductionist theories of mental dispositions, I must insist that, as I am using the term 'reductionist', a reductionist need not be a behaviourist. Surely Hume, if he is a reductionist, is a non-behaviourist one.

My way of marking the distinction between reductionist and realist has the unfortunate effect of imposing an unHumean linguistic character on the investigation. It has, however, the compensating advantages of brevity and clarity.

2.   Commenting on certain 'fictions of the antient philosophy' (*T* 219), Hume makes several remarks that suggest a reductionist theory of mental dispositions. He denies that such terms as 'faculty' and 'occult quality' have a 'secret meaning, which we might discover by reflection'

(*T* 224), that is, that they designate non-empirical or non-observable properties. At one point he even claims that these expressions are 'wholly insignificant and unintelligible' (*T* 224), although I doubt that he intends this literally. Presumably Hume would say of 'faculty', at least, what he earlier says of 'power', 'force', and 'necessary connexion': "tis more probable, that these expressions do here [that is, in certain philosophical theories] lose their true meaning by being *wrong apply'd*, than that they never have any meaning' (*T* 162). The problem is to give a satisfactory account of their meaning strictly in terms of what is observable.

Hume also objects to the use of the concepts of faculties, occult qualities and powers in scientific explanations. Part of his point is that terms such as 'faculty' and 'power' do not designate causal conditions mention of which explains what is to be explained. But his more general point is that such attempted explanations are vacuous. Speaking ironically of the 'antient philosophers' he says: 'They need only say, that any phaenomenon, which puzzles them, arises from a faculty or an occult quality, and there is an end of all dispute and enquiry upon the matter' (*T* 224). Talk of its dormitive power does nothing to explain the effects of opium. Nor does Smith's knowledge of French illuminate his successfully reading a copy of *Le Monde*.

Hume is most explicitly reductionist in his account of powers. 'The distinction', he writes, 'which we often make betwixt *power* and the *exercise* of it, is . . . without foundation' (*T* 171). '[P]ower consists in the possibility or probability of any action, as discover'd by experience and the practice of the world' (*T* 313). '[T]he only *known* difference' between two cases, in one of which we say that *a* cannot perform some action, and in the other of which we say *a* can, is that 'in the former case we conclude from *past experience*, that the person never will perform that action, and in the latter, that he possibly or probably will perform it' (*T* 312).

Several things need to be said about the theory expressed in these passages. First, it is not clear what Hume intends when he says that 'power *consists in* the possibility or probability of any action' (*T* 313, my italics). Given my linguistic way of construing the discussion I shall assume that this is roughly equivalent to: 'To ascribe a power to some entity is *to say nothing more than* that the entity will possibly or probably act in a certain way'.

Second, although Hume is not explicit about this, it is reasonably clear that the possibility or probability he talks of is *conditional*. Thus, I say that my enemy has the power to injure me if it is probable or possible that, given the opportunity and the lack of countervailing motives, he will do so (compare *T* 312).

Third, I do not think one should attach much weight to Hume's failure to include 'certainty' in the formula that expresses his theory of powers. Hume's reason for not doing so here is that there is usually an 'uncertainty of our judgment' (T 313) about the factors that govern a man's behaviour, and thus our expectations about his behaviour are 'attended with uncertainty' (T 124). But if there were not this uncertainty about the factors that govern his behaviour, one's expectations would be 'entirely free from doubt and uncertainty' (T 124). To talk of certainty in such matters, of course, is not to say that it is 'inconceivable' that the person should fail to do what we expect him to do. The certainty in question is not the certainty of what Hume calls 'knowledge' but that connected with what he calls 'proof' (T 124).[1]

Hume's reductionist theory of powers, then, amounts to this: to ascribe to a the power to perform some action is to say no more than that it is possible or probable or certain that, if certain conditions are satisfied, a will perform that action. Omitting the modal or epistemic terms, the point I want to fasten on is that the power is reduced, in a significant way, to a's actions or responses in the appropriate conditions. Consider the sentence forms:

(1) a has P.

(2) If conditions C obtain, a will respond in way R.

(1) provides the form for apparently categorical statements ascribing powers to individuals: statements such as 'Smith can speak French' or 'Jones knows the use of "gibbous"'. (2) provides the form for an overtly hypothetical statement indicating the conditions and response relevant to the power in question. The relation between C and R is to be construed as causal. On the reductionist account of powers that I am here ascribing to Hume, power ascriptions of form (1) are exhaustively analysable into statements of form (2); no overtly categorical statement remains once the analysis has taken place.

Extending what Hume says of faculties, occult qualities and powers to the other mental dispositions mentioned earlier, let us take the general form of statements ascribing mental dispositions to individuals to be:

(3) a has D.

We may now take Hume's reductionist theory of mental dispositions to be: any statement of form (3) may be replaced, without remainder, by a suitable statement of form (2). As nearly everyone who has written on the subject has noticed, the task of actually replacing categoricals with suitable hypotheticals is of herculean difficulty, if not quite impossible. But I shall pass over the problems this raises for a reductionist theory, since they also arise for a realist one.

If apparently categorical ascriptions of mental dispositions are in fact disguised hypotheticals, one role they may play in psychological explanations is that of providing what Ryle has called 'inference tickets'.[2] On such a view, to ascribe a mental disposition to some individual is to express a lawlike statement in terms of which one can both explain and, in principle, predict the psychological responses of that individual. The point to stress, however, is that the explanatory role of the dispositional statement is like that of a law, and not like that of a judgment that certain causal conditions obtain.|

Construed as disguised expressions of causal connection, dispositional statements are subject to the epistemological analysis that Hume applies to any causal statement. Their truth can only be 'discover'd by experience and the practice of the world' (*T* 313); not by 'reflection' (*T* 224). They go beyond the evidence, or the observations that support them, but only in the sense in which any general causal statement goes beyond the evidence; not in the sense of designating some unobserved or unobservable property that *is* the faculty or power or other mental disposition, as the 'antient philosophers' would claim.

3. Before defending my ascription of a realist view of mental dispositions to Hume, it would be well to spell out the principal elements of that view. As a realist, Hume is committed to the claim that an adequate analysis of a mental dispositional statement of form (3) must take the form:

(4) *a* has a more-or-less enduring non-dispositional property the possession of which causes *a* to respond in way *R* if conditions *C* obtain. Several things must be noticed about sentences of form (4). First, they contain an undissolved categorical element, namely, '*a* has a more-or-less enduring non-dispositional property'. It is this, primarily, that marks them off from sentences of form (2), and that thus distinguishes a realist from a reductionist theory of mental dispositions. Second, the view is that a sentence of form (4) *as a whole* replaces an apparently categorical sentence of form (3). It would be a crude mistake to think that a mere part of a sentence of form (4), the undissolved categorical part, replaces a sentence of form (3). To put the point in a different way, the realist does not reduce dispositional to non-dispositional properties. Keeping a firm grip on this fact will help us to avoid some common confusions in the area. Third, a sentence of form (4) contains a hypothetical element that is similar to, but not identical with, that in a sentence of form (2) above. For it contains, in effect, the hypothetical: if *a* has a certain more-or-less enduring non-dispositional property, and circumstances *C* obtain, *a* will respond in way *R*. As with sentences of form (2), this hypothetical expresses a lawlike statement giving (this will be qualified in a moment) causal conditions for *a*'s responding in way *R*.

A fourth, extremely important, point about sentences of form (4) is this: whereas they do specify the circumstances and the response appropriate to a given disposition, they do not specify the more-or-less enduring non-dispositional property ascribed to *a*. The analysis is neutral at that point. Knowing that *a* has a dispositional property *D* one knows *that a* has a non-dispositional property the possession of which explains its responding as it does in circumstances *C*. But *what* specifically that non-dispositional property is, is a matter not for analysis but for empirical enquiry.[3]

Hume's realism about mental dispositions is apparent in his discussion of abstract ideas and general terms. A person who knows the meaning of a general term is said to have acquired a certain 'custom' (*T* 20) or 'habit' (*T* 21); to have 'collected' together those resembling 'ideas' that are associated with the general term in question (*T* 20). These ideas 'are not really and in fact present to the mind, but only in power' (*T* 20). Given acquisition of the custom or habit, the appropriate stimulus, for example, hearing the word, 'raises up an individual idea' (*T* 21). The same stimulus is said to 'revive' the custom or habit, which in turn 'produces' or 'suggests' those other ideas 'for which we may have occasion' (*T* 21). Clearly, these customs or habits are thought to be enduring states of the person to whom they are ascribed. Together with the stimuli indicated they cause certain psychological responses. They are apparently not conscious states but partial causes of certain conscious events. The term 'custom' is perhaps misleading; but it refers not merely to the conditioning process whereby the person acquired the ability in question but also to that enduring state of the individual, also called a 'habit', that results from the conditioning process. Significantly, Hume is puzzled by the customs and habits he invokes here, and expresses this when he talks of 'those very ideas, that are thus collected by a kind of *magical faculty* in the soul' (*T* 24, my italics).[4]

Hume gives an analogous account of moral virtues and character. He distinguishes moral virtues from 'the actions that proceed from them' (*T* 609), and a man's character from those of his actions that are 'sign[s]' or 'indications' of it (*T* 575). In morality, we should consider 'only the quality or character from which the action proceeded' because 'these alone are *durable* enough to affect our sentiments concerning the person' (*T* 575). These 'durable principles of the mind' (*T* 575) are explicitly described as causes, and may exist without having their usual effects if the other necessary conditions are lacking. A man may have a certain 'character, even tho' particular accidents prevent its operation' (*T* 584); his character may fail of its usual effects if there are 'some circumstances wanting to render the cause a compleat one' (*T* 585). In his discussion of the free-will problem Hume criticizes the libertarian for not recognizing that actions cannot be blamed if 'they proceed not from some cause in the characters and disposition of the person, who perform'd them' (*T* 411). Even when a spectator fails to grasp the connection between our character and our actions he judges, rightly, that there is such a connection, and that it would be discoverable 'were he perfectly acquainted with every circumstance of our situation and temper, and the most secret springs of our complexion and disposition' (*T* 408–9).[5]

4. On the face of it, then, there is a serious inconsistency in Hume's expressed views about mental dispositions. To be sure, there are ways in which one can attempt to show that the appearances are merely that. Such whitewashing efforts carry little conviction, however. And it is philosophically much more interesting to try to pin down the reasons

Hume could have for being, on the one hand, a reductionist, and on the other, a realist, about mental dispositions. Let us begin with reductionism.

One possible source of his reductionism is Hume's hard-nosed empiricist theory of meaning. In the opening section of the *Treatise* he lays down his rule about the priority of impressions over ideas: there can be no simple idea without a corresponding, and prior, simple impression; nor can there be a complex idea the simple components of which do not satisfy the rule for simple ideas. Given Hume's views about the relationship between general ideas and the general terms in a language, the meaning of such a term is ultimately a function of the impressions from which one derives the general idea to which the term is linked by association.[6] To explicate the meaning of a complex general term then, one must indicate or specify that complex set of impressions that governs its meaning. Crucially, in specifying those impressions one exhausts the meaning of the general term in question. In somewhat different terminology, the meaning of a complex general term is exhausted by a description of the observations that determine its application. The account is, of course, intended to cover the subclass of complex general terms that now interests us, namely, the various terms designating mental dispositions. But the principal mistake of the 'antient philosophers', on Hume's account, was their contention that dispositional terms designate properties of whose presence one learns by 'reflection', not by observation (including introspection). Clearly, Hume's meaning-empiricism is inconsistent with this 'secret meaning' view. But it is also easy to see that his meaning-empiricism would make Hume very suspicious of the more cautious realist analysis spelled out in the previous section; for when analysing mental dispositional terms the realist requires the introduction of properties with which one may very well not be acquainted. On the realist view, one may know the meaning of 'conscientious', say, or of 'knows French', without knowing what property it is that explains conscientious conduct or the successful perusal of *Le Monde*.

Certain central features of his views about causality and explanation also push Hume in a reductionist direction. A causal generalization (in this case the embedded causal hypothetical about the individual a) in which one of the crucial causal conditions goes unspecified is hardly a typical Humean causal generalization; there is little point to a statement of constant conjunction in which one of the alleged conjuncts is unidentified. It is not possible to support a causal generalization of this kind, in a typically Humean manner, by observing the conjunction of tokens of two types of objects or events. And a purported explanation of a's response in terms of an unspecified property that a possesses is, of course, no explanation at all. This is merely to fill out Hume's point, mentioned earlier, about the vacuous explanations of the 'antient philosophers'. But the difficulties appear to be present also in the realist theory of the previous section. For although one may know what the non-dispositional property in question is, one need not. And on the realist account this lack of knowledge would not prevent one's making, meaningfully and with suitable justification, the partially causal statement that *a* has a given mental disposition. Nor would it prevent one's invoking mental dispositions in explanations of an individual's responses. So it can seem once again that, on Humean grounds, one must eschew the unspecified non-dispositional properties of the realist and make do with a reductionist analysis.

Hume's dualist model of the mind as a bundle of perceptions can also push him towards reductionism. The mind is, Hume says, 'nothing but a bundle or collection of different perceptions, which succeed each other with an inconceivable rapidity' (*T* 252). Let us assume, as a corollary, that for some item to be properly characterized as a mental item it must be a perception. But the dispositions in question are mental dispositions. It may seem to follow that the non-dispositional properties required by the realist analysis must themselves be perceptions. When one attempts to make sense of this suggestion, however, one runs aground. For one thing, the required non-dispositional properties are relatively long-lasting, while Humean perceptions are fleeting. For another, an individual may possess mental dispositions, and thus by hypothesis the requisite non-dispositional properties, even when he has no perceptions. A man continues to be conscientious when soundly asleep. Again, the realist theory admits that one may very well not know the non-dispositional property in question; may not be acquainted with it. If it is a perception, then, it must be possible to have perceptions of a kind with which one is unacquainted. It would be most surprising were Hume to admit such a possibility. All in all, if the realist's non-dispositional properties must be perceptions, Hume must resist the realist theory.

5. If certain important features of his views about causation and explanation constrain Hume to adopt a reductionist analysis of mental dispositions there are other elements in his thinking about these topics that push very forcefully in the opposite direction. Hume is, in fact, deeply committed to a version of the principle of sufficient reason. As is quite clear at many places in both the *Treatise* and the first *Enquiry*, especially the sections on determinism, he subscribes to the principle that every event has a cause, and to the consequence of this, that every event is in principle explicable. As I read Hume, to say that every event is in principle explicable is to say that for every event it is in principle possible both to formulate the empirical law that governs its occurrence and to locate a suitable token of that logically independent set of conditions that would be mentioned in the protasis of the law. Even if there is no known explanation of an event's occurrence there is an explanation to be found: 'chance or indifference lies only in our judgment on account

of our imperfect knowledge, not in the things themselves' (*T* 404). And he is committed to saying that if the conditions purportedly explaining an event of a certain kind can be present without an event of that kind's occurring, one does not have a genuine explanation. The sixth of his 'rules by which to judge of causes and effects' reads:

> The difference in the effects of two resembling objects must proceed from that particular, in which they differ. For as like causes always produce like effects, when in any instance we find our expectation to be disappointed, we must conclude that this irregularity proceeds from some difference in the causes. (*T* 174)[7]

We can see how this bears on Hume's account of mental dispositions by considering the response *R* that an individual *a* makes on a given occasion in circumstances *C*. Now it may seem that we secure a satisfactory explanation of *a*'s response, in the circumstances envisaged, by the (true) ascription of a certain character trait *T*. For, let us assume, a reductionist analysis of the sentence '*a* has *T*' would be: 'If *a* is in circumstances *C*, *a* will respond in way *R*'. So the trait ascription gives us a lawlike statement linking *C* and *R* for *a*'s case, and we already know that circumstances *C* obtain. But this must, from Hume's point of view, be importantly deficient, as can be brought out in various ways.

For one thing, the trait ascription provides us not with a law but merely with a lawlike statement covering only *a*'s responses and not those of the members of a suitable class of individuals. But, if my reading is correct, Hume requires laws for explanation. And if we were to replace this lawlike statement about *a* with a law, by suitable use of a bound variable and the universal quantifier, the result would be clearly false. Since the lawlike statement that is true of *a* is not true of every individual the fact that it *is* true of *a* must be explained. There must be something about *a*, other than that he is *a*, to explain the fact that in circumstances *C* he responds in way *R*. For there is no magic in the mere fact that he is *a*,[8] and in any case, we may assume, individuals other than *a*, but not all other individuals, have the character trait *T*. It is natural to think here of a non-dispositional property the possession of which, together with circumstances *C*, causes *a* to respond in way *R*. If one were to discover what that property is, for example, that it is property *M*, one would be on the way to producing an explanatory law having a chance of being true. The law would run: anything that is *M*, and that is in circumstances *C*, will respond in way *R*. It is considerations such as these, I suggest, that first prompt introduction of the realist's non-dispositional properties, and that lead Hume to talk of customs, habits, powers and the rest as causes of an individual's responses.

But even if one grants that something other than circumstances *C* must be included in the protasis of the law in question, why the seeming mystery-mongering of unspecified, enduring, non-dispositional properties? These seem suspiciously like the occult qualities of the 'antient philosophers'. Why not simply invoke some known, normally observable, kind-property of the entity or entities in question? The difficulties I have just raised for reductionist analyses of sentences such as 'He is conscientious' or 'He is phlegmatic' could be raised also for 'This is water-soluble'. But their straw man character would be displayed, it may be suggested, by replacing 'This is water-soluble' with 'This sugar is water-soluble'. Reference to the kind-property of being sugar enables one to replace the silly 'Anything placed in water will dissolve' with the at least tolerable 'Anything that is sugar and is placed in water will dissolve'. Now, there are general difficulties with this manoeuvre, but for the present it is sufficient to notice that it will not help in the special case of Hume's mental dispositions, such as traits of character or the ability to use some general term. For in such cases what normally observable kind-property would fit the bill? Not the kind-property of being a man, since one can be a man without having the trait or ability in question. And there are no other promising candidates. Hume himself mentions no plausible kind-property in the course of his own analysis. And he seems to believe, when in a realist frame of mind, that even if we cannot identify the requisite additional property of the responding subject we must assume it to be present. If we do not, we admit that its responses are inexplicable in theory as well as in practice.

But can we not produce more satisfactory explanatory laws for such cases by introducing not only normally observable kind-properties but also the conditioning or training undergone by an individual? Such laws might take the form: Any man conditioned in way O will, if in circumstances C, respond in way R. But this will not do the job as long as the purported law remains an empirical one. For two individuals with the same normally observable kind-properties may be conditioned in the same way, and be subjected to the same stimuli, yet differ in their responses. Or a given individual may possess an acquired trait or ability for a certain period of time, then lose it. A satisfactory law must be capable of accounting for the differing responses of similarly conditioned individuals, or for the differing responses of the same individual over a longish stretch of time. And it is difficult to see how these constraints can be met by a law mentioning only normally observable kind-properties and the training or conditioning of individuals of the kind in question.

A connected difficulty is raised by Hume's insistence that a cause must be temporally contiguous to its effect or linked to its effect by a continuous series of temporally contiguous causes and effects.

> [W]hatever objects are consider'd as causes or effects, are *contiguous*; and . . . nothing can operate in a time or place, which is ever so little remov'd from those of its existence. Tho' distant objects may sometimes seem productive of each other, they are commonly found upon examination to be link'd by a chain of causes, which are contiguous among themselves, and to the distant objects; and when in any particular instance we cannot discover this connexion, we

still presume it to exist. We may therefore consider the relation of CONTIGUITY as essential to that of causation. . . . (*T* 75)⁹

The requirement of temporal contiguity reappears in the two definitions of causality that Hume offers towards the end of *Treatise* I iii 14. It follows from the requirement that if past conditioning is to cause or to be part cause of present response there must be a temporally continuous causal series linking it to the response. That the same individual is involved does nothing to meet this requirement; nor does possession of some normally observable kind-property. If temporal continuity is mandatory, then, something in addition to past conditioning, normally observable kind-property and present stimulus is needed to explain the individual's responses.

Another feature of his views about explanation that could lead Hume to adopt a realist approach to mental dispositions is, to put it tendentiously, his deductivism. Hume appears to believe that the object of science is to discover extensive systems of laws the less general members of which are deductively related to the more general. In the first *Enquiry* he remarks that 'it is probable, that one operation and principle of the mind depends on another; which, again, may be resolved into one more general and universal' (*E* 14–15) and that 'the utmost effort of human reason is to reduce the principles, productive of natural phenomena, to a greater simplicity, and to resolve the many particular effects into a few general causes' (*E* 30). '[W]e must', he says in the *Treatise*, 'endeavour to render all our principles as universal as possible, by tracing up our experiments to the utmost, and explaining all effects from the simplest and fewest causes' (*T* xxi. Compare *T* 282). Hume makes little effort to work out the logic of such deductive systems of empirical laws. But he does seem to think that membership in such a system provides a criterion for acceptability as a law of nature.

The relevance of Hume's deductivism to our present question concerning mental dispositions can be brought out by considering the relatively non-problematical physical disposition of water-solubility. We are not inclined to say that having the kind-property of being sugar (defined in terms of such macro-properties as colour, smell and taste) is sufficient, together with immersion in water, satisfactorily to explain an object's dissolving. The reason for this unwillingness is a compelling one; namely, a presumptive law stated only in terms of macro-properties does not have a place in any reasonably extensive system of empirical laws within which possession of just those macro-properties provides a way of deriving that law from some higher-level law in the system. Consider the common assumption among natural scientists that the dispositional properties of objects are to be cashed in terms of the micro-properties of those objects. Thus, the behaviour of gases is to be explained by the micro-properties referred to in kinetic theory. In just this way we may assume that sugar dissolves in water because it has certain structural micro-properties.¹⁰ By at least partial analogy, we may think that mental dispositions are to be understood in terms of properties that are not normally observable but mention of which in a law may enable one to find a place for the law in an extensive system of the kind just described. The analogy with water-solubility suggests that the realist's non-dispositional properties need not be construed as secret properties, on the model of the 'antient philosophers', even if they are not normally observable. The analogy also suggests certain constraints within which postulation of such non-dispositional properties may take place. I shall try to fill out these vague remarks in a moment. But it would be helpful to keep in mind Hume's reference to causes that are 'hid, by reason of their minuteness or remoteness' (*T* 132).

6. I have presented the evidence suggesting that Hume is at times a reductionist about mental dispositions, at other times a realist. I have also tried to sketch the more general philosophical considerations that push Hume in the one direction or the other. I want now to argue that his realism about mental dispositions is compatible with his empiricist premises; more accurately, that the reasons given for his being a reductionist are not compelling ones.

I mentioned three things that, given his views about causality and explanation, might incline Hume towards reductionism: the atypical, and seemingly pointless, character of causal generalizations mentioning, but not identifying, some of the purported causal conditions; the impossibility of supporting such generalizations in the typically Humean manner of observing constant conjunctions; and the seeming vacuity of explanations in terms of unidentified causal conditions. It should be apparent, however, that the realist about mental dispositions can deflect the force of these objections. For, as far as his analysis goes, the realist offers not a causal generalization but, very differently, an incomplete causal generalization with a place-marker to indicate where, and within rough parameters how, the incompleteness is to be made good. His point, negatively, is that the causal conditions specified by the reductionist are not sufficient. Positively, his point is that a more adequate causal law requires discovery of some enduring property of the responding subject, rather than some additional features of his environment.

It should not be surprising that ascriptions of mental dispositions, construed realistically, are not to be justified in precisely the way in which typical causal generalizations are. For their justification requires the recognition that in the absence of some enduring property of the subject his responses are not to be explained. Such recognition is achieved in the way indicated above. The actual character of the enduring property in question can be discovered, of course, only in the ways in which one discovers the causes of things.

To say that an entity must have some property, at present unspecified, because its responses would be otherwise inexplicable is not, of course, to offer a vacuous explanation, for it is not to offer any explanation at all.

It is merely to indicate what kind of explanation is needed and to express confidence that one is to be had. In this connection, it is well to keep in mind Hume's attitude towards the crucial principle of causality. This principle is neither 'intuitively nor demonstrably certain' (T 82), but is nonetheless to be adopted, is in fact adopted, as a 'maxim' (T 132) with a heuristic function: to prompt scientists to search for the explanation of apparently inexplicable events.

We are now in a position to see that Hume's realism about mental dispositions need not conflict with his empiricist theory of meaning. It seems that he must allow meaning to such complex expressions as 'some presently unspecified property' and 'Every event has a cause'. If so, a sentence such as 'Sugar's dissolving in water is caused by its possession of some presently unspecified property' is meaningful, as are statements of similar form about linguistic abilities, traits of character and other mental dispositions. In each case one may meaningfully, if not very informatively, speak of 'springs and principles, which are hid' (T 132) or of the 'secret operation of . . . causes' (T 132).

But, it may be said, the inescapable point of Hume's empiricist theory of meaning, as applied to the case of mental dispositions, is that the unspecified non-dispositional properties must be knowable or observable *in principle*. At the very least there must be nothing in the overall framework of one's analysis to rule this out. This seems to me essentially correct as an interpretation of Hume. Let us pursue the implications.

In considering a possible objection to realism based on a Humean account of the meaning of 'mental' I suggested that the realist's non-dispositional properties cannot cogently be construed as Humean perceptions. It appears to follow that if the use of 'mental' is restricted in the way suggested, and if the 'inescapable' point of Hume's empiricism is allowed, there can be no further hope for a realist theory of mental dispositions. But what if the realist's non-dispositional properties are enduring physiological states in the body of the person to whom the mental dispositions are ascribed?

Construed in this way they can, it seems, meet the requirement of observability in principle. Hume would have to give up the troublesome restriction on the use of 'mental'. For, on the view suggested, physiological states, assuming them to have certain psychological effects in appropriate circumstances, are mental states. But this much can be said to meet the troublesome restriction halfway: the physiological character of the postulated non-dispositional properties (and *a fortiori* their precise physiological character) does not enter into an analysis of the meaning of the mental dispositional terms. So far as meaning goes the realist is committed merely to *some* enduring non-dispositional property causally related to circumstances and response. The property's being physiological becomes germane only when the requirement of observability in principle is invoked *and* one sees the inability of perceptions to meet the requirement. In any case Hume must, if he is a realist about mental dispositions, do *something* to ensure that his empiricist requirement is met.

Some will insist that this is a most unHumean way to understand mental dispositions. If the point is merely that it is unHumean to be a realist I have already argued that Hume is sometimes just that. But the objection may have its roots in an ontologically idealist reading of Hume's views about the physical world. I have argued, in chapters 1 and 2, against such a reading. The objection could also have its origin in non-interactionist interpretations of Hume's views on the mind-body problem. In chapter 2, however, I have shown how far Hume goes in an interactionist direction and how much further he could consistently go. So I am strongly inclined to think that Hume would, and am certain that he could, allow a physiological basis for mental dispositions. This is merely to add some detail to the picture of a person that has begun to emerge in this study of Hume's philosophy of mind. We shall have more occasion, in the next two chapters, to see the fruitfulness of understanding Hume's views about mental dispositions in this physiological way.

Incidentally, the physiological character of the postulated properties explains the fact that they are not normally observable. More importantly, the introduction of physiological properties enhances the likelihood that the causal laws lying behind ascriptions of mental dispositions will satisfy the Humean deductivist criterion; recall the network of physical and psychophysical laws whose form was articulated in the previous chapter. With a physiological basis, explanations in terms of mental dispositions are much more likely to have an established place in an extensive system of laws of that kind.[11]

CHAPTER FOUR

Selves, Substrates and Substances

1. Hume does not deny the existence of selves. Nor does he deny *tout court* that selves are substances. What he does deny is a certain philosophical theory, the substrate theory, that purports to explain or elucidate the fact that selves are substances. We do not 'have . . . any idea of *self*, after the manner it is here [that is, within this philosophical theory] explain'd' (*T* 251). The underlying methodological principle is one employed elsewhere in the *Treatise*, for example, in the discussion of causal necessity:

> [I]n all these expressions, *so apply'd*, we have really no distinct meaning, and make use only of common words, without any clear and determinate ideas. But as 'tis more probable, that these expressions do here lose their true meaning by being *wrong apply'd*, than that they never have any meaning; 'twill be proper to bestow another consideration on this subject, to see if possibly we can discover the nature and origin of those ideas, we annex to them. (*T* 162)

Consonantly with this principle Hume offers, as an alternative to the substrate theory, his own bundle theory of the self. According to this heterodox Humean theory, selves are compound substances constituted by perceptions that are themselves substances.

In this chapter I concentrate on Hume's polemic against the substrate theory of the self and leave discussion of his own theory for chapter 5. My principal concern is to identify and expound the several arguments Hume deploys against this theory, and to argue that only one of his arguments, and that a surprising one, meets with any degree of success. The tasks of articulating and assessing Hume's arguments are worth doing for their own sakes; Hume's is the classical attack on the substrate theory. In addition, scrutiny of his arguments will show how pervasive is Hume's commitment to certain very curious views about the nature of conscious experience.

2. Some preliminary comments are in order. Hume's discussion of the self forms part of a wider examination of the idea of a substance and parallels, in several significant respects, his discussion of physical substances. He claims that several of his arguments against the substrate theory of the self are identical with arguments he deploys against a like theory of physical objects: the notion of substrate-selves 'labours under all the same difficulties' as 'have [been] found impossible to be answer'd

with regard to matter and body', although there are some difficulties that are 'peculiar to' the case of selves (T 232). When we turn to the constructive side of Hume's discussion of substances, the parallels are equally explicit. Of the identity of a self through time and change he remarks: 'to explain it perfectly we must take the matter pretty deep, and account for that identity, which we attribute to plants and animals; there being a great analogy betwixt it, and the identity of a self or person' (T 253).

Largely following Hume's lead, we may distinguish three problems that any theory of substance must solve. One of these concerns the simplicity or unity of substances; a second concerns their identity. To put the matter in linguistic terms: one says things of the form 'A is F and G' and of the form 'A is F and was G'. One may say of a peach 'This is ripe and firm' or 'This is now ripe, but it was hard yesterday'. And a person may say of himself 'I am angry and afraid' or 'I was angry, but am now afraid'. One thereby says that a single thing has several properties either at the same time (Hume speaks of simplicity or unity) or at different times (Hume speaks of identity). And one takes this multiplicity of properties as in no way invalidating the claim that the same individual has the several properties.[1] The philosophical problem is to understand such judgments of simplicity and identity. A more general problem, that of property-instantiation or property-possession, is present in the statement of the other two. For at bottom one must understand what is expressed by a simpler statement of the form 'A is F'.

As characterized by Hume, the substrate theory offers a solution along the following lines. It makes a radical distinction between all the properties that a thing has and something else, a substrate, that has these properties. A self, viewed as something distinct from its experiences and its other properties, is such a substrate. Having a property is analysed in terms of an asymmetrical relation between a substrate and a property: the latter 'inheres in' or 'is supported by' the former. That a given thing has several properties at one time is a matter of these properties inhering, at the same time, in the same substrate. The same thing's having a variety of properties through the course of its career is a matter of a single unvarying substrate enduring through a period of time and having, at different points along the way, the several properties in question.

One of the many variations possible within the substrate theory is especially important for the case of minds or selves. It may be claimed that one has empirical access to that substrate that is one's self. Alternatively, it may be said that whether or not one has empirical access to one's self one can know that one is a self in the sense alleged by the theory.

Hume produces a veritable barrage of arguments against the substrate theory of the self. These are not very tidily assembled, and several are presented in a much too condensed, inexplicit way. Nevertheless he does say two things that provide assistance to the reader and that have affected my interpretation. He distinguishes those arguments that apply to both minds and physical objects from those that apply specifically to minds. He also distinguishes those arguments that concern 'the first origin of ideas' from one that involves, in a way that will become apparent later, a 'definition' (*T* 234). This second division of his arguments corresponds fairly closely to that between the variant substrate theories of the self just mentioned.

So much for preliminaries. Let us turn to the arguments themselves.

3. At *Treatise* I i 6 ('Of modes and substances') Hume directs the following argument against a substrate theory of substance:

> I wou'd fain ask those philosophers, who found so much of their reasonings on the distinction of substance and accident, and imagine we have clear ideas of each, whether the idea of *substance* be deriv'd from the impressions of sensation or reflexion? If it be convey'd to us by our senses, I ask, which of them; and after what manner? If it be perceiv'd by the eyes, it must be a colour; if by the ears, a sound; if by the palate, a taste; and so of the other senses. But I believe none will assert, that substance is either a colour, or sound, or a taste. The idea of substance must therefore be deriv'd from an impression of reflexion, if it really exist. But the impressions of reflexion resolve themselves into our passions and emotions; none of which can possibly represent a substance. We have therefore no idea of substance, distinct from that of a collection of particular qualities, nor have we any other meaning when we either talk or reason concerning it. (*T* 15–16)

There is much that is puzzling in the way Hume here employs the contrast between impressions of sensation and impressions of reflexion.[2] I shall assume that he intends to consider in turn what we observe by means of our senses and what we notice by introspection. Nothing essential to his argument is lost by interpreting the contrast in this way.

Hume's argument for his conclusion combines (a) an empiricist premise about the origin of ideas with the premises (b) that only things of certain specifiable kinds are in fact encountered in experience and (c) that things of those kinds could not be substrates. By sense perception we encounter only such qualities of bodies as their colour, sound or taste. By introspection we are acquainted only with experiences such as emotions, passions, and the like. According to the substrate theory, of course, such qualities and experiences are modifications of substrates, not substrates. It follows that, for Hume, we can have no idea of physical or of mental substrates.

Even granting his empiricist premise Hume's argument is clearly unavailing. His inventory of what we encounter in experience cannot, without begging the question, be taken as exhaustive. Thus the substrate theorist can insist, contrary to (b), that one does have the required experience of substrates. This insistence has some plausibility in the case of minds. It has seemed to many that one does have direct acquaintance with one's own self construed as something distinct from one's experiences. Hume has done nothing so far to discredit this belief. To make out his case he must find some way of displaying its implausibility or incoherence.

4. Hume's first argument merits only brief attention for it fails not only to support his rejection of substrate-selves but also to reveal anything of interest in the assumptions that underpin his inquiry. Of much greater interest are two arguments to which I now turn. Each of these concerns 'the first origin of ideas', but differs from that just examined by being directed specifically against mental substrates or substrate-selves.

The first argument in this group appears at *Treatise* I iv 5 ('Of the immateriality of the soul'):

> As every idea is deriv'd from a precedent impression, had we any idea of the substance of our minds, we must also have an impression of it; which is very difficult, if not impossible, to be conceiv'd. For how can an impression represent a substance, otherwise than by resembling it? And how can an impression resemble a substance, since, according to this philosophy, it is not a substance, and has none of the peculiar qualities or characteristics of a substance? (*T* 232–3. Compare also *T* 234, 251)

Hume's point is that if the substrate theory were true one could not have an experience of one's substrate-self. On Hume's reading a substrate theorist, on pain of contradiction, cannot allow the possibility of experiencing one's substrate-self. Given Hume's empiricist principle it follows that one cannot have the idea of such a substrate.

The novel features of this argument can be summarized as follows: (a) to have an experience of some item one must have an impression that resembles it; therefore to have an experience of one's substrate-self one must have an impression that resembles one's substrate-self; but (b) if the substrate theory is true one cannot have an impression that resembles one's substrate-self, for impressions are not substrates; therefore (c) if the substrate theory is true one cannot have an experience of one's substrate-self. The substrate theory entails that impressions are not substrates; the claim to experience substrates entails that they are.

Underlying this argument is a theory about the nature of experiential awareness that must be made explicit. It is easiest to do this for the special case of the sensory experience of physical objects. The theory maintains that having a sensory experience essentially involves the occurrence of a mental particular, an impression, that is to be construed as a thing in its own right. As a thing in its own right an impression is, in Hume's sense, a substance, although it is not, of course, a substrate. To employ Bennett's helpful expression,[3] the theory reifies impressions rather than viewing them as essentially adjectival on, or as modifications of, the individuals who have them. The theory allows, indeed insists on, the ascription to reified impressions of properties normally ascribed to physical objects, such as colour, taste, shape and size. And it holds that the sensory experience of a physical object is a matter not of direct access to that object but of access to some reified impression that represents and resembles it. Hume's anti-substrate argument assumes that any case of experiential awareness, no matter what the ontological status and the properties of its object may be, must be analysed along the lines marked out for this special case. Quite generally, experiential awareness requires reified impressions that represent and resemble the items of which one is aware.

This theory of experiential awareness, so far as it regards the sensory experience of physical objects, is, of course, the representative theory I attributed to Hume in chapter 1. In its treatment of reification and its ascription to sensations of properties normally ascribed to physical objects, the theory is certainly Hume's. The present argument reinforces my claim that he subscribes to the remaining component of the theory, its representative realism. For the argument reveals how pervasive is the notion of representation in his thinking about experience. Notice what he says about impressions resembling and representing substrates. Notice, too, the intended force of his remark that impressions cannot share with their purported objects the property of being substrates.

Hume's argument rests on the principle that perceptions must have the pertinent properties of their objects, but the principle is absurd. It is absurd to say that my perception of something that is red, sticky, cubical, and cold, and that weighs forty pounds, is itself red, sticky, cubical, cold, and forty pounds in weight. There may be *some* legitimate, perhaps analogical, sense to be attached to such claims, but not the straightforward sense that Hume requires. The same holds true for the suggestion that my experience of my substrate-self, assuming it to occur, must itself be a substrate. The alleged contradiction thus fails to appear. Hume has failed to show that, if the substrate theory is true, the experience of one's substrate-self is impossible.

Hume's endorsement of this absurd principle is intimately bound up with his epistemological idealism and the reification of perceptions. And he might object that one cannot legitimately judge it to be absurd while considering it in isolation from the other integrally related elements in a comprehensive theory of experiential awareness. I am not persuaded by this, but shall let the point go. For attention must then shift from his anti-substrate argument to the theory of experience on which it depends. Hume cannot, so cavalierly as he does, introduce his principle as clearly unobjectionable. Most importantly, he cannot assume the reification of impressions in the construction of his argument. For, as we shall see, it is an essential feature of the substrate theory, whether recognized by its proponents or not, that the reification of impressions is absurd. To assume reification, then, is simply to beg the question.

Another difficulty with Hume's argument may be noticed. Whatever the merits of a representative theory of one's sensory experience of physical objects, if such a theory is extended to introspective awareness the consequences are disastrous. For if experiential awareness of one's own mental states is a matter not of direct access to those states but of access to some impressions that represent and resemble them, how can Hume avoid a vicious regress? And shall we say that the impression that represents and resembles one's emotion is itself an emotion? In any case, within a generally Humean framework, it is scarcely credible that access to one's own mental states is not direct. Whatever considerations might tempt one to think of mental intermediaries in the case of sense perception are simply absent here. But if Hume does not extend his representative theory of experience to introspective awareness, why must it be extended to the purported experience of one's substrate-self? One's substrate-self and one's mental states would appear to be on the same side of the inner/outer divide that is so prominent a feature of representative theories of sense perception.

5. At *Treatise* I iv 6 ('Of personal identity') Hume writes:

For my part, when I enter most intimately into what I call *myself*, I always stumble on some particular perception or other, of heat or cold, light or shade, love or hatred, pain or pleasure. I never can catch *myself* at any time without a perception, and never can observe any thing but the perception. When my perceptions are remov'd for any time, as by sound sleep; so long am I insensible of *myself*, and may truly be said not to exist. And were all my perceptions remov'd by death, and cou'd I neither think, nor feel, nor see, nor love, nor hate after the dissolution of my body, I shou'd be entirely annihilated, nor do I conceive what is farther requisite to make me a perfect non-entity. (*T* 252)

Much the same is said in the 'Appendix':

When I turn my reflexion on *myself*, I never can perceive this *self* without some one or more perceptions; nor can I ever perceive any thing but the perceptions. 'Tis the composition of these, therefore, which forms the self . . . The annihilation, which some people suppose to follow upon death, and which entirely destroys this self, is nothing but an extinction of all particular perceptions; love and hatred, pain and pleasure, thought and sensation. These therefore must be the same with self; since the one cannot survive the other. (*T* 634–5)

The two passages are unsatisfactory in several respects. They do not in any very obvious way invoke the reifying and representative assumptions just noticed, and so are not open to objections on those grounds. But Hume's straightforward assertion that he finds no substrate-self when he introspects is one to which, as we have seen, the substrate theorist has a ready reply. His assumption that the only alternative to a substrate theory is his own bundle theory of the self is one we shall later reject. Finally, the second passage contains an obvious fallacy. 'These [perceptions] therefore must be the same with self; since the one cannot survive the other'. Would Hume similarly argue that mind and body must be the same, if the former cannot survive the latter? Or that the shadow of a man is identical with the man? If the point is that neither can survive the other, the substrate theorist can admit that selves and their perceptions are mutually dependent without identifying them.

Despite these strictures, a line of argument is suggested that, if I am not mistaken, provides a compelling objection to a substrate theory of the self. If not developed explicitly by Hume, it is based on what he says, and is distinctly Humean in character. This line of argument concerns self-identity in the first instance and turns, crucially, on the interruption and cessation of experience.

Let us recall, first, the substrate theory's proposed solution to the problem of self-identity. The same self's having a variety of experiences through a period of time is a matter of a single unvarying substrate's enduring throughout that time and having, at different points on the way, the several experiences properly ascribed to that self. Let us notice, next, Hume's insistence that there are periods in one's life, for example, during sound sleep, when one has no experiences. His position here is that of Locke who remarks that 'every drowsy nod shakes their doctrine who say that the soul always thinks'.[4] In terms of the substrate theory this means that there are periods in the course of its existence when one's substrate-self has no experiences.

The difficulty, now, is to make sense of the claim that a substrate-self can exist when it has no experiences. It surely makes no sense to say that it exists at a certain time but that it has, at that time, no properties. But what properties can it intelligibly be said to possess at a time when, by hypothesis, it has no thoughts, feelings or sensations? Dispositional properties, such as the ability to think, or to feel, or to have sensations, will not suffice for the requisite characterization, for something cannot have dispositional properties without having other, non-dispositional, ones as well.[5] Nor, for the same reason, will purely relational properties do the job. When these have been put to one side there appear to be no candidate-properties by which one might intelligibly characterize a non-experiencing substrate-self. To be concessive, it is, at the very least, incumbent on a proponent of the substrate theory to provide some plausible specification of the characteristics a substrate-self can have during such periods of its alleged existence. Failing such an account, no sense can be attached to the claim that non-experiencing substrate-selves exist. This, I take it, is the legitimate force of Hume's somewhat misleading remark that during 'sound sleep . . . [I] may truly be said not to exist'.[6]

Hume's remarks about death point in the same direction. He claims not that death requires the cessation of experience but that *if* it does the notion of a self surviving death is unintelligible. 'Were all my perceptions remov'd by death . . . I shou'd be entirely annihilated, nor do I conceive what is farther requisite to make me a perfect non-entity'. The cessation of experience is a limiting case of interruption.

We are now in a position to see that for selves of the kind with which we are familiar, that is, sometimes soundly-sleeping ones, the substrate theory collapses. One cannot be identical with a substrate that is the subject of all the experiences one has throughout the course of one's history. For, given the unintelligibility of non-experiencing substrate-selves it cannot be the case that a single substrate is the subject of both the experiences one has before, and those one has after, any gap in one's experience. But by hypothesis all those experiences are one's own. Hence self-identity cannot be a matter of substrate-identity. With the collapse of its account of self-identity, however, goes the collapse of the substrate theory's account of the unity or simplicity of the self, of a self's possession of an experience, and of self-awareness. For, given that one is the subject of experiences before and after periods when one has no experiences, one cannot be identical with that substrate that is alleged to be the subject of all, or any, of one's present experiences. What is obviously true of selves (in the ordinary sense) could not be true of substrates; selves and substrates cannot, then, be identical.

Assuming the unintelligibility of non-experiencing substrate-selves, the only ways out for the substrate theory are (a) to deny self-identity through gaps in experience, or (b) to insist that, although selves are not substrates, experiences are had by substrates, or (c) to deny gaps in experience. (a) and (b) are not so much ways out as blind alleys. What of (c)? Hume, like Locke, appears to rest his claim about gaps in experience on the fact that, when soundly asleep, one is not aware of any experiences. But to this it may be replied that one must distinguish the notions of having and being aware of an experience, and that it does not follow from the fact that I am not aware of any experience during sound sleep that I do not then have any experience. This distinction is problematic.[7] Even if it were granted, the substrate theory would not be much assisted. For to meet the present objection it must hold that, necessarily, one's experience is continuous throughout the course of one's history. And that is surely too strong a condition for the truth of the theory.

In elaborating the present argument I have assumed, with Hume, that any properties properly ascribable to substrate-selves must be non-physical properties. This is the standard version of the substrate theory of the self and the present argument calls for its rejection. But what of a non-standard version of the theory, one holding that a substrate-self is a *psychophysical* substrate that is the bearer not only of one's experiences but also of one's physical properties? Such a theory circumvents the problems posed by gaps in experience; for during the gaps the self could possess unobjectionable physical characteristics. Survival after death would require continuous experience, but that is an issue we can put aside.

Although it gets round the difficulty about gaps in experience the non-standard theory is not yet in the clear. For attention must now focus on the question whether sense can be made of the notion of substrates as the subjects of both experiences and physical properties. And there seem to be special difficulties with the notion of *self*-observation on the part of such a substrate. Unfortunately, Hume does not consider the question of psychophysical substrates. Nor does either of his two arguments against physical substrates appear to be satisfactory.[8] One point is quite clear: if one is to make any sense at all of substrate-selves one must assign them physical properties. It is a short step from this to the more straightforward view that *bodies*, not physical or psychophysical *substrates*, are the proper subjects of experience. It seems to me that Hume has his own reasons for moving in this perhaps surprising direction, and indeed displays some tendency to do so. Defence of these remarks, however, must await the argument of chapter 5.

6. The arguments examined thus far have been directed primarily against the claim of empirical access to substrates, especially substrate-selves. But it may be claimed that, whether or not one has empirical access to substrates, one can know that there are, indeed that there must be, such things; for only by postulating substrates can one render intelligible some fundamental, and agreed, feature of the world of our experience. It is this kind of theory Hume has in his sights when he turns from questions concerning 'the first origin of ideas' to a question of 'definition'. In objecting to this version of the theory, Hume constructs a refutation of an argument offered in its support. I shall call the argument on behalf of substrates 'the Argument' and Hume's reply 'the Refutation'. Both are concerned primarily with the problem of property-instantiation or the possession of experiences, rather than with those of unity (simplicity) or identity. I shall show that the Refutation fails.

The Argument makes a first, oblique, appearance at *Treatise* I iv 3 ('Of the antient philosophy'), in connection with physical objects. 'The notion of *accidents* is an unavoidable consequence of . . . [a certain] method of thinking with regard to substances and substantial forms; nor can we forbear looking upon colours, sounds, tastes, figures, and other properties of bodies, as existences, which cannot subsist apart, but require a subject of inhesion to sustain and support them' (*T* 222). When engaged in this method of thinking we 'infer a dependence of every quality on the unknown substance' (*T* 222). Rejecting the 'conceit' generated by this method of thinking, Hume says: 'Every quality being a distinct thing from another, may be conceiv'd to exist apart, and may exist apart, not only from every other quality, but from that unintelligible chimera of a substance' (*T* 222).

At *Treatise* I iv 5 ('Of the immateriality of the soul') the character of both the Argument and the Refutation is made more explicit; the topic is, specifically, selves and their perceptions:

> If instead of answering these questions [Hume's objections on the score of 'the first origin of ideas'], any one shou'd evade the difficulty, by saying, that the definition of a substance is *something which may exist by itself*; and that this definition ought to satisfy us: Shou'd this be said, I shou'd observe, that this definition agrees to every thing, that can possibly be conceiv'd; and never will serve to distinguish substance from accident, or the soul from its perceptions. For thus I reason. Whatever is clearly conceiv'd may exist; and whatever is clearly conceiv'd, after any manner, may exist after the same manner. This is one principle, which has been already acknowledg'd. Again, every thing, which is different, is distinguishable, and every thing which is distinguishable, is separable by the imagination. This is another principle. My conclusion from both is, that since all our perceptions are different from each other, and from every thing else in the universe, they are also distinct and separable, and may be consider'd as separately existent, and may exist separately, and have no need of any thing else to support their existence. They are, therefore, substances, as far as this definition explains a substance. (*T* 233)[9]

In the 'Appendix', without repeating the Argument, Hume restates his Refutation:

> Whatever is distinct, is distinguishable; and whatever is distinguishable, is separable by the thought or imagination. All perceptions are distinct. They are, therefore, distinguishable, and separable, and may be conceiv'd as separately existent, and may exist separately, without any contradiction or absurdity. (*T* 634)[10]

We can isolate three principal contentions in the Argument. (a) Sensible properties, such as those of being red or round or sticky, are instantiated, and experiences, such as those of having sensations, or emotions, or thoughts, occur. (b) It is not logically possible for experiences, or instantiations of sensible properties, to occur unowned: it is not logically possible that there is an instance of being red that is not a case of something's being red, or that there is a pain that is not someone's or something's pain. Therefore (c) we must postulate the existence of things that bear these properties or have these experiences. These bearers of properties or possessors of experiences are substances understood as substrates.

Hume concentrates his fire on the second premise. His Refutation purports to show that unowned properties or experiences are logically possible. It has three principal components. First, it employs the Cartesian premise that 'whatever is clearly conceiv'd may exist; and whatever is clearly conceiv'd, after any manner, may exist after the same manner (*T* 233). I shall make no comment about this premise. Second, it involves what I shall call Hume's 'separability principle' that, in one of its many formulations, reads: 'every thing, which is different, is distinguishable, and every thing which is distinguishable, is separable by the imagination' (*T* 233). Third, it contains what appears to be the factual claim that perceptions, or alternatively sensible qualities, are in the requisite sense different or distinct.

Some clarifications of the separability principle and of the factual premise are necessary. Taking the latter first, contrast: (1) 'Every quality . . . [is] a distinct thing from another' (*T* 222); (2) '[A]ll our perceptions are different from each other and from every thing else in the universe' (*T* 233); and (3) 'All perceptions are distinct' (*T* 634). For present purposes, the differences between qualities and perceptions are irrelevant; nor is there any interesting difference between the terms 'different' and 'distinct'. Clearly, however, (3) is elliptical: one must know *from what* all perceptions are distinct. If one takes the model provided by (1), and suggested by (3) itself, one gets: 'Every perception is distinct from every other perception'. On the other hand (2) must be read: 'Every perception is distinct from every other perception, and from every other thing in the universe'. Let us call these, respectively, the 'categorially restricted' and the 'categorially unrestricted' versions of Hume's factual premise about perceptions. The intended factual premise is, in either version, trivially true. Its triviality is, however, unimportant in the present connection; we may assume, for any case that arises, that a suitable criterion for distinctness can be provided.

What does the separability principle claim? There are well-known difficulties with Hume's handling of the notions of imaginability, conceivability and possibility, but I shall focus on the notion of separability. Like 'distinct' or 'different', 'separable' is a two-place predicate. So when Hume speaks of separability he must mean something of the form: a is separable from b. And the principle must read: If a and b are distinct from each other then a and b are separable from each other. So much is obvious. But if one examines the numerous places in the *Treatise* at which the principle is introduced[11] it is very difficult to assign a univocal meaning to it. Nonetheless, the relevant contexts make it clear that, for purposes of his Refutation, Hume's principle must be read in this way: If a and b are distinct from each other then the existence of a is compatible with the non-existence of b. Thus, on a categorially restricted interpretation of distinctness, the existence of a given perception, logically speaking, is compatible with the non-existence of any other perception whatever. If distinctness is interpreted in a categorially unrestricted way, the existence of a given perception is compatible, logically, with the non-existence of any other thing whatever. With these clarifications made, let us examine Hume's Refutation.

It should be immediately clear that, if Hume's premise about the distinctness of perceptions is taken in the categorially restricted way the Refutation is wide of the mark. For from the categorially restricted premise, together with the separability principle, one gets: for every perception it is logically possible that it be unaccompanied by any other perception whatever. But the Argument claims not that perceptions unaccompanied by other perceptions are impossible but that there can be no perceptions which are not owned by some substance and thus by some substrate. It is conceivable that there be a mind or mental substrate that has one, and only one, perception, for example, a pain; what is denied is the possibility of a pain that is not someone's or something's pain. Once a distinction is made between accompaniment and ownership, it is clear that Hume cannot get from his categorially restricted premise to the required conclusion that perceptions 'have no need of any thing else to support their existence' (*T* 233). To be sure, it is not surprising that Hume should fail to notice this difficulty, for, when developing his bundle theory for the special case of compound substances, he analyses the notion of ownership in terms of that of accompaniment.[12] They are, nonetheless, distinct notions.

To refute the Argument Hume needs a categorially unrestricted premise, and on at least one occasion he provides it: 'all our perceptions are different from each other, and from every thing else in the universe' (*T* 233). If 'every thing else in the universe' includes substrates in its scope we get a non-fallacious inference from Hume's premises to the logical possibility of unowned perceptions.

But now a number of difficulties emerge. First, in constructing his Refutation Hume tacitly concedes the existence of substrates; for the claim that perceptions and substrates are distinct from one another seems to concede the existence of each. Perhaps, however, this is an illusion. For Hume's point may be that *if* the substrate theory were correct, substrates and perceptions would be different. This, together with the separability principle, would entail the falsity of the main premise of the Argument, that unowned experiences are logically impossible. Hence, whatever else might be said on its behalf, one could not get to the substrate theory via the Argument. Additionally, the substrate theory's characterization of the special asymmetrical relation of inhesion would need drastic revision.

Clearly the crux of the matter is the scope of the separability principle itself. It must be construed in the categorially unrestricted way. Yet it is far from obvious that, taken in this way, it is true. Certainly a proponent of the substrate theory would deny it. Nor need this be a merely *ad hoc* manoeuvre. He may claim that, whatever the principle's legitimacy when categorially restricted, the situation changes radically when categorial restrictions are dropped. A relation is distinct from its terms, but there is no sense in a relation without any terms. Likewise, it may be said, perceptions are different from substrates, but there is no sense in perceptions without substrates.

In any case, to concede the separability principle construed in the categorially unrestricted way is to concede the very point at issue, that perceptions are logically capable of independent existence. That is to say, Hume has no way of moving from non-question-begging premises to a refutation of the substrate theorist's Argument. His contention that perceptions are themselves substances, although not, of course, substrates, amounts to no more than counter-assertion.

The substrate theorist can insist, indeed, that Hume's own admission of 'distinctions of reason' requires a restriction on the scope of his separability principle. Hume is aware of this difficulty, although he glosses over it. Discussing 'the distinction betwixt figure and the body figur'd; motion and the body mov'd' he says:

> The difficulty of explaining this distinction arises from the principle above explain'd, *that all ideas, which are different, are separable.* For it follows from thence, that if the figure be different from the body, their ideas must be separable as well as distinguishable; if they be not different, their ideas can neither be separable nor distinguishable. What then is meant by a distinction of reason, since it implies neither a difference nor separation ? (*T* 24–5)

But if distinctions of reason do require a restriction on the scope of the separability principle it is incumbent on Hume to show that the principle holds nonetheless for the special case of substrates and perceptions. At *Treatise* I iv 5 he argues that a distinction of reason cannot be made between a substrate and its perceptions. Unfortunately, his argument invokes the very principle whose credentials are here at issue. Having defined an 'action' or 'abstract mode' as 'something, which, properly speaking, is neither distinguishable, nor separable from its substance [substrate], and is only conceiv'd by a distinction of reason, or an abstraction' he argues:

> Our perceptions are all really different, and separable, and distinguishable from each other, and from every thing else, which we can imagine; and therefore 'tis impossible to conceive, how they can be the action or abstract mode of any substance [substrate]. (*T* 245)

He does introduce some additional considerations to support his claim, but these appear to rest on a tendentious characterization of the way in which a distinction of reason would have to be made in the present case.[13]

7. This completes my examination of Hume's principal arguments against the substrate theory of the self. We must, however, notice briefly two auxiliary arguments adduced in support of his thesis that perceptions 'may be conceiv'd as separately existent, and may exist separately, without any contradiction or absurdity' (*T* 634), and hence are themselves substances. The first moves from the separability of the members of a certain class of perceptions, that is to say, impressions of sensation, via a premise that all perceptions are alike in nature, to the conclusion that all perceptions are separable. It goes like this:

> When I view this table and that chimney, nothing is present to me but particular perceptions, which are of a like nature with all the

other perceptions. This is the doctrine of philosophers. But this table, which is present to me, and that chimney, may and do exist separately. This is the doctrine of the vulgar, and implies no contradiction. There is no contradiction, therefore, in extending the same doctrine to all the perceptions. (*T* 634)

The second moves from the separability of physical objects, and the premise that what is intelligible of physical objects must likewise be intelligible of perceptions, to the required conclusion about the separability of perceptions. In Hume's words:

In general, the following reasoning seems satisfactory. All ideas are borrow'd from preceding perceptions. Our ideas of objects, therefore, are deriv'd from that source. Consequently no proposition can be intelligible or consistent with regard to objects, which is not so with regard to perceptions. But 'tis intelligible and consistent to say, that objects exist distinct and independent, without any common *simple* substance or subject of inhesion. This proposition, therefore, can never be absurd with regard to perceptions. (*T* 634)

I am concerned not with the defects in these auxiliary arguments but with the light they shed on certain matters broached earlier. We have seen that Hume reifies sensations, construing them as mental particulars that the plain man takes to be physical objects; we have seen that he attributes to sensations a number of properties, such as colour and shape, that are normally attributed to physical objects. As the two auxiliary arguments reveal, Hume takes sensations to be like physical objects in an additional respect; logically speaking, they can be what physical objects are in fact, namely, mind-independent. Although they are not mind-independent there is no contradiction in the suggestion that sensations can be so. This is merely an implication of Hume's separability principle. And the point is one he makes very strikingly elsewhere, when he maintains that a given sensation I now have could go away and return, that, for example, a colour sensation I now have could, logically speaking, be numerically identical with one I had yesterday, though I have had no colour sensations in the interim.[14] Although it is merely an implication of the separability principle, it is instructive to see Hume draw the implication explicitly. As his first auxiliary argument makes clear, he draws it not only for sensations but for any perceptions whatever. In his view not only round red sensations but also emotions and feelings can exist unowned.

Hume takes the reification of perceptions in a bracingly serious way. When one sees what their reification amounts to one sees that it is absurd. The fact that it is absurd strengthens my criticisms of the anti-substrate arguments of sections 4 and 6; it also entails the absurdity of Hume's bundle theory of the self, which has reification as an essential component. As we saw in section 5, however, Hume does have one compelling objection to the substrate theory of the self, at least in its standard version; and a non-standard version promises to fare no better.[15] So we must reject his underlying assumption that the substrate theory and his own bundle theory are the only possible theories of the self. If the problems the two theories are designed to solve are genuine ones there must be an alternative solution.

CHAPTER FIVE

The Idea of One's Self

1. Whatever the success of Hume's polemic against the substrate theory of the self, what are we to make of his own constructive theory, the so-called 'bundle theory'? In so far as this theory involves the reification of perceptions it is, I have claimed, absurd. But there is much more to the theory than this; in particular, there is the account of personal identity advanced especially at *Treatise* I iv 6 ('Of personal identity'). To make any very illuminating assessment of Hume's own theory one must be quite clear about the problem or problems the theory is designed to solve. On a topic so well-worn, it is all too easy to assume one knows just what Hume is up to, and without further ado enter the critical lists. In fact, it is no easy matter to determine just what Hume takes his problems to be. It is only marginally easier to determine the character of his proposed solutions, at least if one insists that they be stated in a hard-edged, well-articulated way.

I shall save for the end of the chapter two commonly noted and especially vexing interpretative problems: the source of the second thoughts about his views of personal identity that Hume expresses in the 'Appendix' to the *Treatise*; and the point of his surprising remarks divorcing 'personal identity, as it regards our thought or imagination' from personal identity 'as it regards our passions or the concern we take in ourselves' (*T* 253). And I shall begin with some interpretative remarks about his empiricist explanation of the very idea of a world of mind-independent physical objects. Justification for this point of departure may await the issue.

I shall leave further comment on Hume's reification of perceptions for chapter 7. I shall also defer until then a detailed characterization and criticism of his position on introspective awareness. This means that my critical assessment of his theory of the self will not be completed until the very end of that chapter.

2. We saw in chapter I that Hume's discussion of the external world at *Treatise* I iv 2 has a constructive as well as a sceptical side. On the constructive side Hume proposes to explain the acquisition of the very idea of a world of physical objects. As required by his empiricist premises he assumes an initial neutrality on the part of those whose beliefs and conceptions are to be explained: in a postulated original situation the items encountered in experience are taken neither as mental nor as physical. Hume's explanation is a causal, associationist one invoking

features both of the items experienced and of the subject's imagination: ideas of physical objects 'arise from a concurrence of some of their [one's impressions'] qualities with the qualities of the imagination' (*T* 194). Importantly, if obviously, the causally relevant features of the items one experiences are features one observes. In his explanation Hume focuses on the mind-independence of physical objects, a property that he takes to be a necessary, though not sufficient, condition of bodies as ordinarily conceived. We have seen all of this before. But we must now take a somewhat closer look at Hume's implementation of this part of his empiricist programme if we are to be aided in our understanding and assessment of his account of the self. In particular, we must look to what he says of the identity of bodies. Perforce, much interesting detail must be omitted; many needed qualifications must go unmade.

To expedite matters let us introduce a battery of technical concepts prompted by an essay of Quine's.[1] Let us distinguish a *time-consuming* from a *momentary* object and say that a time-consuming object is a series of suitably related momentary objects. Since the point is not crucial for our present concerns we may leave the momentariness of momentary objects undefined, allowing our ordinary intuitions or the context to take the place of a definition. Although we may countenance the possibility of *simple* momentary objects let us restrict our attention to *compound* ones. Our concept of a time-consuming object permits both *changing* and *unchanging* time-consuming objects: for an unchanging object each constitutive momentary object is qualitatively identical with every other; for a changing object this condition does not hold. Our concept of a time-consuming object also permits a distinction between *continuous* and *non-continuous* objects. A time-consuming object is continuous if and only if in the interval between its coming to be and its ceasing to be there is no temporal interval that is not filled by a momentary object that is a constituent of that time-consuming object; it is non-continuous if there are unfilled moments during the time of its existence. We may allow time-consuming objects to be *continuously observed* or only *intermittently observed* (or not observed at all, for that matter). Finally, let us distinguish *independent* and *non-independent* time-consuming objects, where the independence in question is independence of some mind.

Thus equipped we can mark out the main lines of Hume's empiricist programme for the case of physical objects. The conception to be explained is that of a world of independent and continuous time-consuming objects.[2] The explanation will point to certain relational properties of the momentary objects we encounter in experience and to certain proclivities of our imaginations. The basic account is given at *Treatise* I iv 2 (194–210), and is supplemented by a discussion at *Treatise* I iv 6 (253–8).

According to Hume, we take only some of the items we encounter in

experience to be physical objects, so a satisfactory explanation of what
we do must pinpoint the respects in which these items differ from the
others: 'since this notion [of distinct and continu'd existence] does not
extend to all of them [impressions], it must arise from certain qualities
peculiar to some impressions' (*T* 194).The qualities he fastens on he
terms 'constancy' and 'coherence' (*T* 194-5). Constancy is, in part, a
matter of the unchanging character of some time-consuming objects,
while coherence is, in part, to be understood in terms of the changing
character of some others. But there is more to the two notions than this.
For one thing, coherence requires some degree of regularity in the
series of changes that a changing time-consuming object undergoes.
More generally, both constancy and coherence must be understood in
terms of a certain gap-indifference³ possessed by one's observation of
some time-consuming objects one encounters.

One may continuously observe both changing and unchanging time-
consuming objects. But one may also intermittently observe time-
consuming objects from either group. Suppose a situation in which one
continuously observes an unchanging object of a certain kind. The
pattern displayed by the constitutive momentary objects one encounters
will be: AAAAA, for some period from t_1 to t_5.⁴ For an intermittent
observation of the same object, or of another of its kind, the pattern of
momentary objects will be: A..AA or .A.AA or AAA.A and so forth
(where the dots indicate moments not observationally filled with a
momentary object). For changing objects the patterns will have the
characters: ABCDE for cases of continuous observation, and AB..E or
A.C.E or ..CDE and so forth for cases of intermittent observation.
The point is that certain kinds of time-consuming objects, both unchanging and changing, allow observational gaps, and what comes after
the observational gaps appears in no way affected by the fact of the gaps.
Of course, the fact that there are gaps on a given occasion, as well as
the fact that certain kinds of objects are gap-indifferent in the way
described, can appear only against a background of 'non-gappy' observations of time-consuming objects of the kinds in question. Roughly,
one's reaction to the intermittently observed case depends on previous
cases of continuous observation.⁵

Hume explains constancy and coherence in this way:

> [W]e ... find, that all those objects, to which we attribute a continu'd
> existence, have a peculiar *constancy*, which distinguishes them from
> the impressions, whose existence depends upon our perception.
> Those mountains, and houses, and trees, which lie at present under
> my eye, have always appear'd to me in the same order; and when I
> lose sight of them by shutting my eyes or turning my head, I soon
> after find them return upon me without the least alteration. My bed
> and table, my books and papers, present themselves in the same uni-
> form manner, and change not upon account of any interruption in
> my seeing or perceiving them ... This constancy, however, is not so

perfect as not to admit of very considerable exceptions. Bodies often change their position and qualities, and after a little absence or interruption may become hardly knowable. But here 'tis observable, that even in these changes they preserve a *coherence*, and have a regular dependence on each other; which is the foundation of a kind of reasoning from causation, and produces the opinion of their continu'd existence. When I return to my chamber after an hour's absence, I find not my fire in the same situation, in which I left it: But then I am accustom'd in other instances to see a like alteration produc'd in a like time, whether I am present or absent, near or remote. This coherence, therefore, in their changes is one of the characteristics of external objects, as well as their constancy. (*T* 194–5)

Gap-indifference, then, is the quality of impressions that contributes to one's forming the idea of independent objects. If a given kind of time-consuming object, whether changing or unchanging, is recognized to be gap-indifferent in the sense described one will take all instances of that kind to be independent, hence physical, objects. If one's experience with a certain kind of time-consuming object does not reveal gap-indifference one will not take objects of that kind to be independent. Hume thinks there are kinds of time-consuming objects that are in fact not gap-indifferent. Such objects, he says, 'we regard as internal and perishing' (*T* 194).

Surprisingly, Hume's discussion of bodily identity is not properly welded to this account of the very belief in physical objects. He does raise the issue of identity when he considers the mind-independence of bodies; but his most helpful discussion of the topic is reserved for *Treatise* I iv 6. He appears to hold that any identity judgment must be a contingent, serial identity judgment. It must be contingent since identity, like causality and spatial or temporal relation, is a relation 'such as may be chang'd without any change in the ideas [which we compare together]' (*T* 69). It must be a serial identity judgment, that is one in which an object existent at one time is identified with an object existent at another time: to understand identity one must 'have recourse to the idea of time or duration' (*T* 200). Hume lays down two further conditions for identity when he says that 'the principle of individuation [identity] is nothing but the *invariableness* and *uninterruptedness* of any object, thro' a suppos'd variation of time' (*T* 201). Interpreting this account of identity ontologically, and in terms of the technical concepts we have introduced, we get the following: a time-consuming object, to satisfy the conditions for identity, must be continuous and unchanging. That is to say, it must be constituted by a continuous series of momentary objects, and the constituent momentary objects must be qualitatively identical.[6]

It is helpful to think of this as Hume's analysis for cases of *strict* identity. As I read him, he allows departures from this strict standard with respect both to invariableness and uninterruptedness. He allows a continuous time-consuming object to change while remaining the same object, the same oak tree, for example. And he allows non-continuous time-consuming objects to preserve their identity; the case, as we shall see, of minds. Moreover, he allows the intermittent observation of identity-preserving, continuous time-consuming objects, a departure from the paradigm of uninterrupted observation.

At *Treatise* I iv 6 Hume isolates three relations between momentary objects that govern the making of physical-object identity judgments: resemblance, contiguity (both spatial and temporal), and causality. Typically, when he speaks of resemblance he means close but not perfect resemblance, in effect distinguishing resemblance from qualitative identity. We can achieve convenient simplification, however, by treating close-but-not-perfect and perfect resemblance as species of resemblance, which would bring his original account of identity judgments for unchanging objects into line with that for changing ones. Spatial and temporal contiguity call for no special comment now, but under the heading of causality Hume includes reciprocal causality, as when we 'add a *sympathy* of parts to their *common end*, and suppose that they bear to each other, the reciprocal relation of cause and effect in all their actions and operations' (*T* 257). By way of illustration he cites our identity judgments about vegetables and animals 'where not only the several parts have a reference to some general purpose, but also a mutual dependence on, and connexion with each other' (*T* 257). Singly or in combination these relations, when recognized to relate the members of a series of momentary objects, give rise to the judgment that the item present is a single time-consuming object.

This is a first approximation. Hume refines the account by indicating some of the ways in which the identity judgments we make about changing objects are relative to a variety of so far unmentioned factors. Addition or subtraction of the constituent parts of physical objects can affect the identity judgments we make. Whether or not they do so depends on a certain relation between the parts and the whole: 'tho' the change of any considerable part in a mass of matter destroys the identity of the whole, yet we must measure the greatness of the part, not absolutely, but by its *proportion* to the whole' (*T* 256). What we do is also relative to the rate of the observed change: 'A change in any considerable part of a body destroys its identity; but 'tis remarkable, that where the change is produc'd *gradually* and *insensibly* we are less apt to ascribe to it the same effect' (*T* 256). More suggestively, the rapidity and extent of change we will tolerate is relative to the kind of object we are dealing with: 'What is natural and essential to any thing is, in a manner, expected; and what is expected makes less impression, and appears of less moment, than what is unusual and extraordinary' (*T* 258). Thus, 'where the objects are in their nature changeable and inconstant, we admit of a more sudden transition, than wou'd otherwise be consistent with that relation [identity]' (*T* 258). To be sure, Hume's handling of questions about the relativity of identity leaves much to be desired. But he does seem to have taken some of Locke's lessons to heart.

What of the other half of Hume's causal story, that is, the proclivities of the imagination that, in response to recognized gap-indifference, generate the notion of independent physical objects? Hume isolates two psychological mechanisms, one of which is at least suggestive, while the other, despite the fond attention he lavishes on it, is quite useless. The suggestive mechanism, which Hume describes only when describing coherence (and thereby changing objects), works somewhat as follows. One's gappy encounters with time-consuming objects, if taken at face-value, contradict one's past experience of non-gappy encounters with objects of the appropriate kind. One finds oneself unable to regularize one's experience if these gaps are allowed to stand. But one dislikes contradictions and has a penchant for order. So one remedies the situation by filling in the gaps; by supposing that the gaps, in fact if not apparently, are filled with suitable momentary objects. 'There is scarce a moment of my life, wherein . . . I have not occasion to suppose the continu'd existence of objects, in order to connect their past and present appearances, and give them such an union with each other, as I have found by experience to be suitable to their particular natures and circumstances' (*T* 197). I overlook Hume's reasons for saying that the suppositions are not instances of causal inferences, as well as his contention that the psychological proclivities cited are 'too weak to support alone so vast an edifice, as is that of the continu'd existence of all external bodies' (*T* 198-9).

Hume shores up this supposedly weak account by introducing a second psychological mechanism, describing its operations for cases of constancy only. Because of the similarity of dispositions of mind when one continuously observes an unchanging object (the paradigmatic case for identity) and when one intermittently observes an unchanging object, one is moved to make an identity judgment in the latter as well as in the former case. More precisely, one judges the momentary object prior to a given observational gap to be identical with the qualitatively identical momentary object that comes after the gap. But the inappropriateness of this stares one in the face: there are, after all, the interruptions. So, one ameliorates the predicament by supposing that the gaps are filled with suitable momentary objects. And, in a characteristically Humean way, one comes to believe the supposition. (Hume provides a summary of all this at *T* 199, and fills in the details at *T* 199-210.)

This ancillary account presumably requires little critical comment. Remarkably, it is the only place at which Hume makes any explicit effort to link questions of identity with those concerning belief in the independence of physical objects. Equally remarkably, he here takes paradigmatic identity judgments to be prior to one's acquisition of a conception of a physical world. And he makes the illusory identification of one momentary object with another a condition for the formation of that conception.

3. In *The Foundations of Empirical Knowledge* A.J.Ayer writes:
    If we agree to say that the objects of which we are directly aware are always sense-data, then we are deciding to treat them and not minds or material things as the units in terms of which we are to describe our perceptual experience. The question, therefore, that we must ask is not how sense-data are to be incorporated in the categories of mind or matter, or whereabouts they are to be located in physical space, but rather how our conceptions of 'mind' and 'material things' and 'physical space' are to be analyzed in terms of them.[7]

There is much in the statement of his question that is peculiar to Ayer's way of doing things. But at one point Ayer's question is identical with one that Hume is committed to asking. For Hume must explicate the notions of both bodies and minds in terms of a neutral starting point. Now that we have examined his account of the notion of bodies, let us turn to the other requisite part of his empiricist programme.

On the face of it, Hume leaves the mental side of the empiricist programme undone. His elaborate attempt to explain the formation of physical-object concepts far surpasses those of Locke and Berkeley. So it is all the more surprising that he fails to give any complementary account for minds. Or perhaps it is not so surprising. For, as I hope to show, he not only does not but could not provide the required account of the concept of a mind, including the conception of one's own mind. Of course it may be doubted that I am right in the claim that Hume *does not* give any explanation of the formation of the concept of a mind. However, the question cannot be readily settled, without seeming to be begged, by simply looking at the text. To make any progress we must proceed by examining the possible manoeuvres that are available to Hume if he is to give an empiricist account of mind. Knowing what is possible should help us to decide what, if anything, Hume does on the topic. Before getting down to business, let us establish the parameters that help to determine the possibilities. These may be conveniently gathered under three headings.

First, there are restrictions imposed by his account of the notion of physical objects. The starting point must be neutral. The account must focus on features of what one observes and of one's imagination. Hume makes this requirement plain enough when he remarks on the close analogies between physical-object and mental judgments of identity. Minds must be taken to *contrast* with bodies in suitable ways. At the very least they must differ on the point of independence.[8] And that means that the observational situations that give rise to the notion of mind cannot possess the gap-indifference that is the mainstay of Hume's account of the idea of bodies.

Second, Hume is concerned to explain the plain man's conception. The elements Hume stresses are these. Minds are things that exist for lengthy periods of time and retain their identity and unity despite often rapid change in psychological state and multiplicity of concurrent psychological states. They are things to which we ascribe sensations, feelings, thoughts, volitions. This conception permits gaps in consciousness: a mind may exist when unconscious. And there may be gaps in what a given mind can recall of its own past mental history. As a plain man one distinguishes one's own self from other selves, and recognizes that others may well exist even if one is not aware of them. One is aware of one's own psychological states in ways in which one cannot be aware of those of others. Minds are, in important ways, quite different from bodies; a mind differs from a body not just as one body differs from another. This delineation of the plain man's views stresses minds to the prejudice of persons, but accords with Hume's own emphasis.

Restrictions of a third kind are imposed by certain elements in Hume's formed metaphysical theory of mind. Most of these we have already had occasion to notice; ascription of the others will be justified shortly. Minds are non-continuous time-consuming objects, the momentary constituents of which are, typically, compound objects. The constitutive momentary objects are perceptions, or momentary collections of perceptions. These momentary objects are bound together by relations to be specified presently, but causality has an especially prominent place. As Hume remarks: 'The true idea of the human mind, is to consider it as a system of different perceptions or different existences, which are link'd together by the relation of cause and effect, and mutually produce, destroy, influence, and modify each other' (*T* 261). Hume is a dualist interactionist. He also holds to a form of epistemological idealism: the only items to which we have direct access in experience are perceptions of one variety or another. It may seem a curious procedure to introduce Hume's mental metaphysics before examining what he says, or would say, about the origin of the idea of mind. But recall that the specific objective is to explain the formation of the plain man's view of things. The plain man need not be a Humean metaphysician. But Hume's explanation of the plain man's view must be consonant with his, that is Hume's, metaphysics.

It seems to me plain that within these parameters Hume cannot successfully account for the idea of a mind, let alone the idea of one's own mind. At least, he cannot do so and at the same time account for the conception of bodies. To comply with Hume's requirements one's observation situation must possess an extraordinary conjunction of properties. (1) One must non-continuously observe a non-continuous, time-consuming object. One's observation must be non-continuous since its purported object is so.[9] (2) This time-consuming object cannot, however, be gap-indifferent, for if it were it would be judged to be independent. (3) Although the time-consuming object may be only one of a kind, that is, only one of many minds, it is the only one of its kind that *I* can observe. (4) This time-consuming object cannot be just one of several time-consuming objects that I observe; for *everything*, every momentary object, that I observe must be a constituent of it. According to Hume's epistemological idealism the only items I directly observe are my own perceptions. So, if I am to get things right, I must take all the momentary objects I encounter to be constituents of the single object that is my self. In any case, if Hume's plain man is right I have sensations as well as emotions, thoughts and volitions. So those *sensations* must be in part constitutive of the object I take to be my mind.

When all this is spelled out, Hume faces a cruel dilemma. If his explanation has the plain man taking everything he observes to be an element in his mind then it flies in the face of the explanation given for the belief in physical objects. For there, some of those very same things (the sensations) were taken to be bodies, and therefore mind-independent. His plain man must believe both that all of what he encounters comprises *one* thing, specifically his own *mind*, and that among the several things he encounters are a number of *mind-independent physical objects,* such as chairs, mountains, and the like; he must, ineluctably, be of two minds about some things. Would Hume welcome this result as further evidence of the unhappy condition of the human understanding? I can find no evidence that he does so.

If Hume's explanation has the plain man taking his mind to be just one of the things he observes he is no better off. On Hume's premises the belief must be false. In any case, he then provides no explanation of the plain man's belief that one's sensations are among one's psychological states. On the present proposal, sensations must be taken to be physical objects or constituents of them.

There is a further deep puzzle here. Hume thinks that, in the case of physical objects, one notices the gaps when one only intermittently observes a given time-consuming object. There is, one might say, a background against which the interrupted observation is made. One observes other momentary objects but not the missing one, as when, in the interval between two glances at one's book, one observes the wall behind the desk. And, of course, there is the background of one's prior continuous encounters with objects of the kind in question. Being in a position to notice the gaps in one's observation, one judges the encountered object to be continuous nonetheless. This judgment is tied in a fairly straightforward way to what one observes.

The contrast between this situation and the present one is striking. One supposedly observes one's own non-continuous mind. Trivially, however, one has no perceptions at those moments that are not filled with momentary objects constitutive of one's self. How then can one observe the gappiness of one's self? According to one recent writer one can not:

A gap in consciousness can . . . never be *experienced* as a gap in consciousness by the person whose consciousness is affected. A person may have the experience of losing consciousness, but that is a conscious experience. No one can be conscious of being unconscious. All we know is that we have the experience of losing consciousness immediately followed by the experience of regaining consciousness. It is only by inference that we know that we have been unconscious, or by being told of this by someone else. In a sense, therefore, consciousness does not record its own interruptions, but gives the impression of being unbroken, although it is not.[10]

And of course Hume cannot fall back on supposed observations of other non-continuous objects, of minds other than one's own, for such observations have been ruled out at the beginning. But if one cannot observe one's own mind as a non-continuous object, if indeed one seems to observation to be continuous, how does one come to conceive oneself as an object which is non-continuous in the required sense?

These difficulties suggest strongly that if one does form the idea of a mind from what one observes one must do so in a much more sophisticated way than that one follows, if Hume is right, in the case of bodies. It cannot be a matter of just observing bodies and one's mind. But the root of Hume's troubles may well be the very assumption that one can observe, in the relevant sense, one's own perceptions, the momentary objects that constitute one's mind. When we examine his views of introspective awareness in chapter 7 we shall see independent reason to think he must give up this assumption. This will provide occasion to notice one way in which he might revise his approach to his empiricist programme.

I claimed, earlier, that Hume offers no account of one's acquisition of the concept of a mind or of one's own mind. Now that we have seen what such an account would have, on Humean principles, to be like, it should be obvious that this is so. There is nothing in the *Treatise* or the first *Enquiry* that fits the bill. Hume may think that what he says of mental identity at *Treatise* I iv 6 supplies all that one could reasonably demand. Unfortunately it does not, even if it does supply much else that is very interesting.

4. Hume's central question in *Treatise* I iv 6 concerns mental id' :itity and may be formulated thus: under what observational conditions does one take the momentary mental objects that one introspects to be constitutive of a single time-consuming mental object? A striking variant of the central question may be formulated in this way: under what observational conditions does one take one's momentary selves to constitute a single, time-consuming self?

Either of these formulations is to be preferred to the more polemical ones suggested by Hume's own best statement of his central question:

'What . . . gives us so great a propension to ascribe an identity to these successive perceptions, and to suppose ourselves possest of an invariable and uninterrupted existence thro' the whole course of our lives?' (*T* 253). Two polemical formulations in particular will not bear serious attention: What observational conditions explain one's identifying one momentary mental object with another? and What observational circumstances explain one's judging that a changing time-consuming mental object undergoes no change?

More interesting, however, are the two questions: (1) What explains one's judging that an observed, changing, mental object has perfect identity? and (2) Under what conditions does one postulate mental substrates? Clearly (1) and (2) are closely linked with each other. But they are linked also with the central question as originally formulated. Hume's answer to the question as first formulated provides at least part of his answers to (1) and (2). Hume believes that one is under an illusion when one ascribes perfect identity to oneself, and under a further illusion when, as a philosopher, one invents a substrate-self to explain that perfect identity. Part of the explanation of these illusions, however, is to be found in the observational circumstances that generate judgments of what he calls 'fictional identity'. The central question concerns the making of a judgment of 'fictional identity' about one's own mind.

The central question has a close analogue in the case of bodies: what leads one to judge that a number of temporally distinct, momentary physical objects constitute a single time-consuming one? It has close analogues, also, for judgments about what Hume calls the 'unity' or 'simplicity' of both bodies and minds. Why is an object with 'different co-existent parts' (*T* 263) judged to be a simple object? Why are 'the colour, taste, figure, solidity, and other qualities, combin'd in a peach or melon . . . conceiv'd to form *one thing*' (*T* 221)? Of course, Hume's answers to all of these questions are, he stresses, very much alike. For example:

> The identity, which we ascribe to the mind of man, is only a fictitious one, and of a like kind with that which we ascribe to vegetables and animal bodies. It cannot, therefore, have a different origin, but must proceed from a like operation of the imagination upon like objects.
> (*T* 259)

What has been said of 'our notion of identity, as apply'd to the human mind, may be extended with little or no variation to that of *simplicity*' (*T* 263).

Judgments of mental and physical-object identity 'proceed from a like operation of the imagination upon like objects' (*T* 259). What operation of the imagination has he in mind? Writing of physical-object judgments he mentions a 'succession of related objects' [a series of suitably related, momentary physical objects] and claims that 'the relation facilitates the transition of the mind from one object to another, and renders its passage as smooth as if it contemplated one continu'd object' (*T* 254). When he turns to minds he remarks: 'our notions of personal identity, proceed entirely from the smooth and uninterrupted [*sic*] progress of the thought along a train of connected ideas, according to the principles above explain'd' (*T* 260). In what respect are one's momentary objects alleged to be alike in the two cases? In the case of physical objects, the causally relevant feature of one's momentary objects is their being observed to be related to one another by resemblance, spatial and temporal contiguity, and causality. Something very similar is true in the case of mental identity:

> The only question ... which remains, is, by what relations this uninterrupted progress of our thought is produc'd, when we consider the successive existence of a mind or thinking person. And here 'tis evident we must confine ourselves to resemblance and causation, and must drop contiguity, which has little or no influence in the present case. (*T* 260)

I shall comment later on Hume's unexplained elimination of contiguity from the list of causally relevant relations between perceptions. Having noticed the extent of the purported parallels between the mental and the physical cases, let us work out the details of Hume's answer to his central question.

The role of resemblance is described in a single, quite extraordinary, paragraph:

> To begin with *resemblance*; suppose we cou'd see clearly into the breast of another, and observe that succession of perceptions, which constitutes his mind or thinking principle, and suppose that he always preserves the memory of a considerable part of past perceptions; 'tis evident that nothing cou'd more contribute to the bestowing a relation on this succession amidst all its variations. For what is the memory but a faculty, by which we raise up the images of past perceptions? And as an image necessarily resembles its object, must not the frequent placing of these resembling perceptions in the chain of thought, convey the imagination more easily from one link to another, and make the whole seem like the continuance of one object? In this particular, then, the memory not only discovers the identity, but also contributes to its production, by producing the relation of resemblance among the perceptions. (*T* 260-1)

Having said this, Hume simply remarks: 'The case is the same whether we consider ourselves or others' (*T* 261).

I take it that Hume's point is that what goes on when one thinks of one's own identity parallels what would occur, in thinking about the mental identity of another, if one were able to 'see into his breast'. But why does the account go *that* way? Why does Hume begin with the third-person case? Some recent philosophers recommend doing that, of course, but Hume's own premises, and his almost exclusive concern with judgments of self-identity, surely urge the opposite course. And Hume *must* intend his description of the third-person case to be counterfactual. He does not think, after all, that one can see into another's breast, or that one's actual judgments of the mental identity of others require that one do so. Does he perhaps think his exposition will prove more perspicuous if done in this curious way? If so, why? As we shall see, there is a deep reason for Hume's unusual procedure.

Overlooking the obvious difficulties in his procedure, however, let us get clear about the picture that controls his thinking about the link between resemblance and judgments of identity. For the third-person case the picture is this. One person (call him the *observer*) notices a resemblance between certain past and present perceptions had by another person (call him the *subject*). The resemblance in question is specifically that between the subject's present recollection of some past perception and the past perception that the subject recalls. On noticing this resemblance, the observer comes to view the subject's perceptions as 'the continuance of one object'. That is to say, the observer comes to view those resembling momentary objects as constituting a single enduring thing. This, of course, requires both that the observer be aware of the subject's present recollection and that the observer himself recall the subject's past perception. For the simplest case, then, four perceptions are involved: two belong to the subject (his past perception; his present recollection of that past perception); two are the observer's (his awareness of the subject's present recollection; *his* recollection of the subject's past perception). Hume's account assumes awareness of a number of such pairs of resembling perceptions, but for brevity's sake I focus on a single instance.

Distinguishing between the subject's and the observer's recollections of the subject's past perception does, I think, help us to understand Hume's quite obscure remark that 'memory not only discovers the identity, but also contributes to its production' (*T* 261). Hume says that memory 'contributes to its production, by producing the relation of resemblance among the perceptions' (*T* 261). I take this to mean that since a recollection resembles the perception recalled, memory provides the resemblance, the noticing of which gives rise to the judgment of identity. He explains the meaning of 'memory ... discovers the identity' when he discusses judgments of self-identity based on causality: 'In this view, therefore, memory does not so much *produce* as *discover* personal identity, by shewing us the relation of cause and effect among our different perceptions' (*T* 262). I take this to mean that only if one recalls a past perception can one notice its causal connection with present perceptions, and thus be moved to think of the successive perceptions as constituting one object.[11] If this is Hume's meaning, however, it is clear that memory must play its discovering role *whatever* relation between successive perceptions is in question, and thus for the case of resemblance as well as for that of causality. But if this is so it can be only the *subject's* memory that 'produces' personal identity, and the *observer's* memory that 'discovers' it. For it is the subject's memory that provides the necessary resemblance, and the observer's memory that enables the observer to note the resemblance.

Now if this picture is applied to judgments of *self*-identity (and if it is not then, of course, Hume has offered no explanation of such judgments), the consequences are fairly obvious. A distinction must be drawn between the self as subject and the self as (self-) observer. More precisely, a distinction must be drawn between those resembling perceptions that provide the basis for one's judgment of self-identity and those perceptions that in some way constitute one's awareness of the former perceptions and of their resemblance to one another. Once again four perceptions are needed. As subject one must both have had a past perception and now recall that past perception; as self-observer one must now be aware of the subject's present recollection of some past perception *and* one must now recall that past perception. It is one's perceptions as subject that 'produce' the thought of one's identity by providing the resemblance upon which this thought is based. It is one's perceptions as self-observer that constitute the awareness of these resembling perceptions. As self-observer one comes to view oneself as a subject identical through change.

This, I take it, is Hume's uncompromisingly third-person picture of one's thinking of oneself as identical despite change.[12] It must be admitted that Hume does not draw out the implications of his picture in this explicit way. His remarks are much too cursory for that. But if we do read Hume this way it is readily understandable that he begins the discussion with his counterfactual characterization of identity judgments made about other minds. One can also make much greater sense than one otherwise could of the parallels that Hume insists obtain between judgments about physical objects and judgments about one's own mental identity. And, although there are quite extraordinary difficulties in the idea, Hume makes it fairly plain that he here accepts *some* distinction between the resembling or causally related perceptions and other perceptions that are perceptions of the former ones. (The distinction between the subject's recalling a past perception and the self-observer's being aware of this recollection would be a special case of this distinction.) He asks 'whether it [identity] be something that really binds *our several perceptions* together, or only associates *their ideas* in the imagination' (*T* 259, my italics), and adopts the latter alternative: 'identity is ... merely a quality, which we attribute to *them* [these different perceptions], because of the union of *their ideas* in the imagination, *when we reflect upon them*' (*T* 260, my italics). And in the 'Appendix' he cites with at least partial approval the view of 'most philosophers' that 'personal identity *arises* from consciousness; and *consciousness is nothing but a reflected thought or perception*' (*T* 635, most italics mine).

Hume's explanation of judgments of self-identity based on *causal* connections among one's perceptions presumably parallels that of judgments based on resemblance. Memory's discovering role must be

stressed, and one must distinguish the subject's causally related perceptions from the self-observer's perceptions of them. As with the earlier
account of physical-object identity, however, one must assume that
Hume's notion of causality here encompasses complicated variants such
as reciprocal causality. It is the special cases of plants and animals that
are said, on two occasions, to provide the analogy. This point, as well as
the rapidity of change that is permitted by one's concept of mind, comes
out forcefully when Hume writes:

> As to *causation*; we may observe, that the true idea of the human
> mind, is to consider it as a system of different perceptions or different
> existences, which are link'd together by the relation of cause and
> effect, and mutually produce, destroy, influence, and modify each
> other. Our impressions give rise to their correspondent ideas; and
> these ideas in their turn produce other impressions. One thought
> chaces another, and draws after it a third, by which it is expell'd in
> its turn. (*T* 261)

5. It should be plain enough that, whatever the merits of Hume's
central question, the part of his answer that invokes resemblance and
memory cannot be right. If Hume's third-person picture is to have
application to the case of *self*-identity it must be possible for a given
person to have, at a given time, two numerically distinct recollections
with the same content. Two numerically distinct recollections are
necessary; if this requirement is not met the subject/observer distinction
is lost, and there is no way of introducing, in the way Hume needs, both
the resemblance between present recollection and past perception and
the awareness of this resemblance. The two recollections must be had
by a single person; for otherwise we do not have a case of self-identity.
The recollections must occur at the same time (or at least must overlap
for a stretch of time); for if the subject's recollection ceases before the
self-observer's begins, the self-observer cannot link the subject's past
and present perceptions;[13] and if the temporal ordering is reversed the
self-observer will no longer recall the subject's past perception when
he is alleged to notice its resemblance to the subject's present recollection. Finally, the two recollections must have the same content, they
must be of the same past perception; failing this the whole point of an
explanation in terms of resemblance is lost. As Hume must realize were
he to think it through, however, these several conditions cannot be
jointly satisfied, for there can be no way of individuating two numerically
distinct recollections in the circumstances envisaged. It follows that his
explanation in terms of memory and resemblance must be rejected.[14]

If Hume cannot use resemblance and memory in the way he does to
answer his central question what is the upshot? Is there nothing at all
to the idea that memory, resemblance and the consciousness of one's
own identity are significantly linked? To be sure, memory and resemblance come into play for judgments of identity in other-person cases.

Jones appears to remember having done such and such; I recall some-one's having done just that; I take Jones and that someone to be the same. (All this, of course, without seeing into his breast!) Presumably it was the possibility of just such cases that led Hume's reflections along the lines we have laid out. However, such an account cannot work when observed and observer are the same. Nor can the mere fact of resemblance between recollection and perception recalled serve Hume's official purposes.

Suppose we alter the roles assigned to memory and resemblance. We, reading Hume narrowly, have taken the relevant resemblance to be that between recollection and past perception, a resemblance that can be used, if at all, only by an external observer. Suppose, however, that the relevant resemblance obtains between one's present perceptions, other than one's recollections, and the past perceptions one recalls. Suppose, to broaden the scope, we think in terms of a resemblance be-tween one's present and one's remembered past self or selves? (One's recollections, viewed as present occurrences, come into the story, but not as items to be compared with what is remembered to have happened in the past.) One notices similarities between the thoughts, feelings, inclinations and desires that one now has and those that one remembers having had. Perhaps one also notices causal connections between one's past and these present perceptions. Were Hume to think along these lines he could assign a role to both memory and resemblance in the formation of judgments of one's own identity, bypassing the objections I raised a few paragraphs back. There seem to be no intractable diffi-culties with the idea that I may compare my past and present psycho-logical states; why could not Hume use this idea to help explain the sense of one's identity?

It will be objected that there could be no question to which such facts might provide an answer. Since I remember those past perceptions, and perhaps even remember them as my own, it cannot be a genuine question whether I and the person who had them are the same. (Here I assume the memories are veridical. It is a striking fact that Hume makes that assumption throughout his discussion of personal identity.) Even if the past and present perceptions were utterly dissimilar I must take them all as my own, so the point about resemblance becomes otiose. Indeed, in posing his central question, Hume himself assumes that the percep-tions of which one is aware, or that one recalls in the requisite way, are, perhaps necessarily, one's own. Since there is no question here of *acquiring* the concept of a mind, or of one's own mind, what conceivable question remains?

This objection brings home the severe limits within which Hume is working. Despite these limits, he seems to have raised a legitimate, indeed fundamental, question on which our revised account of resem-blance may well have some bearing. It may be that to settle some of the baffling questions that arise when we philosophize about personal identity we must adopt a way of thinking proposed in a now classical paper of Derek Parfit's.[15] *Very* roughly, Parfit's conception admits a distinction between one's past, one's present, and one's future selves. The distinction is not merely one of temporal location, for my self of yesterday need not, according to Parfit's conception, be merely a past self of mine. These several selves are related by a relation that he calls, provisionally, 'psychological continuity', that includes causal continuity.[16] This relation is one of degree. If what one recalls experiencing, doing, and the like is *closely* psychologically continuous with one's present psychological state one may talk of those past psychological states in a straightforwardly first-personal way; for example: 'I began to think that the problem is difficult', 'I was angered by his remark', 'I decided to try again'. As the distance, measured in terms of degree of psychological continuity, increases between one's present psychological state and what one remembers, one might move to locutions such as 'A past self of mine was angered by his remark', and 'One of my past selves was in love with her'. Beyond a certain limit one might need to speak of the feelings and doings of some merely 'ancestral self' of one's own.[17]

For our purposes, three points are especially significant. First, Parfit's 'psychological continuity' has close affinities with Hume's (revised) account of resemblance and causal connection. Second, Parfit insists that the relations between my several selves are strictly matters of degree. It is a mistake to think of the link between my past and present selves as an all-or-nothing affair. Third, and connected with this, is the point that different individuals in perfect agreement about the facts may well differ in the descriptions they take to be appropriate. I may think it appropriate to say that I was in love with her; others may think it better to say that some past self of mine was in love with her. There is, in Parfit's view, no way other than decision of settling the question in such cases.

Parfit's theorizing arises from a concern to understand a number of extraordinary possibilities such as fusion, fission and the like. Hume, unlike both Parfit and Locke, pays no attention at all to the question whether Socrates might be identical with the Mayor of Quienborough, or the past prince with the present cobbler. But Parfit urges that his conception illuminates not only the philosopher's curious cases but also the actual state of things. And I suggest that Hume's central question, as well as his (revised) answer to it in terms of resemblance and causality, may be usefully viewed as an anticipation of Parfit's account. Indeed, it seems that Hume's central claim is the same as Parfit's: what is important in what we call cases of personal identity is merely a matter of degree, and thus boundary disputes concerning one's past and present selves have no correct answer. For Hume the identity of minds is just like that of bodies; in each case it is a matter of relations, which may be more or less close, obtaining between more or less momentary objects. In the normal run of things there are, of course, natural, agreed-upon groupings of such momentary objects. When one thinks accurately, however, one sees that should one care to raise boundary questions one may not be assured of an answer, even when all the facts are in. Hume says, 'the nice and subtle questions concerning personal identity can never possibly be decided, and are to be regarded rather as grammatical than as philosophical difficulties . . . as the relations, and the easiness of the [mind's] transition may diminish by insensible degrees, we have no just standard, by which we can decide any dispute concerning the time, when they acquire or lose a title to the name of identity' (*T* 262).

Even if Hume were right in all of this, difficulties would remain. For in the ordinary course of events one's sense of one's identity through change (a sense which is built into one's past-tense self-ascriptions) seems not to be based on what one observes or even on facts of which one is introspectively aware. Ordinarily, one does not move from recognized relations between given perceptions to the notion of identity. So it seems that Hume's central question, *as he poses it*, rests on a false assumption. That question, it will be recalled, concerns the *observational circumstances* that give rise to judgments of one's own identity. As we shall see, the notion of introspective observation is especially problematic. But the present problem remains even if it is not observation but some more generous, although recognizably Humean, notion of introspective awareness that is invoked.

To meet this difficulty, let us amend Hume's picture of things in a fairly drastic way by reconstruing the relation between one's sense of identity and those circumstances (the relations of resemblance and causality among one's several perceptions) that purportedly explain one's sense of identity. Let us assume that the sense of one's identity is a product of the fact that those circumstances obtain and *not* of one's being aware of that fact. What we are concerned with, we may say, are the causally effective truth-conditions for one's commonly made and correct judgments of self-identity when it is assumed the conditions may be effective without one's being aware of them. Some may say that if the truth-conditions for one's judgments enter causally into one's making those judgments that is tantamount to one's being aware that the conditions obtain. But that, I shall assume, is not a move that would recommend itself to Hume.

Other difficulties now stare us in the face. We may take it that, in the now much revised Humean view, the truth-conditions for mental identity judgments involve the relations of resemblance (including the resemblance between recollection and item recalled) and causality between perceptions. Let us look first at causality. As we have seen, Hume holds that minds are non-continuous collections of causally related perceptions. Indeed, he stresses causality at the expense of resemblance. He also assumes that one retains one's identity (albeit 'fictional identity') despite, for example, one's sometimes soundly sleeping. In addition, however, he maintains that causal series are continuous ones. It follows that if causality is to play the extensive role demanded of it, if it is to link all of one's perceptions and especially those occurring before and after gaps in consciousness, Hume must postulate intervening causal links that are not themselves perceptions. Given all that has gone before, of course, we may assume that he would think of these intervening causal links as physiological states or events in an individual's body.

Surprisingly, Hume does not make the point himself even though a near relative of it provides him with his only sound objection to the substrate theory of the self.[18] Indeed, he remarks without explanation that contiguity 'has little or no influence in the present case [personal identity]' (T 260). Perhaps, on the ground that at least some perceptions do not have spatial properties, he means merely to deny that *spatial* contiguity has much scope here ? Perhaps he is thinking of gaps in consciousness, and hence of the fact that one cannot get a temporally continuous series of perceptions through the life of a given individual, but does not think through the ramifications of that fact ? Whatever the explanation of this remark may be, Hume needs temporal continuity if his causal account of mind is to work. And he cannot get it, at least on his own premises, without the intervention of a body.

Were he to introduce a person's body to secure causal continuity for 'that chain of causes and effects, which constitute our self or person' (T 262) he could use the body to serve other purposes as well. Though I shall not rehearse the well-known arguments here, there is compelling reason to think that exclusively psychological characteristics must be insufficient to explicate the individuation of persons and perceptions or to provide conditions for personal identity. Were Hume to concede this he might partially endorse Ayer's claim that 'personal identity depends upon the identity of the body, and . . . a person's ownership of states of consciousness consists in their standing in a special causal relation to the body by which he is identified'.[19] Whether the notion of dependence on bodily identity can be construed laxly enough to permit at least some varieties of cases outside the normal range is a fundamental question, but one that I shall simply not pursue.

To avoid misunderstanding two points must be noted about the suggestion at hand. First, Hume's adopting this suggestion need not prevent his posing and answering his central question in the manner that anticipates Parfit. For both I and others could still wonder whether the past perceptions I remember and those of which I am now aware are sufficiently continuous psychologically to legitimate my saying 'I did that' rather than 'Some past self of mine was the culprit'. Hume's more extreme version of this question could likewise have a place. Second, the present suggestion does not require that one use bodily criteria as the basis for one's self-ascriptions. One need mention one's body only when spelling out the causally effective truth-conditions for one's judgments of self-identity, where 'truth-conditions' is used as above. As

Ayer remarks: 'I am not maintaining . . . that this is how one actually becomes aware of one's own experiences, but only that the fact that they are one's own, or rather the fact that they are the experiences of the person that one is, depends upon their being connected with this particular body'.[20]

Hume's inclusion of the body in his causal account of mental identity will also help him to deal with what we may call 'the permanent-self objection'. This expression covers a family of objections, some of which are difficult to state clearly, that have in common the claim that Hume's theory of the self requires something with which it is incompatible, that is, some continuant 'behind' the perceptions that officially constitute one's mind. Price's version of the permanent-self objection is particularly interesting since it displays the extent of the damage done to his general philosophy if Hume is unable to meet the objection.

> [I]t may be doubted whether his [Hume's] theory of the Self is consistent either with his theory of Inductive Inference or with his theory of the External World. For 'the imagination', which plays so prominent a part in the two last, seems uncommonly like the permanent self which he has rejected; or at least it seems to be permanent in a sense in which a series of impressions and images is not. Indeed there is the same difficulty within the section on *Personal Identity* itself. His account of the identity of continuants in general is not easily reconciled with his account of the identity of the self in particular. A continuant, he says, is a series of numerically and qualitatively diverse particulars along which the imagination makes a smooth transition. The identity of a continuant is therefore a 'fictitious', or as others might say, a 'constructed' identity. But if the imagination is to make this smooth transition from item to item, must not it itself have an identity which is *not* fictitious or constructed? If it is itself a series of particular imagings, what can we mean by saying that it makes a smooth transition along some other series of particulars? Perhaps there is some way of answering these questions without reintroducing the Pure Ego that Hume has officially rejected. But it is clear that the theory needs pretty drastic reformulation if his fundamental contentions are to be preserved.[21]

Price elsewhere develops his objection in connection with memory.[22]

Hume's reply to the objection can be straightforward enough. His ontology admits continuously existing objects whose states or properties can be invoked to answer Price's questions. He admits bodies that are distinct from minds, and not in any sense reducible to minds, whose acquired properties may explain both the recollection of events and the retention of what one has inductively acquired in the past. Features of bodies may also be used to underpin Hume's explanation of belief in physical objects, including one's own body, and even the sense of one's identity through time, interruption and change. To be sure, there are difficulties in Hume's account, so far as he gives one, of the nature of bodies. But these difficulties in no way affect the present question. The permanent-self objection seems unanswerable on the assumption that Hume is a neutral monist, say, or a subjective idealist. (Significantly, Price asserts that Hume *is* a neutral monist.[23]) With these assumptions scrapped, however, Hume's reply is plain.

Hume apparently thinks of a man's mind and his body as causally linked, but distinct, compound substances or time-consuming objects, one of them, the body, continuous in the sense defined earlier, the other not so. Of course, when discussing personal identity he focuses almost exclusively on intramental matters partly, I take it, for methodological reasons. It is the mental, not the physical, side of things that is the proposed subject-matter of his so-called science of human nature. The narrowing of focus is also a function of his interest in questions of self-consciousness rather than of personal identity more broadly construed. Not surprisingly, with the exception of the startling remark about seeing into another's breast, he conducts his discussion of personal identity without any consideration of the identity of other persons.[24] Again not surprisingly, things do not go very smoothly.

Let us give the kaleidoscope one further turn. Although Hume appears to view a person as a team of two compound substances he could view him, in an interestingly different way, as an embodied mind, or as a single psychophysical substance. Persons, construed as psychophysical substances, would be continuous even if not always conscious. Why should we say they are single substances? For one thing, Hume can have no objection to a single thing having properties of very different kinds. For another, given his doctrine of the relativity of identity, one can as reasonably and naturally raise identity questions about things of this kind as about purely physical things or purely mental ones. Most importantly, the states and properties of such single substances can satisfy the most stringent conditions for ('fictional') identity that Hume imposes. Like the properties of purely physical things, the states and properties, both mental and physical, of psychophysical substances can display 'a *sympathy* of parts to their *common end*' (*T* 257), and can 'bear to each other, the reciprocal relation of cause and effect in all their actions and operations' (*T* 257). We have seen something of how this works, in chapters 2 and 3.

To look at Hume this way is, to be sure, unusual. But the suggested view of persons is one that Hume could recognize as his own. In his discussion of mental identity he writes that 'the same person may vary his character and disposition, *as well as* his impressions and ideas, without losing his identity' (*T* 261, my italics). Character and disposition are contrasted with the perceptions that constitute one's mind. Yet both character and perceptions bear on one's personal identity. It is easy to work this out if persons are psychophysical substances; not so easy otherwise. 'Bodily pains and pleasures', Hume says, 'are the source of many passions, both when felt and when consider'd by the mind; but arise originally *in the soul, or in the body, whichever you please to call it,* without any preceding thought or perception' (*T* 276, my italics). This obscure remark may turn one's thoughts to an identity theory, perhaps to a double-aspect theory, of mind, but neither of these is at all likely to be Hume's view. Perhaps Hume means to convey Descartes' point that 'I am not only lodged in my body as a pilot in a vessel, but . . . I am very closely united to it, and so to speak so intermingled with it that I seem to compose with it one whole'.[25] Mention of Descartes turns our thoughts to two substances again, but the ideas of close union and intermingling suggest one thing with two sets of states and properties. And *that* view of the matter comes right to the surface when, writing of pride and humility, Hume claims that they 'have the qualities of our mind and body, that is *self*, for their natural and more immediate causes' (*T* 303).

6. Hume does not remain satisfied with his discussion of personal identity for very long. '[U]pon a more strict review of the section concerning *personal identity*', he writes in the 'Appendix' to the *Treatise*, 'I find myself involv'd in such a labyrinth, that, I must confess, I neither know how to correct my former opinions, nor how to render them consistent' (*T* 633). Surprisingly, it has proved uncommonly difficult to determine his reasons for dissatisfaction.

Some things that he says suggest that the difficulties parallel those encountered in his discussion of the external world. He implies that his 'theory of the intellectual world' is subject to 'those contradictions, and absurdities, which seem to attend every explication, that human reason can give of the material world' (*T* 633), and hence he seems to retract the claim that 'the intellectual world, tho' involv'd in infinite obscurities, is not perplex'd with any such contradictions, as those we have discover'd in the natural' (*T* 232). He also says explicitly that 'there are two principles, which I cannot render consistent; nor is it in my power to renounce either of them, viz. *that all our distinct perceptions are distinct existences*, and *that the mind never perceives any real connexion among distinct existences*' (*T* 636), a statement that echoes the sceptical conclusion to his discussion of belief in an external world. Although tempting, this rendering of Hume's second thoughts about personal identity cannot be correct: the suggested parallels are all wrong, and the two principles that seem to pinpoint the difficulty neither are, nor could they be thought by Hume to be, inconsistent in any strict sense of the word.

That the suggested parallels are all wrong is readily seen. Hume's examination of belief in an external world has three principal parts. (1) He rejects a substrate analysis of physical substances, the fiction of 'an unknown something, or *original* substance and matter, as a principle of union or cohesion' (*T* 221). (2) He offers an elaborate causal explanation, within the framework of his associationist psychology, of the plain man's beliefs about physical objects. In the first instance, he explains the belief in independent objects. Additionally, he explains identity beliefs with respect to such objects. (3) He argues for an ineradicable antinomy resulting from equally natural operations of the human imagination. One acquires an ineradicable belief that there are independent physical objects; but one can also construct an irrefutable argument whose conclusion is that this ineradicable belief is false. Importantly, Hume remains satisfied with all of this. There are no retractions in the 'Appendix'. The antinomy argument is repeated in the first *Enquiry*. The only difficulties he admits are difficulties in the nature of things (in the nature of the imagination), not in his account of the nature of things.

What parallels may be suggested between this account of bodies and what Hume says, in the 'Appendix', of his account of minds? He continues to reject a substrate theory of the self. That is the point of his reiterating that all our distinct perceptions are distinct existences, and it involves no change of mind. Perhaps by the time he writes the 'Appendix' he is persuaded that the imagination is antinomic not only with respect to bodies but also with respect to minds? But if this is so, what is the ineradicable belief about minds that can be shown, by irrefutable philosophical argument, to be false? Not, obviously, that one's mind is an independent object in the sense in which a body is. Is it that the mind is a single thing that endures despite change and interruption? But that belief may well be true if 'fictional' identity is in question. Is it that one's self has perfect identity? Hume nowhere suggests that this belief is ineradicable. Is it that one's self is a substrate? The belief is hardly ineradicable, and in any case is a philosopher's, not a plain man's, belief. Perhaps it is that minds are continuous in the sense defined earlier? This would amount to a belief that minds are continuously conscious. But Hume thinks that this belief is not even widely held, so it can hardly be ineradicable. This exhausts the likely interpretations. But the basic objection to this reading of Hume is a more obvious one. Were Hume to determine that the imagination is antinomic in relation to one's beliefs about minds he would surely relish the result, not complain of it. The defeat would be for the mind, not for Hume's theory of the mind. It seems clear that his second thoughts do not concern antinomies.

If there are parallels, then, they must concern Hume's associationist explanations. Once the question of such parallels is raised, however, it should be perfectly obvious what Hume's point is in the 'Appendix'. By the time he writes the 'Appendix' he realizes that he has failed to do, for the case of minds, what he still believes he has successfully done in that of bodies. He has failed to give a satisfactory associationist explanation of the plain man's beliefs. The defeat is for Hume, not for the mind.

His own words are quite clear. His argument has led to the view that 'we only *feel* a connexion or determination of the thought, to pass from one object to another' and that 'the thought alone finds personal identity, when reflecting on the train of past perceptions, that compose a mind,

the ideas of them are felt to be connected together, and naturally introduce each other' (*T* 635). This accords with the view of 'most philosophers' that 'personal identity *arises* from consciousness; and consciousness is nothing but a reflected thought or perception' (*T* 635). So far his
account has a 'promising aspect' (*T* 635). His troubles begin when he
attempts to give the associationist explanation: '[W]hen I proceed to
explain the principle of connexion, which binds them [that is, our
particular perceptions] together, and makes us attribute to them a real
simplicity and identity; I am sensible, that my account is very defective'
(*T* 635). Here, he gives a footnote reference to that point in the original
discussion where, having argued that an associationist account of
personal identity must be given, he writes:

> The only question . . . which remains, is, by what relations this un-
> interrupted progress of our thought is produc'd, when we consider
> the successive existence of a mind or thinking person. And here 'tis
> evident we must confine ourselves to resemblance and causation.
> (*T* 260)

Is the failure one of principle or one of execution merely ? Hume leaves
open the latter possibility: the difficulty may not be 'absolutely insuper-
able' and others, or even he himself, may, with further thought, discover
a satisfactory 'hypothesis' (*T* 636).

If Hume tells us that it is his associationism that is at fault he does not
tell us his reasons for this assessment. Save to satisfy our biographical
curiosity, however, this does not greatly matter; we have discovered
quite sufficient reasons on our own. Still, two points are worth noting.
First, the reasons we have discovered would explain the differing final
assessments Hume makes of associationism for the case of bodies and
associationism for the case of self-consciousness. Most of the difficulties
we have discovered stem from the associationist's need to distinguish
observer and observed, a distinction easily made in the former case, but
problematic in the latter. The other difficulties we have raised concern
individuation and continuity, issues that are more-or-less readily handled
when one considers bodies but are quite intractable if one's attention is
riveted on intra-mental occurrences. A second point to notice is this.
We have devised ways in which Hume might alter his account in
response to our objections, while remaining a causal theorist, if not an
associationist, about consciousness of mental identity. If these responses
are adequate, Hume's seemingly vain hope for a more satisfactory
'hypothesis' is not vain after all.

Hume unwittingly leaves a false scent when he says that he cannot
render 'consistent' the two principles cited earlier; for he can hardly
think that they are logically inconsistent with one another. The first
amounts to the claim that perceptions are logically capable of independent existence. The second claims, in effect, that causal judgments do not
have the character of logical necessity. Either or both of these may be
objectionable, even if Hume clearly does not think so. But what possible

reason could *Hume* have to think them *incompatible* with one another ?

His conclusion seems rather to be that, with the apparent failure of his associationist account, he can conceive of no way to explain the judgments of mental identity we make. Three candidates present themselves. Mental identity is a function either of an underlying substrate or of causal connections among the perceptions that constitute a mind. If the latter, it is a function either of a real causal tie among the perceptions themselves or merely of the mind's associating ideas of those causally related perceptions. Hume rejects the first two alternatives; the first because of his views about substance ('all our distinct perceptions are distinct existences'); the second because of his analysis of causality ('the mind never perceives any real connexion among distinct existences'). The third is the associationist alternative but Hume discovers, to his chagrin, that it, too, will not work. Thus he confesses himself stymied in his efforts to understand mental identity.[26]

As I remarked at the beginning, the question of Hume's second thoughts is one of two especially vexing problems of interpretation. The second of these concerns his unexplained statement that 'we must distinguish betwixt personal identity, as it regards our thought or imagination, and as it regards our passions or the concern we take in ourselves' (*T* 253). Some view this as an admission that the theory of the self provided in Book I of the *Treatise* is incompatible with the view of the self he adopts when theorizing about the emotions in Book II. They find confirmation for their view in the fact that, when discussing sympathy, Hume appears to vacillate on a question of fundamental importance when he speaks of 'the idea, or rather impression of ourselves' (*T* 317). Surely this is a half-hearted retraction of his earlier denial of an impression of the self ? Not at all. The apparently vacillating remark need imply no more than the recognition that self-awareness requires both present awareness (hence 'impression') and memory (hence 'idea'). Hume says, quite explicitly, that the object of pride and humility is 'self, or that succession of related ideas and impressions, of which we have an intimate memory and consciousness' (*T* 277).

What then is Hume's point in distinguishing self, as regards the thought and imagination, from self, as regards the passions ? Two possibilities suggest themselves. Were Hume concerned with the requirements for an empiricist explanation of the idea of a mind, or of one's self, his point might be that, in general, one's emotions cannot be among the neutrally construed data from which one begins; for the simple reason that many of one's emotions are causally dependent on one's already possessing a conception of one's self and of others. Pride and humility, love and hatred, and many other emotions, depend, in Hume's view, on one's having certain beliefs about the doings, qualities, and the like, of both other persons and one's self. However, Hume does not in fact address himself to an empiricist construction of the concept of the self. So it is unlikely that this is the intended force of his unexplained remark.

Fortunately, another, simpler reading is available. In a passage quoted earlier Hume says that 'pride and humility have the qualities of our mind and body, that is *self*, for their natural and more immediate causes' (*T* 303). A theory of the self that is adequate to an understanding of the emotions must, that is to say, treat the self as a compound of mind and body or as a psychophysical substance. The explanation of self-awareness at *Treatise* I iv 6, however, is explicitly restricted to awareness of one's mental identity. Hume is well aware that questions of merely mental identity are narrowly restricted ones. He seems equally aware that posing such questions is compatible with recognizing that there are other questions about selves that must be posed as well. His language is obscure. But his point, by now at any rate, should be plain enough.

CHAPTER SIX

Concept, Thought and Judgment

1. In this and the next chapter I propose to examine a number of utterly fundamental topics in Hume's philosophy of mind, topics having to do with his detailed characterization of the items that constitute minds and that are the mental participants in mind-body transactions. Hume is, or inclines to be, a reductionist on many matters. We have seen his reductionist proclivities with respect to mental dispositions, his reduction of minds to bundles of perceptions and his reductionist reification of perceptions. As we shall see in the present chapter he is also a reductionist in his analysis of concept-exercise, of thought and of judgment. (We shall see that there is a reductionist thesis attributed to him that he does not hold.) He attempts to explicate thinking exclusively in terms of introspectible, determinate, concrete, antiseptically construed mental particulars and the causal relations in which they stand both to other such mental particulars and to objects and events in the physical world. The salient features of this part of Hume's empiricist and reductionist project, and its success or failure, are my present concern.

I begin by providing an extended account of Hume's views about concept-exercise or the use of so-called 'abstract ideas'. The detail is needed lest we overlook the surprising complexity of Hume's views and the seriousness of his efforts in a reductionist direction. It is tempting to soften Hume's doctrine at several points; to do so, however, would be to lose the benefits of close scrutiny of the genuine empiricist article. Having depicted the genuine article I shall argue that, at least in its Humean guise, it must be rejected. Despite the constraints within which he operates, Hume succeeds in isolating several crucial features of judgments. I shall indicate these in section 4. Even here, however, his reductionist objectives prevent the satisfactory deployment of his discoveries. The critical point of the present chapter is that an adequate theory of concept-exercise, of thought and of judgment requires, on some of Hume's own premises, a much richer ontology than Hume is prepared to accept. As we shall see in chapter 7 one also requires an analysis different from the one Hume provides for the mental items that his ontology does admit. It is not to be thought that ontological and methodological questions are quite independent. Only by examining Hume's views about introspective awareness shall we get to the bottom of his philosophizing about mind. But that is to look too far ahead; we must look, first, at his philosophizing about thought.[1]

2. Let us begin by reflecting on two passages from the *Treatise*:
   Suppose a person present with me, who advances propositions, to which I do not assent, *that* Caesar *dy'd in his bed, that silver is more fusible than lead, or mercury heavier than gold*; 'tis evident, that notwithstanding my incredulity, I clearly understand his meaning, and form all the same ideas, which he forms. My imagination is endow'd with the same powers as his; nor is it possible for him to conceive any idea, which I cannot conceive; or conjoin any, which I cannot conjoin. (*T* 95)
   If one person sits down to read a book as a romance, and another as a true history, they plainly receive the same ideas, and in the same order; nor does the incredulity of the one, and the belief of the other hinder them from putting the very same sense upon their author. His words produce the very same ideas in both; tho' his testimony has not the same influence on them. (*T* 97–8)

Leaving the question of belief or assent till later, let us focus narrowly on the picture Hume here presents of successful communication between speaker and hearer, or writer and reader. Indeed, for brevity's sake let us consider only the speaker-hearer case; the points I want to stress can be readily adapted to that of writer and reader.

According to Hume's picture, the speaker means something in what he says and the hearer puts a sense on what the speaker says. The utterance of 'Silver is more fusible than lead' expresses the speaker's thought of silver's being more fusible than lead. That, one might say, is what he means in what he says. The hearer, understanding the speaker's meaning, likewise has the thought, whatever his attitude to it, of silver's being more fusible than lead. In more Humean language, both speaker's meaning and hearer's understanding are matters of ideas, indeed of the very same ideas. And both speaker and hearer have, so far as the relevant ideas go, the very same powers or abilities. The picture requires that we distinguish at least four causally related items, taking each as an occurrence: the speaker's thought of silver's being more fusible than lead; the utterance that expresses that thought; the hearer's hearing that utterance, and the hearer's thought of silver's being more fusible than lead. The utterance is a public occurrence; the thoughts of speaker and hearer, however, occur *in foro interno*.[2] Hume apparently takes the thoughts to be complexes or conjunctions of ideas.[3] Surely he also thinks the utterances in question have constituents; in particular, they involve tokens of what he calls 'general terms'.

Taking a lead from Hume's reference to powers, we may say that both speaker and hearer have the ability to have certain complete thoughts, such as the thought that Caesar died in his bed, or the thought that silver is more fusible than lead. The ability follows trivially from the fact of having these thoughts. They also have certain complex linguistic abilities: the ability to express these thoughts by certain English sentences, and the ability to construe the utterance of certain English sentences as the expression of these thoughts. Recalling the suggestion that these thoughts are complexes, as well as the fact that Hume singles out general terms for extended discussion, we may go further. Speaker and hearer have the ability to have the constituent thought of silver, say, or of death, as well as the corresponding subsentential linguistic abilities to use or construe the general terms 'silver' and 'death'. Introducing some non-Humean terminology, I shall take the ability to have such constituent thoughts of silver as identical with having a concept of silver, and having such a thought of silver as identical with exercising that ability, or employing that concept. I shall by-pass the question whether, in Hume's view, one can exercise concepts without having complete thoughts.

Several things should be noted about this way of viewing the situation. A concept, or the having of a concept, is to be understood as a psychological property that is dispositional in character. As such, a concept is subjective in one sense (one may speak of Smith's concept), and intersubjective in another (Smith and Jones may have the same concept or ability). In the present context, of course, communication of thoughts cannot take place unless both speaker and hearer have the same relevant conceptual abilities. Concepts are abilities exercised in thoughts, that is, in occurrences taking place *in foro interno*. As such they are distinct from, though they may be intimately related to, certain linguistic abilities. For the present I want to leave the notion of an exercise of a concept otherwise uninterpreted. Only thus can we use the notion to get some purchase on Hume's thinking without at the same time distorting his thinking out of all recognition.

Making use of the terminology just introduced, we may express one of Hume's most famous doctrines in this way: concepts are acquired by a process of abstraction. One comes to notice the repetition of features in one's environment; to sort out these features from other accompanying ones. Having 'found a resemblance among several objects' (*T* 20) one comes to grasp or recognize these objects as 'of . . . [a] particular species' (*T* 17). This, I take it, marks the onset of a conceptual ability. There are complications, of course, but the basic doctrine is clear.

Acquiring both a concept and the linked ability to use a general term requires a double process of abstraction. That abstraction is involved is clear: 'When we have found a resemblance among several objects, that often occur to us, we apply the same name to all of them, whatever differences we may observe in the degrees of their quantity and quality, and whatever other differences may appear among them' (*T* 20). That abstraction is involved twice over is also clear:

> When ev'ry individual of any species of objects is found by experience to be constantly united with an individual of another species, the appearance of any new individual of either species naturally conveys the thought to its usual attendant. Thus because such a particular idea is commonly annex'd to such a particular word,

nothing is requir'd but the hearing of that word to produce the
correspondent idea. (*T* 93)

Acquiring the use of 'blue', say, requires both that one take different
utterances of 'blue' as 'individuals of a species' and that one take different occurrences of the requisite visible quality in one's environment as
'individuals of a species'. Additionally, of course, items of each of the
two species must be suitably conjoined in one's experience. For Hume's
is an associationist account of language learning. By associative conditioning, requiring repeated encounters with conjoined items of the two
species, one acquires a certain 'custom' (*T* 20), a certain 'habit' (*T* 21,
22). More accurately, one acquires both a concept and an ability to use
or construe an appropriate general term.[4]

What happens when one has thus acquired both concept and linguistic
ability? Using the more-or-less uninterpreted notion of concept-
exercise introduced earlier, what happens is this: hearing a suitable
sound prompts an exercise of the related concept; and exercising a
concept disposes one to utter the related sound. The hearing of 'blue',
for example, causes an exercise of the concept of blue; and the thought
of blue things disposes one to utter 'blue'. It is plausible to view the
transition as perfectly constant in the hearer's case; on hearing, one may
say, one automatically understands. Thus Hume writes that, having
heard a word, "twill scarce be possible for the mind, by its utmost
efforts, to prevent that transition' (*T* 93).

Concepts and their associated linguistic abilities, viewed as dispositional properties, must be understood, in part, in terms of a pattern
of stimulus and response. In effect, I have just indicated how Hume
would fill in such a pattern for the knowledge of a general term. When
one isolates concepts from linguistic abilities, however, things are not
very clear; Hume has made no systematic attempt to catalogue and
characterize the stimulus-response pattern for non-linguistic cases. We
may assume, however, that an adequate account must countenance at
least each of the following as a thought in which the concept of blue is
exercised, and thus as a response of the kind required: recognizing some
object present in one's environment as blue; recognizing some object,
whose image just pops into one's head, as blue; imagining a blue object
(just for the fun of it, say, or in response to a psychologist's request);
recalling some object as having been coloured blue; and thinking that
blue cars are more common than orange ones. We may assume, also,
that an adequate account must include the presence of a blue object or
the presence in recollection or imagination of a blue object, in its list of
stimulus conditions. But such an account must also accommodate cases
where no blue objects, whether actual or merely imagined, are present.
For one with the appropriate linguistic ability, of course, the sound
'blue' would be stimulus enough, but there are other cases to be handled
as well. I shall have occasion as we proceed to note some of the difficulties that are masked by Hume's failure to spell out systematically the

details of his stimulus-response view of conceptual abilities.

Whatever his views about the range of thoughts in which concepts may be exercised and about the character of the requisite stimulus conditions, what has Hume to say of the thoughts themselves? What, to put it crudely, does he think transpires *in foro interno* when one exercises the concept of blue or some other concept? How would he interpret the expression 'the exercise of a concept', which has already proved its usefulness for the articulation of his views? To answer these questions we must look more closely at what Hume actually says when discussing so-called 'abstract ideas'. That is to say, we must take a further look at his characterization of the acquisition and exercise of linked conceptual and linguistic abilities. It is on such cases that Hume concentrates his attention. But we must assume that the interpretation of concept-exercise offered for these cases suits the non-linguistic cases as well.

Hume holds that when one employs a general term, or understands another's use of it, one has an idea, that is to say, an image, of a particular object. '[']T]is certain *that* we form the idea of individuals, whenever we use any general term' (*T* 22). '[T]he image in the mind is only that of a particular object' (*T* 20); 'the imagination conceive[s] it [the object] with all its particular circumstances and proportions' (*T* 20). This thesis splits into at least two sub-theses: that one has an image whenever one uses, or grasps another's use of, a general term; and that the image one has is of a particular object. Hume argues for the latter thesis by arguing the more general point that any image one has is an image of a particular object. In his own words: '[T]he mind cannot form any notion of quantity or quality without forming a precise notion of the degrees of each' (*T* 18). Hume could hold the former thesis on quite limited grounds: for example, that one must employ tokens of an object of a given kind whenever one thinks of objects of that kind. I take it, however, that the thesis is merely part of an empiricist and reductionist restriction on the possible constituents of mental occurrences. I shall return to this point shortly.

It is worth noting, however, that Hume's associationist theory of language learning provides further motivation for the view that one has a suitable image whenever one uses, or grasps another's use of, a general term. Learning the use of 'blue' is a matter of the repeated conjunction of seeing something blue and hearing an utterance of the sound 'blue'. The something blue is an instance of one 'species of objects', the utterance of 'blue' is an instance of another. And the point is that once the 'habit' or 'custom' has been acquired, an encounter with another *instance* of the one species of objects gives rise to an *idea* (*image*) *of an instance* of the other species. Unless this takes place one would not have *another* instance of the appropriate sound/object *pair*, and there would be nothing for an associationist explanation to explain. To repeat:

> When ev'ry individual of any species of objects is found by experience to be constantly united with an individual of another species,

the appearance of any new individual of either species naturally conveys the thought to its usual attendant. (*T* 93)

Similarly: 'After we have acquir'd a custom of this kind, the hearing of that name revives the idea of one of these objects, and makes the imagination conceive it with all its particular circumstances and proportions' (*T* 20).

To talk of uttered sounds prompting images of particular objects is not to tell the whole of Hume's story. For, as Hume points out, the same term may be linked with images of resembling particular objects that are nonetheless different in many respects, and images of the same object may be linked with different terms. Despite this we are able to reason without mistake and to speak intelligibly and correctly. Thus, although our image is of a particular equilateral triangle, we do not say that the three angles of a triangle are equal to each other. Likewise, although we image 'an equilateral triangle of an inch perpendicular' (*T* 21) when reasoning about figures, rectilineal figures, regular figures, triangles, and equilateral triangles, we manage to reason correctly in these several situations. The explanation, according to Hume, must be found in the custom or habit we have acquired. Besides giving rise to an image of a particular object upon the hearing of a given sound, the custom ensures that one will not think or say things incompatible with the meaning of the term in question. Custom exerts a similar control in non-linguistic settings. It does this by guaranteeing that images of other particular objects from the appropriate range will come to mind should occasion require. Thinking of a linguistic case Hume writes:

Thus shou'd we mention the word, triangle, and form the idea of a particular equilateral one to correspond to it, and shou'd we afterwards assert, *that the three angles of a triangle are equal to each other*, the other individuals of a scalenum and isosceles, which we overlook'd at first, immediately crowd in upon us, and make us perceive the falsehood of this proposition, tho' it be true with relation to that idea, which we had form'd. (*T* 21)

When one has acquired the appropriate custom or habit, hearing a word both causes the occurrence of an image of a particular object from the range of objects designated by that term, and puts one in readiness to image other particulars from that range as required. In Hume's words:

After we have acquired a custom of this kind, the hearing of that name revives the idea of one of these objects, and makes the imagination conceive it with all its particular circumstances and proportions. But as the same word is suppos'd to have been frequently applied to other individuals, that are different in many respects from that idea, which is immediately present to the mind; the word not being able to revive the idea of all these individuals, only touches the soul, if I may be allow'd so to speak, and revives that custom, which we have acquir'd by surveying them. They are not really and in fact present to the mind, but only in power; nor

do we draw them all out distinctly in the imagination, but keep ourselves in a readiness to survey any of them, as we may be prompted
by a present design or necessity. The word raises up an individual
idea, along with a certain custom; and that custom produces any
other individual one, for which we may have occasion. But as the
production of all the ideas, to which the name may be apply'd, is in
most cases impossible, we abridge that work by a more partial
consideration, and find but few inconveniences to arise in our
reasoning from that abridgement. (*T* 20–1)
Hume's revival of custom is Price's sub-activation of a capacity.[5]

Hume's rather casual use of the expressions 'abstract idea' and
'general idea' obscures the presentation of his views. That it dissipates
this obscurity is some confirmation of the interpretation that I have
offered. Hume says that 'in forming most of our general ideas, if not all
of them, we abstract from every particular degree of quantity and
quality' (*T* 17). This is consistent with Hume's Berkeleyan thesis about
the determinateness of ideas, in the sense of images, if we take the
general idea to be a concept in the sense introduced earlier. Hume
remarks that 'the idea of time . . . will afford us an instance of an abstract
idea, which . . . is represented in the fancy by some particular individual
idea of a determinate quantity and quality' (*T* 34–5). The abstract idea
in question is best construed as a concept; the idea representing it in the
fancy is an image of a particular object. Of course, there are passages
where Hume clearly intends the expressions 'abstract idea' and 'general
idea' to designate images. He says that 'all abstract ideas are really
nothing but particular ones, consider'd in a certain light; but being
annexed to general terms, they are able to represent a vast variety, and
to comprehend objects, which, as they are alike in some particulars, are
in others vastly wide of each other' (*T* 34). Compounding the difficulty
he says that 'a general idea . . . [is] nothing but a particular one consider'd in a certain view' but goes on, in the very same sentence, to refer
to a 'particular idea, by which we represent a general one' (*T* 425).
Once again, however, we can interpret these passages in a way consistent with the Berkeleyan thesis. When 'abstract idea' or 'general
idea' is used to designate an image, rather than what I have called a
concept, the abstractness or generality in question is a relational, not an
intrinsic, property. That is to say, an image is an abstract or general idea
on condition that it occurs in the appropriate causal setting involving,
at least for linguistic cases, associative conditioning, ability to use a
general term, suitable stimulus, revived custom, and so forth. It is an
abstract or general idea if it serves in the exercise of a concept. This use
of 'abstract idea' and 'general idea' occurs when Hume writes that 'all
general ideas are, in reality, particular ones, attached to a general term,
which recalls, upon occasion, other particular ones, that resemble, in
certain circumstances, the idea, present to the mind' (*E* 158n).

In expounding Hume I have used the expression 'the range of objects designated by a general term'. This usefully colourless expression, which is not Hume's, deflects attention from a number of deep difficulties in the interpretation of Hume that must be mentioned even if they are not pursued. Hume writes both that general terms 'represent' or 'express' ideas and that they 'represent' or 'express' objects. Although these claims may be rendered consistent without turning Hume into an onto-logical idealist Hume has not, I think, done the needed job of untangling them. At times Hume assumes that a general term used by a given speaker represents only objects previously encountered by that speaker (T 20). But he is also prepared to say, with much greater plausibility, that 'we seldom or never can exhaust . . . [the] individuals' that fall within 'the compass of that collection, which it [the mind] intends to express by the general term' (T 22), that 'we can . . . form a notion of all possible degrees of quantity and quality' (T 18), and that ideas 'can become general in their representation, and contain an infinite number of other ideas under them' (T 24). Hume expresses his agreement with Berkeley's thesis about the determinateness of images in ways that are not, on the face of it, equivalent. I have preferred Hume's 'idea of a particular object' to such other expressions as 'individual idea' (T 21), ideas that are 'in themselves individual' (T 20), or ideas that are 'parti-cular in the mind's conception of them' (T 17). In doing so, it is clear, I have avoided quite fundamental problems that any more thorough-going examination of Hume's doctrine of abstract ideas must tackle.

Even without settling these several issues we have discovered that Hume's theory of abstract ideas has more, and more interesting, internal detail than is usually supposed. But we have yet fully to answer our earlier question about what transpires *in foro interno* when one thinks or exercises a concept. Just how, in Hume's view, do images enter in? Exercise of one's mastery of a general term is linked, by complicated causal ties, to the exercise of a concept *in foro interno*. One's use, or grasp, of a general term on a given occasion is similarly linked, by com-plicated causal ties, to the having of an image. The exercise of a concept in a non-linguistic setting involves the occurrence of images. But what precisely is the relation between the exercise of a concept *in foro interno* and the having of an image in a suitable linguistic or non-linguistic causal setting? Is the relation that of identity? And are complete thoughts constituted by such images, or exhaustively analysable as concatenations of them? In short, is Hume a thoroughgoing imagist about concept-exercise and thinking?

It is possible to stress images and yet not be a thoroughgoing imagist. Indeed one may hold that a concept is exercised when, and only when, an image is had in a suitable causal setting, and at the same time refuse to identify the two. For one may consistently hold that there are or must be further goings-on *in foro interno* when one exercises a concept; goings-on that are integrally related to the images one has but that none-theless are to be distinguished from these.[6] I cannot, however, believe

that Hume is prepared to countenance such additional items. He nowhere mentions them; and he certainly thinks he has presented an
adequate rendering of what happens when one thinks. He intends to
present an empiricist and reductionist theory of concept-exercise, and
thus of thinking, a theory that requires only Humean perceptions and
those dispositional properties that, in context, he calls 'customs' and
'habits'. In order that the theory should not be trivial the perceptions in
question must be construed antiseptically; they must be viewed as
determinate, concrete, introspectible items about whose occurrence
in foro interno it is assumed there is agreement on all hands. The point of
Hume's emphasis on the controlling role of one's dispositional properties, that is to say one's concepts, is that, given this role, one has no
need of items other than images as constituents of what transpires *in foro
interno*. The interest of the theory lies precisely in its attempt thus to
make do with images-cum-dispositions. Were Hume not a thoroughgoing imagist he would have provided no theory of thinking at all.

3. Once the imagist aspect of Hume's interestingly causal theory of
abstract ideas or concept-exercise is made fully explicit its many defects
become apparent. Some of these bear mention here; most are well
known.

There is, first, the difficulty of concept-exercise in the presence of an
object of the relevant kind. A linnet flies past and I say 'That is a linnet'.
In thus exercising my concept of a linnet must I have linnet-images in
addition to the sensations prompted by the linnet's passing? Surely not;
but if not, how are we to accommodate this case within the theory we
have sketched out? Some, perhaps, think of abstract ideas as ideas used
only in the absence of objects of the kind in question and thus in abstraction from them. I can find no evidence that Hume holds this view. Were
he to do so, however, he either must deny that in recognizing a linnet
one exercises one's concept of a linnet or he must admit that he has
made no attempt to explicate a large and central set of cases.

Hume's choice of examples assists the construction of his imagist
theory but, notoriously, there are numerous concepts that have no
straightforward links with one's abilities to image instances. The concepts of negation and existence are perhaps controversial examples;
but, as we shall see, there are pressures within Hume's own theory of
judgment to countenance these as concepts. Even in the case of initially
more promising colour concepts and physical-object concepts it is
simply false that concept-exercise requires images of appropriate
colours or objects. Can non-instantiative imagery, for example an
auditory image of the word 'cow', substitute for the otherwise required
instantiative image of a cow in otherwise intractable cases? Whatever
its own merits the suggestion runs counter to Hume's associationist
requirement that there should be instances of each species of object in
the associated word/object pairs. At one place Hume appears prepared

to make do with incomplete instantiative imagery: 'we do not annex distinct and compleat ideas to every term we make use of, and . . . in talking of *government, church, negotiation, conquest,* we seldom spread out in our minds all the simple ideas, of which these complex ones are compos'd' (*T* 23). At another place he seems to admit the possibility of concept-exercise without any relevant imagery at all: 'it . . . [is] usual, after the frequent use of terms, which are really significant and intelligible, to omit the idea, which we wou'd express by them, and to preserve only the custom, by which we recal the idea at pleasure' (*T* 224). His willingness to allow radical departures from his elaborate paradigm is, I take it, a product of his confidence that the much-emphasized operations of revived customs can take up the theoretical slack. Clearly, however, if Hume's exercises of concepts are to be occurrences *in foro interno*, cases involving only words and customs fail to fit the bill.

The problems facing Hume's imagism that I have mentioned so far narrowly concern the question of concept-exercise. But his imagism generates equally deep difficulties when the task is to explicate complete thoughts, which are the topic of the next section. Hume's imagism distorts his presentation of a correct and fundamentally important thesis about the nature of judgment. It leaves him with nothing of interest to say about the psychological analogue of predication; it prevents his giving any illuminating account of mental representation and of the complexity and logical structure of thoughts. There is, however, no need to expand on these and like objections here.

Despite its transparent implausibility an imagist theory of concept-exercise must prove irresistibly attractive to an empiricist such as Hume; images have the allure of the concrete and, or so it seems, the introspectively observable. There is point, then, to the conclusion that Hume's theory fails even for the cases it seems best equipped to handle: those in which, in exercising a concept, one images an object of the appropriate kind. There are various such cases. One may recall, with vivid imagery, the smithy's shop of one's youth, or imagine oneself being awarded a gold medal at the Olympic Games, or recognize the image that pops into one's head as the image of a Pomeranian; one may use the image of an equilateral triangle in the course of one's geometrical reflections, or image the upshot of the experiment one is conducting. Hume's theory must handle such cases if it is to handle any at all. When one looks closely, however, one sees that it cannot handle even these.

For one's imagings to count as exercises of concepts one must recognize what one images: the imaged shop as the shop of one's youth, the triangle as a triangle. To image with recognition, within even Hume's framework, is more than merely to image. In effect we have seen that Hume must distinguish having an impression with, and having one without, recognition; failure to do so renders his empiricist programme otiose, for there can be no need of concept-formation if one recognizes one's impressions from the beginning. But if ideas, construed as images, are merely pale replicas of impressions, differing from them only in vivacity, what guarantees that one recognizes one's images?

To image with recognition does not require that one say what is imaged or even that one be linguistically equipped to identify or describe the object imaged. In many cases recognition and linguistic expression go hand in hand; and it is surely true that the recognition of some kinds of objects is impossible without appropriate linguistic skills. But as Hume must insist, the capacity to recognize may outstrip the ability to report or describe, indeed it may be present when linguistic capacity is completely absent. Hume, after all, insists on the conceptual capacities of speechless infants and animals (compare T 176–7). Again, to image with recognition it is not necessary, or sufficient, that one's images have an aura of familiarity. Essentially, if not very informatively, to image with recognition is, in Hume's own words, to view the item imaged as an object 'of . . . [a] particular species' (T 17). Imaging with recognition is akin to face-to-face recognition of the things one encounters in experience.

Let us assume that Hume proposes to analyse imaging with recognition in terms of the occurrence of images in the appropriate causal settings, which are described above. Such an analysis, at first glance, can seem plausible enough. Consider a linguistic case. As hearer one has an image of a pineapple precisely because one hears 'pineapple' and because one has been conditioned by the repetition of pineapple / 'pineapple' pairs to respond as one does. Surely to image a pineapple in that setting is to image it with recognition? Consider the speaker's perspective. The speaker images a pineapple and is at least disposed to utter 'pineapple'. Surely nothing more is involved in his imaging a pineapple with recognition? After all, he is disposed to utter the name of what he images.

On Hume's own premises, however, this must be an illusion. The individuals in question may well image with recognition; but their doing so is not to be understood solely in terms of images and linked linguistic dispositions. Recall that, in Hume's view, having a concept and having the ability to express exercises of that concept by the use of a suitable general term are not to be identified, even if the abilities are intimately linked. Acquiring linked conceptual-cum-linguistic abilities requires a double process of abstraction and associative conditioning. Thoughts, and hence exercises of concepts, are occurrences *in foro interno*, and are to be distinguished from any public verbal expression they may receive. The picture of speaker-hearer communication with which we began is clear on the point: the speaker gives expression to a thought; the hearer, upon hearing the utterance, comes to have the same thought. The speaker, exercising his concept of a pineapple in some complete thought, gives expression to what he thinks; the hearer, who has mastered the use of 'pineapple', is thereby prompted to have a thought of, that is, exercise his concept of, a pineapple.

Against this background it is plain that the occurrence *in foro interno* that finds expression in speech, or that is prompted by another's utterance, if it involves imagery at all, must itself be an occurrence of imaging with recognition. That is to say, the element of recognition must be an intrinsic feature of the inner occurrence, not an extrinsic property that accrues to the image in virtue of its verbal or other causal accompaniments. It is thoughts, not mere images, that cause and are caused by utterances spoken and heard; and if in a given case we take the thought to be an imaging with recognition it is that imaging with recognition, and not a mere image, that is causally tied to public utterance. To be sure, the causal setting enters in; but it does so by explaining how one comes to link thought and sound, which is not to be confused with the linking of sound and mere image.

Similar considerations apply to the non-linguistic case. One exercises a concept, if in imagery at all, only in imaging with recognition. It is possible, if Hume is right, to specify a causal setting for such exercises of concepts; the causal story would need to mention abstraction, present non-linguistic stimulus, thoughts prompted by the thought in question, and perhaps resultant behaviour as well. But the intervening link in all of this, the occurrence in which one exercises a concept *in foro interno*, must have intrinsic features, in addition to those present when one merely has an image. One must recognize the upshot whose image is prompted by one's present experiment. It is only if one takes what one images to be a triangle that it can assist one's further reflections about triangles. It is not until one has recognized what one images as a Pomeranian that one has exercised the concept of a Pomeranian in connection with the image that popped into one's head. The underlying point is so simple that it may seem trivial: to image with recognition is to exercise a concept with respect to what is imaged. Although the point needs some qualification, we may say that imaging provides the raw material for concept-exercise and cannot itself constitute, even in an elaborate causal setting, the exercise of a concept.

Hume has not explicated imaging with recognition, and so has not provided a satisfactory interpretation for the notion of concept-exercise, for the seemingly more tractable cases. On his own premises we are left with the question of what must be added to images, and in what way or ways, if recognition, and hence thinking, is to come on the scene. More generally, we are left without any plausible way of construing the inner occurrences in which, within Hume's theory, exercises of concepts must consist. It is clear that Hume can do nothing to assist us within the limits of his ontological resources. His philosophy of mind countenances dispositional properties, antiseptically construed perceptions, and the public behaviour, including utterances, of bodies. But if concept-exercise takes place in occurrences *in foro interno* it seems that we must enrich this austere empiricist ontology with entities, or characteristics of entities, of a most unHumean variety. There is more to thinking than meets the introspectionist's or the behaviourist's eye.

4. The two passages that provided our starting-point in section 2 explicitly concern complete thoughts and judgments. Having examined Hume's views about concept-exercise it is time to turn to these more inclusive matters. As we shall see, Hume's account of the character of complete thoughts is hopelessly undeveloped. Certain features of his doctrine of judgment have none but a historical interest. These failings are connected with the imagism we have seen reason to reject. Despite these failings, Hume defends a thesis of fundamental importance about the nature of judgment and the relation between judgment and thought. I shall make a more-or-less uninterpreted use of our expression 'exercise of a concept', ignoring the imagist reading that, as I have argued, Hume in effect gives to it. By doing so we can isolate the fundamental thesis about judgment that his imagism has obscured.

I shall begin obliquely by examining David Pears's claim that Hume 'reduce[s] all complete thoughts to single ideas', that he 'treat[s] the composite product [a complete thought] as if it were a single unit'.[7] Pears holds that Hume argues for this reduction of complete thoughts to single ideas (hereafter, the reductionist thesis) in an important footnote to *Treatise* I iii 7 ('Of the nature of the idea or belief'). Against Pears I shall argue that this footnote is designed not to support the reductionist thesis but to make a very different point about the nature of judgment. As we shall see, Hume reduces some complete thoughts, namely simple existential ones, to single ideas. *Pace* Pears, however, he does not reduce all complete thoughts to single ideas. There is a tangle of issues here that needs sorting out.

In the terminology introduced earlier, Pears holds that Hume reduces each complete thought to the exercise of a single concept. Despite Pears's stress on Hume's imagism I shall assume, following the policy indicated above, that the present reductionist issue may be examined independently of questions about the interpretation of 'the exercise of a concept'. Construing the issue in this way makes better sense of Pears's own position. Pears holds that the reductionist thesis is a mistake: a complete thought, he says, 'is necessarily composed of at least two ideas'.[8] But Pears is no imagist and, as his discussion of existence makes clear, he takes the controversy to concern the possibility of complete thoughts involving only one concept.

Fortunately there is no need here to identify the conditions that are necessary or sufficient for something's counting as a single complete thought. We may take as examples the thoughts expressible by the following sentences and their negations: 'God exists', 'Caesar died in his bed', 'Silver is more fusible then lead', 'In war the weaker have always recourse to negotiation', 'The three angles of a triangle are equal to each other'. The examples are Hume's own.

But what is supposedly at issue between Hume and Pears? The controversy can have nothing to do with Hume's distinction between simple and complex ideas. Hume's own example of a complete thought that is reducible to a single idea is the thought that God exists; but the idea of God is, for Hume, a complex one. Reduction to single ideas is not reduction to simple ones; nor, of course, is the admission that a complex concept is exercised in a judgment an admission that more than one concept is exercised. Eschewing the needed qualifications, I suggest that the controversy concerns the need to admit a psychological analogue of predication in one's analysis of complete thoughts and of judgments. In Pears's view, judgment essentially involves a psychological analogue of predication; which is to say it involves the propositional linking of at least two concepts. The judgment that silver is more fusible than lead involves the propositional linking of the concept of being more fusible than lead with the concept of silver; the judgment that God exists involves the propositional linking of the concepts of God and existence. In the view Pears attributes to Hume there is no room for an analogue of predication. To reduce complete thoughts to single ideas is precisely to eliminate this feature of judgment. This construal of the controversy will be justified by our subsequent discussion. For brevity's sake I shall refer to this propositional linking of concepts, this psychological analogue of predication, as, simply, predication.[9]

Does Hume endorse the reductionist thesis? Straightforward textual evidence is not decisive in the matter, but let us begin with it. Save where otherwise indicated, I shall read 'idea', in the passages cited, as 'concept' or as 'exercise of a concept', as required.

Hume certainly holds that some complete thoughts, and hence some judgments, involve the exercise of only one concept. He says just this about existential judgments: "'tis far from being true, that in every judgment, which we form, we unite two different ideas; since in that proposition, *God is*, or indeed any other, which regards existence, the idea of existence is no distinct idea, which we unite with that of the object, and which is capable of forming a compound idea by the union' (*T* 96n). But, to turn a point of Pears's on its head,[10] one must be wary of generalizing from what Hume says about existential judgments to what he would say of non-existential ones. After all, he has distinctive views about the idea of existence. To be sure, there are places where he uses the singular term 'idea' in connection with non-existential judgments, as when he says: 'When I am convinc'd of any principle, 'tis only an idea, which strikes more strongly upon me' (*T* 103). In such a passage, however, I am inclined to think Hume's versatile word 'idea' is roughly equivalent to 'complete thought', and imports no commitment on the reductionist question.

What of the textual evidence on the other side? Throughout *Treatise* I iii 1 ('Of knowledge') Hume is concerned with two classes of relations: 'such as depend entirely on the ideas, which we compare together, and such as may be chang'd without any change in the ideas' (*T* 69). Of course, his attention is here sometimes directed to cases of inference, and therefore to cases involving a plurality of ideas in the sense of complete thoughts; but he is equally attentive to single judgments, and throughout he uses the plural 'ideas'. Elsewhere, he says that 'a person, who does not assent to a proposition you advance; after having conceiv'd the object in the same manner with you; immediately conceives it in a different manner, and has different ideas of it' (*T* 95); that 'belief consists not in the nature and order of our ideas, but in the manner of their conception' (*T* 629); that when one understands a speaker's proposition one 'conceives the ideas according to the proposition' (*T* 95). Again, we may 'perceive any repugnance among the ideas' involved when, for example, we say something such as 'In war the weaker have always recourse to conquest' (*T* 23).

Prima facie these are cases of thoughts involving more than one idea or concept. Since the textual evidence that Hume allows single complete thoughts to involve more than one idea may be resisted in a variety of ways, however, let us look at the footnote on which Pears bases his interpretation. I shall show that the footnote not only does nothing to support Pears's interpretation but is also *prima facie* inconsistent with it. Hume refers to 'a very remarkable error, which being frequently inculcated in the schools, has become a kind of establish'd maxim, and is universally received by all logicians' (*T* 96n). 'This error', he says, 'consists in the vulgar division of the acts of the understanding, into *conception, judgment* and *reasoning*, and in the definitions we give of them' (*T* 96n). The definition of 'reasoning' is at present irrelevant, but in what way are the definitions of 'conception' and 'judgment' faulty? 'Conception is defin'd to be the simple survey of one or more ideas: Judgment to be the separating or uniting of different ideas' (*T* 96n). And the difficulty is that ''tis far from being true, that in every judgment, which we form, we unite two different ideas; since in that proposition, *God is*, or indeed any other, which regards existence, the idea of existence is no distinct idea, which we unite with that of the object, and which is capable of forming a compound idea by the union' (*T* 96n). '[W]e can thus form a proposition, which contains only one idea' (*T* 96n–97n). Hume continues:

> What we may in general affirm concerning these three acts of the understanding, is, that taking them in a proper light, they all resolve themselves into the first, and are nothing but particular ways of conceiving our objects. Whether we consider a single object, or several; whether we dwell on these objects, or run from them to others; and in whatever form or order we survey them, the act of the mind exceeds not a simple conception; and the only remarkable difference, which occurs on this occasion is, when we join belief to the conception, and are perswaded of the truth of what we conceive. This act of the mind [belief] . . . is only a strong and steady conception of any idea, and such as approaches in some measure to an

immediate impression. (*T* 97n)

Pears maintains that Hume here argues for the reductionist thesis; citing this footnote he says that Hume 'uses the example of God's existence in order to reduce all complete thoughts to single ideas', and that he 'extended his over-simplified account of existential thoughts to other thoughts'.[11] It is imperative, then, to be clear about Hume's main concern in the footnote, and to grasp just how Hume's remarks about existence address these concerns. I suggest that the main point of the footnote, which is appended to Hume's positive account of belief or judgment,[12] is to display the inadequacies of what Hume takes to be the traditional theory of judgment, and thus to display the need for a theory of judgment such as that which Hume develops in the body of the text. The focus is on the question what makes a judgment a judgment. It must be admitted that Hume does not conduct his argument in the most felicitous way. The position for which he argues is this. One must distinguish merely having the thought that *p* from judging or believing that *p*. One must distinguish merely having the thought of God's existing, or of Caesar's having died in his bed, from judging or believing that God exists or that Caesar died in his bed. Let us say that one must distinguish mere conception from judgment. One who has a mere conception merely 'conceives the ideas according to the proposition' (*T* 95); his 'imagination reposes itself indolently on the idea' (*T* 115). Judgment involves something further. Of course there is something common to the mere conception that *p* and the judgment that *p*, namely the thought that *p*. Whether I merely conceive of Caesar's having died in bed, or I judge that he did so, I have the thought of his having died in bed.

What is the difference between merely conceiving that *p* and judging that *p* ? In Hume's view the difference lies in the 'manner of conception'. '[T]here is a great difference betwixt the simple conception of the existence of an object, and the belief of it, and . . . this difference . . . lie[s] in the *manner*, in which we conceive it' (*T* 94-5). '[A]n opinion or belief is nothing but an idea, that is different from a fiction . . . in the *manner* of its being conceiv'd' (*T* 628). We may leave the characterization of this manner of conception until later. On the traditional view, by contrast, the difference between mere conception and judgment is that in the latter, but not in the former, one separates or unites different ideas or concepts. That is to say, the traditional view identifies judgment with what I have called predication. In judging, but not in merely conceiving, one predicates something of something. One predicates existence of God, or having died in bed of Caesar, or being more fusible than lead of silver. Hume's point in the footnote is to show that this will not do as a general account of judgment, and thus to eliminate his only live competitor.

His argument against the traditional theory is, if unsound, perfectly straightforward. Judgment cannot be identical with predication for there are cases of judgments, namely, all existential ones, which do not involve predication. In Hume's language, judgment cannot be identical with the separating or uniting of different ideas since there are cases of judgments, namely existential judgments, that involve only one idea. If existential judgments cannot be accommodated within the traditional theory, however, we must look elsewhere for a satisfactory theory of judgment; at least we must do so if we want a general theory of judgment, one that will cover all agreed cases. Hume's argument rests, of course, on his previously argued views about existence.[13]

Clearly, Hume's argument does not require him to hold that *no* judgments involve more than one concept, or that judgment *never* involves predication. He needs only to argue that *some* judgments do not. His language indicates that he is well aware of this. '['T]is far from being true, that in *every* judgment, which we form, we unite two different ideas' (*T* 96n, my italics). '[T]he idea of existence is no distinct idea, which we unite with that of the object, and which is capable of forming a compound by the union' (*T* 96n). The language suggests that the idea of existence is peculiar in that it can not, whereas other ideas can, form a compound by its union with some other idea. 'Whether we consider a single object, or *several*; whether we *dwell on these objects*, or run from them to others' (*T* 97n, my italics): the words, in their context, suggest that judgments may involve the exercise either of one or of more than one concept. It is quite illegitimate to assume that Hume's theory for the peculiar case of existentials is extrapolated to cover all cases of simple judgments; there is no evidence in the footnote that Hume does this.

Hume's concern is not to eliminate predication but to distinguish it from the making of a judgment, on the grounds that one may have either without the other. Judgment cannot in general be identical with predication; for although some judgments involve predication others do not. Nor is judgment identical with predication for those cases that do involve predication, or the separating or uniting of different concepts. Mere conceptions can comprise exercises of more than one concept; but mere conceptions are not judgments. Although we 'dwell on these objects' we do not judge until 'we join belief to the conception, and are perswaded of the truth of what we conceive' (*T* 97n). Predication comes on the scene (in non-existential cases) with the element that is common to the mere conception that *p* and the judgment that *p*, namely, the thought that *p*.

To secure a better purchase on Hume's position about judgment and predication let us consider the following depictions of the thoughts or judgments that God exists and that silver is more fusible than lead:

(1) (God's existing);
(2) J (God's existing);
(3) (Silver's being more fusible than lead); and
(4) J (Silver's being more fusible than lead).

Each of items (1) to (4) depicts a psychological occurrence *in foro interno*, whether a mere conception or a judgment. The gerundial expressions within parentheses represent the contents of the mere conception or judgment in question, that is to say the complete thought that is either merely conceived or judged to be the case. The presence or absence of judgment is marked by the presence or absence of the symbol 'J'. Given our conventions, (1) and (3) depict complete thoughts that are mere conceptions; (2) and (4) depict judgments. (1) and (2) have the same content, as do (3) and (4). On my reading of Hume, (1) and (2) do not involve the joining or separating of distinct ideas, and therefore do not involve predication, whereas (3) and (4) do; (1) and (2) are existential thoughts, and (3) and (4) are not. The concept or concepts involved in these thoughts are represented by what appears within the parentheses; predication, for the cases in which it occurs, is likewise a matter of what appears within the parentheses. The symbol for judgment indicates something quite different in character from either the exercise of a concept or predication. Predication, we may say, is present prior to the introduction of judgment. There are, to be sure, crucial questions concerning the interpretation of these formal depictions of occurrences *in foro interno*. We have already examined the difficulties in Hume's account of concept-exercise; we have yet to consider the interpretation to be assigned to predication and to the element of judgment. Before pursuing these and related matters, however, let us return briefly to Pears's account and criticism of Hume.[14]

Pears argues, correctly, that existential judgments do not involve only one idea. One must, he says, recognize 'existence as an idea of a higher order – viz. the idea of an idea's having a correspondent impression or impressions, or the concept of a concept's having an instance or instances'.[15] So existential thoughts involve predication; Hume is simply mistaken when he denies this.[16] It follows that his footnote argument by counterexample cannot succeed; Hume cannot in his way show the unacceptability of the traditional theory of judgment, and hence the need for a theory such as his own. Hume may nonetheless be correct, indeed I think he is correct, on the main point: judgment and predication are not to be identified. Even if judgment requires predication the two must be distinguished: witness the case of mere conception. Even were he to allow that the thought of God's existing involves uniting the idea of God with the higher-order idea of a concept's having an instance he could insist that that union does not yet constitute judgment.

Hume does not, in general, deny the role of predication; indeed he appears to hold that predication is an element in non-existential thoughts and judgments. He is, however, almost wholly silent about its character. He makes incidental remarks, referring, for example, to the 'form or order [in which] we survey' the objects of our thinking (*T* 97n), to the 'order of . . . [the] parts' (*T* 628) of an idea which we believe or to which we subscribe, and to the 'order of our ideas' (*T* 629). But these provide little help. Having as it were placed parentheses around the gerunds that we have taken to represent complete thoughts he proceeds to treat everything within the parentheses *en bloc*. Perhaps he thinks that our thoughts display their structures on their faces; his imagism would encourage this. But to take this route is lazy and unilluminating. More importantly, it is difficult to see how Hume *could* give an account of predication within the constraints of his imagist theory of concept-exercise. Any attempt, it seems, must collapse the propositional linking of two concepts into the having of a single complex image, albeit an image in a suitable causal setting. Hume has isolated predication from judgment; that, I take it, is a significant achievement. But he has not provided, and I should say cannot provide, any satisfactory account of what predication involves.

Although his imagism, once again, must stand in the way of a developed interpretation of the situations envisaged, it is well to notice a further dimension of Hume's theory of judgment; namely, his distinction between the absence of judgment in the case of mere conception and the making of a negative judgment. In a passage that confirms the reading I have offered thus far Hume writes of the 'difference betwixt incredulity and belief':

> 'Twill not be a satisfactory answer to say, that a person, who *does not assent* to a proposition you advance; after having conceiv'd the object in the same manner with you; immediately conceives it in a different manner, and has different ideas of it. This answer is unsatisfactory; not because it contains any falsehood, but because it discovers not all the truth. 'Tis confest, that in all cases, wherein we *dissent* from any person; we *conceive both sides of the question*; but as we can believe only one, it evidently follows, that the belief must make some difference betwixt *that conception to which we assent*, and *that from which we dissent*. We may mingle, and unite, and separate, and confound, and vary our ideas in a hundred different ways; but 'till there appears some principle, which fixes one of these different situations, we have in reality no opinion: And this principle, as it plainly *makes no addition to our precedent ideas*, can only change the *manner* of our conceiving them. (*T* 95–6, my italics, save for 'manner' in last sentence)

Consider an occasion on which one understands another's claim that Caesar died in his bed, wonders whether the claim is true, and comes to believe or judge that it is not. This can be represented in terms of the relations between:

(1) (Caesar's having died in his bed);
(2) (Caesar's not having died in his bed); and
(3) J (Caesar's not having died in his bed).

In understanding the other person's claim, without yet assenting to it or dissenting from it, one has the mere conception represented by (1). In order to 'conceive both sides of the question' one must also have the mere conception depicted by (2). (3) depicts one's ultimate dissent from the speaker's claim; one comes to judge that the negative thought is true. Had one come instead to agree with the speaker, one's judgment would have been represented by:

(4) J (Caesar's having died in his bed).

Judgment and negation, then, are elements of very different kinds: judgment or its absence is revealed, in our model, by the presence or absence of 'J'; negation is a matter of what appears within the parentheses.

This account requires admission of a concept of negation; the prospects for a satisfactory imagist rendering of this concept are slim. Having noted this, let us consider another quartet of thoughts:

(5) (God's existing);
(6) (God's not existing);
(7) J (God's existing); and
(8) J (God's not existing).

As before, (5) and (6) represent mere conceptions in which one 'conceives both sides of the question', and (7) and (8) represent judgments. The trouble is that the situation represented by (6) seems to be ruled out by Hume's claim that 'Whatever we conceive, we conceive to be existent' (*T* 67), a claim that Hume takes to be an implication of his thesis that 'the idea of existence is no distinct idea' (*T* 96n). How, given this, can one have the mere conception of God's not existing? How can one consider both sides of the question before judging that he does, or that he does not, exist?

A way out is suggested by Hume's early remark that 'no two *ideas* are in themselves contrary, except those of *existence* and *non-existence*, which are plainly resembling, as *implying both of them an idea of the object*; tho' the latter excludes the object from all times and places, in which it is suppos'd not to exist' (*T* 15, my italics; compare *T* 70). Existence and non-existence are ideas but they are not 'distinct' ones. They are ideas 'implying' other ideas; ideas 'implying' ideas of the objects that one either conceives to exist or conceives not to exist. This is remarkably like the view of existence that Pears says that Hume should, but does not, have. Holding firm to such a view would enable Hume to construe existential thoughts as, after all, thoughts that involve the exercise of more than one concept. To highlight the distinctive character of the concept of existence, and to accommodate more recent philosophical usage, he could insist that existential judgments do not involve predication; but he could hold that, nonetheless, they require the propositional linking of exercises of concepts. I suspect that Hume's imagism contributed to the textual tangle about existence. Surely his imagism will in no way assist him in the formulation of what I take to be the more promising of the two views of existence suggested by the text.

5. To complete this selective survey of Hume's views about concepts, thoughts and judgments we must briefly consider the interpretation he

would give to the judgment-indicator, 'J', in our model.

The feature indicated by 'J' must be distinguished from predication or the propositional linking of ideas. As Hume makes plain in the 'Appendix', it is not an isolable perception, whether idea or impression. Interpreting 'idea', we may say that the feature of judgments that is represented by the judgment-indicator is neither an image nor an exercise of a concept. Hume denies that 'belief is some new idea, such as that of *reality* or *existence*, which we join to the simple conception of an object' (*T* 623); he denies that 'belief ... consists in some impression or feeling, distinguishable from the conception' (*T* 625). The feature in question is not 'only [that is, 'merely'] annex'd to it [the conception believed], after the same manner that *will* and *desire* are annex'd to particular conceptions of good and pleasure' (*T* 625); it is 'no distinct or separate impression attending' the ideas I believe (*T* 625). In terms of our schematic model for at least non-existential judgments, the feature in question is a property of a psychological complex; a complex somehow constituted by exercises of concepts. It is not another element in that complex, but a property that the complex as a whole possesses. It cannot exist without the psychological complex that it modifies, although that complex can exist without it: judgment requires a complete thought, but not every complete thought is a judgment. The essentially dependent status of the feature that 'J' represents is, I take it, part of Hume's point when he says that belief is a 'manner of conception'.

Although it does not involve a separate feeling or impression, judgment is, in Hume's view, a matter of feeling. The 'manner of conception' is, fundamentally, a matter of the way certain thoughts feel to their owners. Belief 'only modifies the idea or conception; and renders it different to the feeling' (*T* 627); it is 'only a strong and steady conception of ... [an] idea, and such as approaches in some measure to an immediate impression' (*T* 97n). Is a more specific or illuminating characterization of this non-independent feeling available?

> [W]hen I wou'd explain this *manner*, I scarce find any word that fully answers the case, but am oblig'd to have recourse to every one's feeling, in order to give him a perfect notion of this operation of the mind. An idea assented to *feels* different from a fictitious idea, that the fancy alone presents to us: And this different feeling I endeavour to explain by calling it a superior *force*, or *vivacity*, or *solidity*, or *firmness*, or *steadiness*. This variety of terms, which may seem so unphilosophical, is intended only to express that act of mind, which renders realities more present to us than fictions, causes them to weigh more in the thought, and gives them a superior influence on the passions and imagination. . . . And in philosophy we can go no farther, than assert, that it is something *felt* by the mind, which distinguishes the ideas of the judgment from the fictions of the imagination. It gives them more force and influence; makes them appear of greater importance; infixes them in

the mind; and renders them the governing principles of all our actions. (*T* 629; compare *T* 624–7)

In his efforts to characterize that feature that distinguishes judgment from mere conception Hume cites both causal and phenomenological properties. David Armstrong, discussing 'Hume's Problem' of the difference between belief and mere thought, writes:

> He [Hume] wavers between looking for an internal difference between the two, such as the superior 'vivacity' of the idea that is the belief; and a difference in characteristic effects, as when he says that beliefs are, and mere thoughts are not, 'the governing principles of all our actions'. His philosophical approach inclines him to look for the internal difference, his acumen to look for the effect of beliefs upon behaviour.[17]

Armstrong is right to emphasize the effects of belief on behaviour, but one must add to this the effects of belief on other psychological states as well. The move from mere conception to belief not only renders certain thoughts 'the governing principles of all our actions' (*T* 629) but also gives them 'a superior influence on the passions and imagination' (*T* 629). The causal account must, of course, be further qualified so as to square with Hume's views about the need to mention the passions in the explanation of actions; but these further qualifications are easily introduced.

Hume's explicit recognition of the causal properties of judgments or beliefs enables one to make more ready sense of two prominent further elements in his theory of belief. He has a notion of degrees of belief or assent. The relation of contiguity, he says, often 'encreases the belief by encreasing the vivacity of the conception' (*T* 111). He writes of 'imperfect belief' (*T* 135), of a 'gradual encrease of assurance' (*T* 180), and of expectations 'which are entirely free from doubt and uncertainty' (*T* 124). Hume's language, at least in the first passage quoted, is that of the phenomenological reporter; but the phenomenon, it is clear, must be understood in causal terms.

Hume also has a notion of ersatz, even if sincere, belief. He asks whether people 'really believe what is inculcated on them, and what they pretend to affirm' (*T* 114). The question concerns the common man's belief in immortality and, despite the use of 'pretend', sincerity is not at issue. Hume claims that the common man does not really believe in immortality. His explanation of the ersatz phenomenon invokes the faintness of the relevant ideas; his criterion for the distinction however concerns, as it must, connections between purported belief and actual conduct. One is reminded of Hume's later distinction between the violence and the strength of a passion: a passion's violence is a matter of introspectible internal characteristics, that is, the degree of agitation or emotion involved; its force or strength is a matter of its causal properties, specifically the extent of its influence on one's behaviour. That is his point when he says that we 'must . . . distinguish betwixt a calm and a weak passion; betwixt a violent and a strong one' (*T* 419).

Citation of their causal properties is not, however, to be viewed simply as one of two alternatives between which Hume wavers when it is time to characterize the differences between beliefs and mere conceptions. Hume's admittedly vain phenomenological description is not an alternative to the causal one; it is rather an attempt to capture those intrinsic features in virtue of which beliefs have the causal properties they do. In Hume's view the causal properties of judgments are dependent on those intrinsic features that, in the last analysis, distinguish them from mere conceptions. On this point he is surely correct. But this brings us back to the question whether we may identify the requisite intrinsic features of beliefs with the phenomenological characteristics on which Hume himself settles. As one might expect, Hume's imagism exerts pressure in a most unpromising direction; at times he writes as if belief is merely a matter of vivid images in a suitable causal setting. Provided his imagism is put to one side, however, there is something to be said for Hume's phenomenological description of belief, where beliefs are viewed as occurrent judgments. There are times when one does have a feeling of conviction (an expression no better, I suppose, than any of Hume's own candidates). Nevertheless it is clear that the phenomenological account is not up to the task of explicating the peculiar feature of judgments that we have indicated by 'J'. For one thing, the cases of judgments in which it is plausible to speak of a feeling of conviction are far too few. For another, something akin to the judgment-indicator must appear in the analysis of imperative thoughts, for example, that expressed by 'Shut the door'; but to speak of a feeling of conviction or sincerity in each of these very different cases sheds no illumination at all. Again, one must be suspicious of the proposed partial analogy with impressions. The 'impression' cannot usefully be compared to a sensation, for sensations have not got the needed conceptual complexity. But if judgment is thought to be analogous not to sensation but to perceptual awareness, to the awareness, for example, that a boat is in the water or a typewriter is at the tips of one's fingers, the purported explanation is no explanation at all. For perceptual awareness in the sense intended is no less a judgment than is the judgment that the sun will rise tomorrow. If the point is that a non-perceptual judgment is analogous to a perceptual one we are left still seeking the feature that makes either of them a judgment. The phenomenological interpretation of 'J' must be rejected.

As with concept-exercise, so with judgment. Hume's concern is to provide a theory of judgment that is consonant with an ontology of bodies, dispositional properties and mere perceptions. I have suggested that he succeeds in distinguishing judgment from both mere conception and predication, and that he says some promising things about the analysis of negative and even of existential judgments. But his more specific characterization of judgment, presented within the constraints of his ontology, must be judged a failure. Granted that 'the phenomenon of belief . . . is merely internal' (*T* 102), neither a phenomenological nor a phenomenological-cum-causal account suffices. There seems to be no way in which the lack can be made good within the ontological resources that Hume permits himself to draw on. There must be more to judgment, just as there must be more to concept-exercise, than meets the introspective or the behaviourist eye. It is time to look more closely at the concept of introspection.

CHAPTER SEVEN

Introspection and Sensory Awareness

1. To say that there is more to thinking *in foro interno* than meets the introspective eye appears to concede the existence of objects that do meet one's inner gaze. It appears to concede that there are introspectible images; by an obvious extension it appears to concede that there are introspectible items from Hume's two other classes of perceptions, namely, impressions of sensation (sensations) and impressions of reflection (feelings or passions). That there are such introspectible entities, and that they alone are introspectible, are, of course, two elements of Hume's imagism; and the two claims are inextricably involved with other central theses in Hume's philosophy of mind. The concession that there are such entities, however, is mistaken. More narrowly, Hume provides, and can provide, no adequate defence of them. Indeed their admission fits ill with other things he wishes to say.

There are really two issues here. The first is the existence of items such as sensations, feelings and images, construed in the Humean way as reified mental particulars. I have already given reasons for rejecting this view of Hume's, and I shall return to the question at the end of the present chapter. The denial of such things should not be taken as a denial that sensing, feeling or imaging take place *in foro interno* or that the description of these occurrences requires mention of qualitative characteristics such as colour, shape or sound. None of my arguments is designed to support *these* denials. The second issue is that of the introspectibility of sensations and their like, and is the issue that will exercise us through the bulk of the chapter. In sections 2, 3, 4 and 5 I shall be concerned to discover and assess Hume's views about the nature of introspective awareness and judgment, including his views about the possibility of introspective mishap.

My examination of Hume on introspection is quite narrowly focused but has, at least in intent, broad ramifications. The examination concerns, exclusively, the cases of present sensation, feeling and imagery. Any adequate general theory of introspection must range over many more cases than these; but we may assume that if Hume's theory proves inadequate for the minimal, if on his view central, cases it cannot explicate the more complicated ones. Moreover, given the role assigned, throughout Hume's philosophy of mind, to awareness of present sensations, feelings and images irreparable damage here must prove extensively damaging to the whole. That there is such extensive damage is the theme of the closing pages of the chapter.

Having rejected Hume's imagist theory of concept-exercise I shall use the phrase 'exercise of a concept' in a more-or-less uninterpreted way, as before.[1] When I use the Humean expression 'perceptions' I shall intend to designate only the reified mental particulars, that is the sensations, feelings and images, that, as Hume construes them, provide the building-blocks for his theory of mind.

2. Our first main task is to discover the broad outline of Hume's views about the nature of introspection. We shall be much aided in our inquiry by noting a few preliminary distinctions to which Hume is committed and some restrictions of scope that, I take it, he would find agreeable.

A crucial first distinction is that between awareness of a perception with, and awareness of a perception without, the exercise of concepts. Leaving aside the possibility of mere conception, as defined in the previous chapter, for introspective cases, we may distinguish *mere awareness* of a perception from an *introspective judgment* concerning a perception. As the tags suggest, in the former one is aware of a present perception without exercising any concepts with respect to it, and hence without making an introspective judgment. Introspective judgment requires both awareness and concepts. The distinction is imposed by the requirements of Hume's empiricist programme. If all concepts are acquired by the performance of certain operations on the data provided by sensation and feeling, that is to say on the perceptions that are the objects of one's awareness, then at least some of one's perceptions must be objects of mere, because pre-conceptual, awareness.[2] Now Hume does not mark this essential distinction as clearly and consistently as he should; a tendency to blur it may explain some of the more puzzling passages we shall have to examine. He must make it nonetheless.

Hume's introspective judgments, in the restricted sense intended here, may be psychological or non-psychological. Psychological judgments about present perceptions employ psychological concepts; non-psychological introspective judgments employ only non-psychological concepts. For our purposes, a judgment is introspective not in virtue of its content but in virtue of the ontological status of the objects that it concerns. A judgment, concerning a present image, that it is red is no less introspective than the judgment that it is an image.[3]

Although not restricted to psychological content the introspective judgments with which we are concerned are restricted in tense; they are present-tense judgments about perceptions of which one is presently aware. We may take it that the most primitive verbal expression of one of these judgments has the form of the demonstrative sentence 'This is F'. We may take it, too, that these judgments are somehow directly linked with the perceptions they concern; their status is not the indirect status of judgments based on evidence or testimony.

What account does Hume offer of introspective awareness and judgment for this restricted range of cases? Surprisingly, it is very difficult to say. One cannot discover, by simple scrutiny of the texts, any un-equivocally expressed and reasonably determinate theory of intro-spection that one can attribute with confidence to Hume. He says a great deal, in one connection or another, about introspection, but it is impossible to piece together all that he says if one proceeds in a purely inductive manner. I propose, then, to make heuristic use of the very tempting idea that Hume is committed to a doctrine of inner sense. As we shall see, the textual evidence accords with this reading even if it does not require it. Not to use some such device to regiment the textual evidence is to give up hope of understanding what Hume says. Of course, to speak of inner sense is to speak analogically; we shall have to pin down the respects in which and the extent to which Hume, as an inner sense theorist, would liken introspection to outer sense or the per-ception of physical objects. Since variant inner sense theories are con-ceivable we shall need to identify those that are more-or-less Humean in character. The interpretative exercise must be in large measure con-structive, even if there is much to circumscribe our constructions.

On my reading of Hume, the inner sense account applies to percep-tions of each of the three kinds Hume distinguishes; namely sensations, feelings and images. One would expect this to be so, for perceptions of the three kinds are ontologically on a par. Images differ from sensations and feelings in vivacity, but this should make no difference to the account. In any case, in Hume's view images share with sensations those properties, such as colour, texture and shape, that, we may conjecture, suggest the inner sense story in the first place. The text suggests that a single account, whatever its detailed character, is to be given for all perceptions. Hume says not only that 'sentiments' and 'agitations of the passions' but also that 'operations of the understanding' are 'surveyed by reflection' (*E* 60); only sensations fall outside the scope of this remark. No restriction is hinted at when he says, with at least partial approval, that 'consciousness is nothing but a reflected thought or per-ception' (*T* 635). Likewise his coverall expression 'operations of the mind', which on the face of it includes sensations in its scope, suggests that all perceptions are 'intimately present to us . . . [and may] become the object of reflexion' (*E* 13). Incidentally, in intimating that a single account will do for perceptions of the several kinds Hume anticipates Ryle's distinction between one's ordinary consciousness of one's psychological states and one's purposive introspective scrutiny of them.[4] We can 'reflect upon' an 'act of the mind, with which we are sufficiently acquainted' (*E* 69), and there are 'operations of the mind, that, though most intimately present to us, yet, whenever they become the object of reflexion . . . seem involved in obscurity' (*E* 13). In connection with this last passage Hume links the notions of 'reflexion' and 'enquiry' (*E* 13).

Of course there must be some differences in the accounts offered of introspective awareness for each of our three classes of perceptions. As we shall see, Hume identifies having a perception with having mere awareness of it. So, differences in the causal explanation of one's coming to have a perception amount to differences in the causal explanation of one's mere awareness. But in Hume's view the causal explanation of one's having a given perception must vary for the three kinds of perceptions. All have physiological causes, as we saw in chapter 2. But whereas, in general, feelings and images have psychological causes, sensations do not. Sensations require the operation of the senses; feelings and images do not. Moreover, the causation of the passions is rather different, in Hume's view, from the causation of images. Despite all this, the analysis of mere awareness could well be the same for the three cases. Indeed it must be the same if mere awareness is understood in terms of ownership, for Hume has only one analysis of the latter notion.

One can be misled by the fact that differences in aetiology are marked in Hume's language even when his topic is ostensibly the analysis of mere awareness of perceptions. He contrasts 'impressions of reflection' with 'impressions of sensation', and the language suggests a difference in the modes of introspective access. Clearly, however, we must interpret 'of reflection' and 'of sensation' in a causal way; the passions are caused by reflection, while sensations have the operations of the senses as their proximate causes. As Hume says, 'the new impressions of desire and aversion, hope and fear . . . may properly be called impressions of reflexion, *because derived from it*' (*T* 8, my italics).

To be sure, Hume often links the contrast between passions and sensations with that between inner and outer perceptions. He contrasts an 'impression, which presents itself to the hearing or any other of the senses' with an 'impression, which the mind by reflection finds in itself' (*T* 36). He contrasts 'sensation' and 'reflection' (*T* 157) or 'sensation' and 'consciousness' (*T* 158), in contexts that, on the face of it, do not concern the causation of the perceptions in question. Discussing Spinoza, Hume marks what is presumably the same contrast in this way: 'whatever we discover externally by sensation; whatever we feel internally by reflection' (*T* 240). We also find the reiterated contrasts of the 'senses' and 'internal perception' (*T* 108), of 'the internal and external senses' (*E* 47), of what is *felt*, either by our external or internal senses' (*E* 62), of 'outward sense and inward sentiment' (*E* 74), of what 'appears to the *outward* senses' and any 'sentiment or *inward* impression' that 'the mind feels' (*E* 63).

These numerous passages reveal Hume's willingness to speak of sense and perception in each of the two cases, but they can seem to further suggest a substantive contrast between inner and outer sense, with consequent substantive variations in the accounts to be offered of awareness of one's passions and of one's sensations. They can seem to suggest that only the passions are objects of inner sense. These appearances, I submit, are misleading. Passions and sensations have ontological parity within Hume's philosophy; so there is no reason for them to differ in mode of access. And alternative readings are available for the inner/outer contrast. We have already seen that there are differences in causation. Hume would also insist that items from the one group do, items from the other do not, play a central role in the plain man's perceptual judgments about the external world. In the same vein he would distinguish those of his perceptions that the plain man takes to be items in the external world from those that he takes to be merely mental or internal.

As we have just seen, there are numerous passages in which Hume uses 'reflection' of the passions but not of sensations, and in which 'reflection' appears not intended to refer merely to the causal antecedents of the passions. In this use of the term Hume appears prepared to speak of both images and passions as objects of 'reflection'. The passions, he says, are items 'which the mind by reflection finds in itself' (*T* 36), which we 'feel internally by reflection' (*T* 240). In such contexts 'reflection' is associated with 'consciousness' and contrasted with 'sensation' (compare *T* 157–8). Speaking of ideas or images he says that an idea is 'a real perception in the mind, of which we are intimately conscious', glossing this with the comment that 'the mind reflects upon it, and is assur'd of its present existence' (*T* 106). As noted earlier, 'operations of the understanding', like 'sentiments' and 'agitations of the passions', are 'surveyed by reflection' (*E* 60). Shall we take this as evidence that, in Hume's view, introspective access to one's feelings and images takes one form, namely 'reflection', and access to one's sensations takes some other?

As before, the ontological parity of the items in question suggests that we not do so. If we take this suggestion we are, of course, left with the problem of dealing with Hume's selectivity in his use of 'reflection'. Hume often uses 'reflection' in a way roughly synonymous with 'thinking', 'thought' or 'reasoning'.[5] Perhaps in the passages that seem to select passions and images for common and distinctive treatment Hume is merely displaying a rather murky recognition of the need to distinguish mere awareness and introspective judgment? Of course this distinction does nothing to segregate feelings and images from sensations. In fact, however, Hume's use of 'reflection' has affinities with perceptual as well as cognitive terms, which suggests that we should not put much weight on his rarely using 'reflection' with respect to sensations. Hume speaks of passions being *felt* by reflection (*T* 240). In so far as he adopts a representative theory of perception one would expect him to think of the relation between perceptions and physical objects as akin to that between objects and their physical reflections. Since, as was indicated in chapter 4, on at least one occasion Hume adopts a representative theory of inner experience, it is not past belief that he uses 'reflection' in this patently metaphorical way in introspective contexts as well. When 'reflection' is so read, of course, there is no way of distinguishing sensations from other perceptions. I can think of no obvious explanation of the distribution of Hume's uses of 'reflection'. However, we are not required to infer a radical difference, in the matter of introspective access, between passions or images and sensations.

Although Hume tends to cluster images with passions via his use of 'reflection' he eschews talk of sense, inner or outer, in the case of images or ideas. Does he intend a substantive difference between the mode of introspective access for images and that for passions and sensations? Does he intend to reject an inner sense theory for images? I can see no serious reason for thinking so. He does, after all, speak of 'acquaintance' and being 'intimately conscious', when discussing ideas, and these two expressions have complicated links with his more perceptual vocabulary. Then, too, there is the consideration of ontological parity. And if images are merely less vivid sensations and feelings what motive could there be to reject inner sense in the one case while admitting it in the others? Hume might well have reason for denying that one has access by inner sense to one's thoughts, for, despite his imagism, Humean thoughts are more than mere images. But this would go no way at all towards requiring rejection of an inner sense doctrine for images themselves.

The status of Hume's volitions is not very clear (compare *T* 399). If we take volitions to be perceptions, however, Hume's comments about one's access to them are especially interesting, given the direction of our discussion thus far. Volitions are, Hume says, 'surely . . . act[s] of the mind, with which we are sufficiently acquainted' (*E* 69), and are 'known by an inward sentiment or consciousness' (*E* 66). They are presumably to be included when Hume writes of 'reflecting on the operations of our own mind' (*E* 64); they are 'impression[s] we feel and are conscious of' (*T* 399). The casual linking of 'reflection', 'consciousness', 'acquaintance', 'feeling' and 'sentiment' suggests that one should put little weight on the presence or absence of such expressions in the more-or-less incidental things Hume says when the context is introspective awareness of one's ideas.

My heuristic hypothesis is that Hume's is an inner sense theory of introspective access to one's perceptions, that is, to one's sensations, feelings and images. As remarked earlier, however, an inner sense theory is fundamentally an analogical one. What then are the points of analogy that Hume must have in mind when he likens introspection to the perceptual awareness of physical objects? For the present we need do no more than list prospective points of likeness; when we examine his views about introspective mishap in section 3 we shall be in a much better position to determine just where, in Hume's view, the analogies lie.

To begin with, the characteristic objects of perceptual awareness, namely physical objects, have such properties as colour, shape, texture and taste. They are distinct from the psychological states or occurrences that constitute awareness of them. States of perceptual awareness may involve only mere awareness or, more usually, may be states of conceptualized awareness. States of perceptual awareness concern objects present to the senses; objects that stand in causal relations to one's perception of them. Characteristically, if not invariably, sense perception requires the operation of sense organs. Sense perception further requires the presence of sensations that somehow present the object of awareness to the perceiver. Avoiding intractable issues of philosophical theory we may say that sensations present the objects to which, in perceptual judgments, one assigns various properties. Perceivers are fallible; mishaps of various kinds are possible. For example, one may remain simply unaware of various objects or events in one's environment. One may also be subject to illusion or hallucination. If one is led, in such cases, to make mistaken perceptual judgments,[6] one's mistake has a special character. Commonly, in such cases, the appearance of the object prompts one's mistaken judgments about it; the appearance of the green coat under fluorescent lighting prompts the misjudgment that it is black. Underlying such perceptual mistakes is a form of mishap I shall call 'misawareness', involving a discrepancy between appearance and reality. Although appearances do the deceiving, the mistake is not about the appearances but about the object that appears.

The reader may well object to some of the items in this list. And it is not to be thought that decisions about items to be included depend in no way on one's philosophical theory of perception. The list provided does, I think, accord with Hume's own views about sense perception. In any case, some such list of features must underpin an analogical theory of introspection; and our actual list has only a heuristic function. Putting further discussion of the question of analogies to one side for the moment, let us distinguish three variant theories of introspective awareness, each of which is a possible Humean theory in that each is, to all initial appearances, faithful to the main lines of his philosophy. Careful characterization of these variants will greatly assist the progress of our investigation.

A certain account of the ownership of perceptions is common to these variant theories: for a mind M to have or own a perception P is for P to stand in suitable relations (Hume mentions causality and resemblance) to the other members of that temporally extended collection of perceptions that, together with P, constitutes M. According to our first variant theory, *Theory A*, mere awareness of perception P requires that M have, in addition to P, a second-order perception P*. P*, understood as a second-order sensation, stands in an asymmetrical relation to P such that P is the object of P* or P* counts as an awareness of P. P and P* are to be construed, in straightforwardly Humean fashion, as distinct perceptions; the existence of each is logically independent of the existence of the other. Numerous further questions arise about the detailed characterization of the relation between P and P*, but we may let these go. According to Theory A, introspective judgment concerning P involves the addition to P* of the exercise of relevant concepts, such as the concept of being red, or that of being an image. Given Hume's failure to explicate predication, there is no point in raising questions about the tie between P* and the exercise of the concepts in question.[7] But two crucial matters must be noted. On this theory, the complex comprising P* and the specified exercises of concepts constitutes the conceptualized introspective awareness of P; this complex constitutes the introspective judgment in which such-and-such properties are assigned to P. This judgment as a whole is the inner counterpart of the statement expressible by, for example, 'This is red' or 'This is a red image', austerely construed. P* is to be viewed as the inner counterpart of the demonstrative pronoun; it presents P for the purpose of property-ascription. The second crucial matter is that the first-order perception P and the second-order introspective judgment that has P* as a constituent stand to one another as distinct existences, in Hume's sense; the existence of each is logically independent of the existence of the other. Theory A is, it should be noted, an inner sense analogue of a standard representative theory of external perceptual awareness and judgment.

Both *Theory B* and *Theory C* avoid the introduction of second-order perceptions such as P*. Each takes the mere awareness of P to be identical with the having of P, thus eliminating the need for second-order perceptions to explain mere awareness. What of introspective judgment? According to Theory B an introspective judgment concerning P is a complete thought, logically distinct from P, in which such-and-such properties are ascribed to P. Having rejected P* Theory B takes the constituents of the second-order introspective judgment to be, exclusively, exercises of concepts. It must do so unless it countenances, as possible constituents of judgments, items other than perceptions and exercises of concepts.

Theory C is simpler still. Theories A and B are alike in taking introspective judgments to be complete thoughts that are logically independent of the perceptions they concern, and that are of a higher order than those perceptions. According to Theory C, an introspective judgment is of the same order as the perception it concerns. Indeed an introspective judgment concerning P has P as a constituent; and the remaining constituents of the judgment do not, by themselves, constitute a complete thought. For a case where a single concept is exercised with respect to P the sole constituents of the introspective judgment are P and the exercise of the concept in question. We may take it that, in the likely Humean version of Theory C, P and the exercise of a concept are, with respect to one another, distinct existences.[8]

As we shall see, Theory C is the theory of introspective awareness and judgment that Hume must prefer. To see this, however, we must first take a close look at what he says of introspective mishap.

3.   In the light of our distinction between mere awareness and intro-

spective judgment we must distinguish a variety of ways in which introspection may go awry. At least we must distinguish a variety of questions
about the possibility of introspective mishap. Consider the four following claims:

  (1) If M judges that p, then p;
  (2) If p, then M judges that p;
  (3) If M has mere awareness of P, then M has P;
and
  (4) If M has P, then M has mere awareness of P.

Let 'p' stand for some introspective judgment from the restricted range
of such judgments as we are here concerned with; let 'P' stand for some
perception, in our austere sense of 'perception'. (1) claims that if some
mind M makes an introspective judgment that p, then what M judges is
true; (2) claims that if some introspective judgment concerning M's
present perceptions is true, then M makes the judgment in question.
(1), I shall say, denies the possibility of *introspective mistake*, whereas
(2) denies the possibility of *introspective ignorance*. Someone might, of
course, wish to deny the possibility of introspective ignorance, or
mistake, or both, for only certain kinds of introspective cases, but we
may ignore this complication for the moment. (3) claims that mere
awareness of a perception guarantees M's actually having that perception. We may say that (3) rejects the possibility of *misawareness*. (4)
denies the possibility of one's being *unaware* of some perception one has.
Propositions (1) to (4) may be viewed, singly or severally, as logically
necessary or as merely contingent claims. Notice that only (1) and (2),
which concern introspective judgment and not mere awareness, introduce considerations of truth and falsity. This accords with Hume's way
of viewing the matter. '[N]othing', he says, 'can be contrary to truth
or reason, except what has a reference to it, and . . . the judgments of
our understanding only have this reference' (*T* 415–6). The level of
mere awareness is not the level of truth and falsity.[9]

We are now in a position to pose a number of quite specific questions
about Hume's views on the matter of introspective mishap. Does he
subscribe to propositions (1) to (4)? Does he subscribe to any of them?
Does he subscribe to any or to all of them for any appropriate substitu-
tions for 'p' and 'P'? Would he limit the scope of any of them? If he
subscribes to any or to all of them, or to restricted variants of them,
what logical status does he assign to them? There is good reason to
think that Hume would not allow (2) without qualification; one may
have and be aware of some perception P yet not possess the concepts
requisite for making the introspective judgment in question. Would he
subscribe to (2) if it were amended to meet this difficulty?

If Hume endorses any of the three variant theories of introspective
awareness and judgment identified at the end of section 2 he must hold
that (1) and (2), even if true, are not true necessarily or as a matter of
logic. Theories A, B and C, in their varying ways, incorporate Hume's

doctrine of distinct perceptions in their analyses of the relation between a perception and an introspective judgment concerning that perception. It must follow, for Hume, that no introspective judgments are necessarily correct, and that there are no perceptions to which one must necessarily assign some property in introspective judgment. In the case of any perception introspective ignorance and mistake are logically possible. What are we to say of propositions (3) and (4), concerning the level of mere awareness? If Hume adopts Theory A, with its distinction between P and P*, he must view (3) and (4) as, if true, only contingently so. Given Theory B or Theory C, however, and the identification of mere awareness with ownership, (3) and (4) are trivial consequences.

If Hume is committed to the logical possibility of introspective ignorance and mistake, for any perception, what is his view of the contingent facts of the matter? Does he think that one never makes a mistake, and never fails to make appropriate correct judgments, about one's perceptions? Does he think, more plausibly, that there are some situations in which introspective ignorance and mistake are genuine possibilities, and other situations in which they are not? What kinds of introspective judgments can he distinguish, where the distinctions bear intelligibly on the implied differing probabilities of mishap? One possibility is to distinguish judgments concerning intrinsic features of one's perceptions from those concerning their extrinsic, especially causal, features. On the face of it, mistake or ignorance is more likely in the latter case. Paralleling the intrinsic/extrinsic distinction Hume can distinguish classificatory from explanatory judgments; he can claim that explanatory mishaps are more likely than classificatory ones.[10] Of course, there are classifications and classifications; some employ relatively ordinary concepts, for example, colour concepts or the concept of a sensation, while others employ technical concepts whose proper place is within a scientific or philosophical theory. Similarly there are differences between ordinary and scientific explanations. Hume can hold that differing accounts must be offered of the plain man's and the psychologist's difficulties. He can also draw attention to differences in the situations in which one's introspective judgments are made, plausibly suggesting that, in the ordinary run of things, there are numerous kinds of interfering factors that can generate either ignorance or mistake. But it is time for conjecture to give place to a survey of what Hume says. In looking to what he says, it is well to note that we shall continue to focus quite narrowly on Humean perceptions; the intended range of Hume's actual remarks may not be thus severely circumscribed.

Hume admits the empirical, not merely the logical, possibility of introspective ignorance and mistake, whether the judgments in question are classificatory and thus concerned with intrinsic properties, or explanatory and thus concerned with extrinsic, especially causal, features; at least he does so for scientific contexts. In the first *Enquiry*, commenting on the difficulties to be met with in an introspective science of the mind, he writes:

> It is remarkable concerning the operations of the mind, that, though most intimately present to us, yet, whenever they become the object of reflexion, they seem involved in obscurity; nor can the eye readily find those lines and boundaries, which discriminate and distinguish them. The objects are too fine to remain long in the same aspect or situation; and must be apprehended in an instant, by a superior penetration, derived from nature, and improved by habit and reflexion. It becomes, therefore, no inconsiderable part of science barely to know the different operations of the mind, to separate them from each other, to class them under their proper heads, and to correct all that seeming disorder, in which they lie involved, when made the object of reflexion and enquiry. This talk of ordering and distinguishing, which has no merit, when performed with regard to external bodies, the objects of our senses, rises in its value, when directed towards the operations of the mind, in proportion to the difficulty and labour, which we meet in performing it. And if we can go no farther than this mental geography, or delineation of the distinct parts and powers of the mind, it is at least a satisfaction to go so far. (*E* 13)

In the *Treatise*, having laid down the 'rules by which to judge of causes and effects', Hume says:

> [T]he utmost constancy is requir'd to make us persevere in our enquiry, and the utmost sagacity to choose the right way among so many that present themselves. If this be the case even in natural philosophy, how much more in moral, where there is a much greater complication of circumstances, and where those views and sentiments, which are essential to any action of the mind, are so implicit and obscure, that they often escape our strictest attention, and are not only unaccountable in their causes, but even unknown in their existence? (*T* 175)

The *Treatise* passage, which follows a discussion of the canons of induction, has plainly to do with difficulties in explanation. In the later *Enquiry* passage Hume has trimmed his associationist sails and concentrates on difficulties of a classificatory sort, on difficulties in 'mental geography'. Whether in explanatory or classificatory contexts, however, it is possible, as these passages indicate, to be introspectively ignorant and to make introspective mistakes.

Hume says a few vague things to account for the possibility of ignorance and error. The objects of introspective scrutiny are 'too fine'; they come and go with great rapidity; they are 'implicit and obscure'; the circumstances of their occurrence are extraordinarily complex. The very attempt to secure suitable items for introspective investigation produces distortion (*T* xxiii). Problems of classification are exacerbated by the close similarity of some intrinsically distinct mental phenomena (*E* 60). Hume also makes some vague suggestions about what is needed to overcome one's ignorance and avoid mistake in scientific contexts: the utmost constancy and sagacity; the strictest attention; the development of various observational skills. To meet the problems of introspective distortion he even makes the non-introspectionist recommendation that we 'glean up our experiments in this science from a cautious observation of human life' (*T* xxiii).

In the *Treatise* passage just cited Hume makes a remark that, because of its obscurity and its possible ramifications, must be noted. He refers to 'views and sentiments, which are essential to any action of the mind ... [but which are] unknown in their existence'. Is Hume here conflating the levels of mere awareness and judgment and admitting perceptions that one has but of which one is simply unaware? Is he rather thinking of perceptions of which one has mere awareness but about which one fails to make introspective judgments, perhaps because one cannot make them? Is he making the very different claim that, in the case of some perceptions, one is somehow prevented from making any but causal judgments? He does, after all, say that these 'views and sentiments' are essential to the mind's activities. Is he perhaps thinking not of perceptions as such but of some other mental operations, for example, complicated causal sequences, about which one remains in ignorance? The *Treatise* passage does not force any of these readings on us; it is best not to force any reading upon it.

Hume admits the empirical possibility of introspective mistake and ignorance in ostensibly non-scientific contexts as well. He cites several instances of mistaking some perceptions for other, closely resembling, ones. We may 'confound . . . sentiments [that] are, in themselves, distinct' (*T* 472). '[E]very action of the mind, which operates with the same calmness and tranquillity, is confounded with reason by all those, who judge of things from the first view and appearance' (*T* 417). Some passions have been taken to be operations of reason: 'Their nature and principles have been suppos'd the same, because their sensations are not evidently different' (*T* 417). How are such mistakes to be avoided or corrected? In words reminiscent of the earlier 'superior penetration' Hume says that 'a man of temper and judgment may preserve himself from these illusions' (*T* 472). There is also some suggestion that causal theorizing may play a role in preserving oneself from, and in correcting, introspective error: 'certain calm desires and tendencies . . . are more known by their effects than by the immediate feeling or sensation' (*T* 417).

At several places Hume writes as if impressions as a group, but not ideas, have a feature in virtue of which it is empirically impossible to be ignorant of or mistaken about their intrinsic features. Impressions, he says, 'are all so clear and evident, that they admit of no controversy'; by contrast 'many of our ideas are so obscure, that 'tis almost impossible even for the mind, which forms them, to tell exactly their nature and composition' (*T* 33). In the *Enquiry*, introducing his 'new microscope or species of optics', Hume writes:

> Produce the impressions or original sentiments, from which the
> ideas are copied. These impressions are all strong and sensible. They
> admit not of ambiguity. They are not only placed in a full light them-
> selves, but may throw light on their correspondent ideas, which lie
> in obscurity. (*E* 62)

Against these passages, however, one must set Hume's remark that 'the
confusion in which impressions are sometimes involv'd, proceeds only
from their faintness and unsteadiness' (*T* 19), and his recognition of 'the
natural infirmity both of our imagination and senses, when employ'd on
such minute objects' (*T* 41–2). Hume can render these passages consistent if he holds that one cannot be ignorant of or mistaken about
certain impressions, provided, at least, that one has them in certain
advantageous circumstances.

Several passages from the *Treatise* are especially interesting in the
present context, for they not only contribute to our developing picture
of Hume's views about introspective mishap but also have a direct
bearing on his presumptive theory of inner sense. In several of these
passages Hume's subject is the perception of physical objects; given his
views about sense perception, however, they illuminate his thinking
about introspective access to sensations. In each passage Hume employs
a notion of the understanding's correcting the senses or one's sentiments.

Consider the following statement:

> All objects seem to diminish by their distance: But tho' the appear-
> ance of objects to our senses be the original standard, by which we
> judge of them, yet we do not say, that they actually diminish by the
> distance; but correcting the appearance by reflexion, arrive at a
> more constant and establish'd judgment concerning them. (*T* 603)

There are obvious traps laid by Hume's language here, but the main
point is clear enough. Our judgments about physical objects are objective; we do not take such objects to vary in their properties with variations in their relations or appearances to us. Though they seem to
diminish as we move away from them we do not judge that they do
diminish. In this sense, at least, we 'correct the appearance by reflexion'.
Such objectivity of judgment is a prerequisite of the use of language:
'Such corrections are common with regard to all the senses; and indeed
'twere impossible we cou'd ever make use of language, did we not
correct the momentary appearances of things, and overlook our present
situation' (*T* 582). The point, we may say, is not that one corrects the
appearances but that one corrects *for* the appearances. In the wrong
circumstances, perhaps, just these appearances could mislead an
observer about the physical objects themselves. Such correcting for the
appearances imports, of course, no mishap or mistake. But has Hume
more in mind than this? Does he think that in correcting the appearances we mistake the appearances themselves, and thus make mistaken
judgments about *their* qualities? If so, the case is one of introspective

mistake. Alternatively, does he think that correction alters the appearances of the appearances? If so, we have, possibly, a case of misawareness at the level of mere awareness. Hume's intentions, it must be said, are not here perspicuous.

Elsewhere Hume's meaning is plain on at least one of these two last issues. '[T]he understanding corrects the appearances of the senses, and *makes us imagine*, that an object at twenty foot distance *seems even to the eye* as large as one of the same dimensions at ten' (*T* 632, my italics). Again:

> 'Tis universally allow'd by the writers on optics, that the eye at all times sees an equal number of physical points, and that a man on top of a mountain has no larger an image presented to his senses, than when he is cooped up in the narrowest court or chamber. 'Tis only by experience that he infers the greatness of the object from some peculiar qualities of the image; and *this inference of the judgment he confounds with sensation*, as is common on other occasions. (*T* 112, my italics)[11]

In these passages, I suggest, Hume envisages mistaken judgments about the appearances of physical objects, and not about the objects themselves. In a Humean context such appearances are impressions caused by the physical objects. In judging that these mental items have properties other than those they actually have, for example, in judging that a visual impression has dimensions that *it* does not have, but that are rather the dimensions of the physical object represented by the impression, one makes an introspective mistake.

There is some hint, as well, of introspective misawareness. Note the expressions 'makes us imagine' and 'seem even to the eye', and the remark about confounding inference with sensation. If Hume does intend to invoke misawareness his point would be that, on some occasions, the understanding's correction of appearances produces misleading appearances of perceptions.

In an interestingly ambiguous passage Hume cites with approval the view 'that all bodies, which discover themselves to the eye, appear as if painted on a plain surface, and . . . their different degrees of remoteness from ourselves are discover'd more by reason than by the senses' (*T* 56). Does Hume think that the things that the plain man directly sees appear to him to have visual depth despite their being two-dimensional? If so he must allow an appearance/reality distinction, and hence misawareness, for at least visual impressions. Does he mean that visual sensations appear, as they really are, two-dimensional? If so, there is no need for an appearance/reality distinction to accommodate misawareness, but Hume is surely wrong about the facts of the case. Does he perhaps believe that, given the operation of the understanding, visual impressions are, as they appear, three-dimensional? On this reading, of course, the understanding's correcting appearances neither generates nor remedies any mishap; it brings about a change in what is seen. Is

Hume's point merely that one judges the very things one sees, one's visual sensations, to be three-dimensional although they appear in their true colours as two-dimensional? Construed this way, we have merely a case of introspective misjudgment.

Whatever be the case with misawareness, Hume appears in these passages, and elsewhere, to be firmly wedded to the empirical possibility of introspective misjudgment. Do these passages reveal anything of significance about its character? In particular, do they reveal introspective misjudgment to be akin to perceptual illusion? We must first ask what these passages reveal about perceptual illusion in the basic case, that of sense perception of physical objects. It is clear enough that Hume here, and especially in the first of the passages cited, holds a view of perceptual illusion like that we sketched in section 2. He seems to hold that perceptual illusion about physical objects is prompted by misleading features of the appearances of those objects, and that such perceptual mistakes are nonetheless mistakes not about the appearances but about the objects that appear. In perceptual illusion things seem to be what they are not and it is their appearances that deceive. On one of these points, quite plainly, there is a disanalogy between the standard case of perceptual illusion and the case of introspective mistake; in the passages in question introspective mistake is prompted not by the appearances of one's perceptions but by the operations of the understanding. It is not a perception's appearing to be of one size that causes one to judge it to be of another size; at least its appearing to be of one size is not, on Hume's rendering, the significant factor to be mentioned in an explanation of introspective misjudgment. On the more fundamental point, of course, the evidence thus far is quite ambiguous. At bottom, perceptual illusion requires the possibility of an appearance/reality distinction. If introspective mistake is to be understood by analogy with perceptual illusion a distinction between appearance and reality at the level of mere awareness must be possible. To be analogous to perceptual illusion introspective misjudgment must rest on misawareness. If it does not, the proposed inner sense/outer sense analogy is drastically attenuated.

The textual evidence for Hume's allowing or rejecting mishap at the level of mere awareness is thus far ambiguous at best. It seems to me, however, Hume is quite firmly committed to the view that such mishaps are not possible. In the *Treatise* he takes the very strong line that it is not 'conceivable that our senses shou'd be more capable of deceiving us in the situation and relations, than in the nature of our impressions' (*T* 190). In context, this amounts to the claim that the senses may deceive us neither about the nature nor about the situation and relations of our impressions. In explanation, he says that 'since all actions and sensations of the mind are known to us by consciousness, they must necessarily appear in every particular what they are, and be what they appear' (*T* 190). On the previous page he writes, of sensations at least, that they are 'felt by the mind, such as they really are' (*T* 189). In the first *Enquiry* the crucial assemblage of points is made with striking economy: 'consciousness never deceives' (*E* 66). The central point is not one about introspective ignorance or mistake; it amounts rather to the denial of the possibility of mishap at the level of mere awareness. Additionally, however, Hume draws the consequence that we have come to expect: if misawareness is not possible then mishap at the level of mere awareness cannot be the origin of introspective mistake. As we have seen, this treatment of introspective mistake undercuts the proposed inner sense analysis of introspection.

At one place Hume writes that 'the perceptions of the mind are perfectly known' (*T* 366). The occurrence of 'known' suggests that he is here concerned with the level of judgment, not with that of mere awareness. If this is so the statement as a whole seems to contradict the Humean picture of introspective ignorance and mistake that has emerged thus far. Perhaps Hume is in fact contradicting himself. Perhaps, however, the absence of a suitable technical vocabulary, or the failure to get a secure grip on the mere awareness/judgment distinction, merely contributes to the appearance of a contradiction. If the statement does concern introspective judgment it is, it should be noted, very obscure. Is Hume addressing the question of ignorance or that of error? If the former, the passage is inconsistent with Hume's recognizing a level of pre-conceptual awareness; at best the claim must be restricted to cases where the requisite concepts are possessed. What of 'perfectly'? Is Hume claiming that one has exhaustive knowledge of one's perceptions? This is very strong, surely false, doctrine and transparently at odds with Hume's own insistence on the multiple sources of introspective mishap. At best, ignorance of intrinsic properties of perceptions can be ruled out, with some show of plausibility. Even so, Hume must reckon with his own display of the effects of bias, haste and the like on one's knowledge of one's own perceptions. Is Hume concerned, in this troublesome passage, not with ignorance but with error? This seems most unlikely for he can then provide no reading for 'perfectly', at least on the presumptively Humean view that knowledge is not a matter of degree.

It is preferable, I suggest, to take this passage as providing an especially strong, if somewhat misleading, expression of the thesis that mishap at the level of mere awareness is impossible. If one has mere awareness of a perception P then one has perception P. It is this side of the story on which I have placed most stress. If one has perception P then one has mere awareness of P. This side of the story has been told, if not in so many words, in previous chapters. Signs of it are also present in several of the remarks just examined. It is hardly far-fetched to think that this is a main part of Hume's point when he writes of perfect knowledge of one's perceptions.

If Hume does deny the possibility that one is unaware or misaware of any of one's perceptions he is thereby committed to the more fundamental disanalogy, noted above, between introspection and outer sense. Without room for an appearance / reality distinction at the level of mere awareness there is no room for perceptual illusion. Without room for perceptual illusion there is little, if any, room for a doctrine of inner sense. Of the possible points of analogy between inner and outer sense that we listed earlier the only remaining substantive one concerns the purported similarity of the objects of both inner and outer sense: both Humean perceptions and physical objects have properties such as colour, shape, texture and felt temperature. With the list of like features reduced to this minimum, it seems clear there is little to recommend an inner sense theory of introspection, whether as a philosophical theory or as a theory seriously to be attributed to Hume. As we shall see shortly, even this last purported point of analogy must be rejected.

The texts that reveal Hume's thinking about introspective mishap, even if they are somewhat more illuminating than those that evidence his views about the analysis of introspection, are, it must be said, not especially perspicuous. They can fall into various configurations, no one of which, perhaps, is indisputably preferable to the others; still, I have presented a set of views that can be ascribed to Hume with a reasoned measure of confidence. He admits the logical possibility of introspective error and mistake but denies the possibility of mishap, whether mis-awareness or unawareness, at the level of mere awareness of percep-tions. He allows the empirical possibility of introspective ignorance and mistake, in both scientific and ordinary contexts, for both classificatory and explanatory judgments, and for both intrinsic and extrinsic pro-perties. He explicates ignorance and mistake by citing such features as bias, haste, lack of attention, close resemblance between intrinsically different perceptions, and the lack of perceptual vividness. He suggests that, knowing the sources of mishap, one can take preventive, if not necessarily foolproof, measures of various kinds. For some judgments about some perceptions, in some circumstances, there is no serious prospect of one's going wrong. Roughly, and unsurprisingly, the less one claims, and the more careful one is not to get things wrong, the more likely one is to be successful. Circumscribing the content of one's intro-spective judgments, and taking quite extraordinary pains in their making, can effectively insulate one from ignorance and mistake. Hume epito-mizes this view of the matter in his cautiously restricted dismissal of the supposition that 'even where we are most intimately conscious, we might be mistaken' (*T* 190). On my reading of Hume, however, ignor-ance and mistake in such cases is logically possible.

4. Although no introspective judgments come with logically airtight guarantees some suitably cautious and circumscribed ones have the highest degree of empirical reliability and merit one's full confidence. This, I take it, is the philosophical setting in which to understand Hume's remark that the 'only existences, of which we are certain, are

perceptions, which being immediately present to us by consciousness, command our strongest assent, and are the first foundation of all our conclusions' (*T* 212). Consciousness 'presents' perceptions that in turn command our assent; the framework assumed is one that distinguishes mere awareness from judgment. Is the point that in every case in which one has, and thus has mere awareness of, a perception, the judgment one makes has the highest reliability, and thus commands one's strongest assent? In the light of what has gone before, the point must rather be that only in the case of judgments about perceptions does one reach the highest degree of reliability and assurance achievable in empirical contexts. That some introspective judgments merit this degree of assurance does nothing, of course, to show that all do. Not to recognize that Hume allows some introspective judgments to merit our strongest assent, however, would be to radically misconstrue his position.

There are two likely sources of misgiving about my reading of the passage we are considering. First, the 'first foundation of all our conclusions' may be thought to require some logically guaranteed infallibility, not just empirical reliability and the highest degree of assurance. This is not, however, Hume's view of the matter. To be sure Hume's is a foundationalist epistemology of some description. He appears to hold that there is a level of naturally most primitive beliefs about one's perceptions and that these primitive introspective beliefs provide the infrastructure for one's formed beliefs about physical objects and about minds. Much more needs to be said, of course. For one thing, one needs an account of the move from foundations to formed beliefs. For another, it is not clear whether Hume takes primitive judgments as the foundational elements or whether (and the passage under discussion suggests this) he takes non-conceptual states of mere awareness as the foundational elements.[12] Let us overlook the first of these questions; let us also assume, to simplify things, that the foundational elements are introspective judgments.

In Hume's epistemology foundational judgments are assigned two tasks, neither of which requires infallibility. They are to provide a level of beliefs that are not dependent on other beliefs. If there were no such foundational beliefs, Hume thinks, one would be trapped in a vicious regress. Further, they are to provide not only a starting point for inference but also an explanation of the fact that the conclusions to one's inferences are believed. This is simply an application of Hume's general thesis that belief in one's conclusions is 'communicated' from belief in one's premises (compare *T* I iii 8).

It is helpful to reflect on two passages in which Hume writes of the foundations of belief, but where the foundational beliefs are not from the most primitive level. Discussing ordinary historical inferences he writes:

> [W]ithout the authority either of the memory or senses our whole reasoning wou'd be chimerical and without foundation. Every link

of the chain wou'd in that case hang upon another; but there wou'd not be any thing fix'd to one end of it, capable of sustaining the whole; and consequently there wou'd be no belief nor evidence. (*T* 83)

He also writes: '*belief* or *assent*, which always attends the memory and senses ... constitutes the first act of the judgment, and lays the foundation of that reasoning, which we build upon it, when we trace the relation of cause and effect' (*T* 86). The point is plain enough. To explain inferred beliefs without regress one must take some beliefs as uninferred. But this does not entail a need for logically infallible beliefs. Indeed we know that in the two passages just cited Hume does not view the foundational beliefs as infallible; they are ordinary beliefs about persons and things.

But, it may be said, the situation changes when one moves to the level of rock-bottom foundations; to the level of the introspective judgments that provide the foundation for *all* of one's inferred beliefs about bodies and minds. In ordinary inferences, for example, ordinary historical inferences, one's foundational beliefs are themselves the product of inference; that is why they are not infallible. Their foundational status is merely a courtesy status; for practical purposes they are taken to have a property they do not really have. But when one moves to the beliefs that provide the foundations for *all* of one's inferred empirical beliefs the foundational beliefs must be logically infallible; otherwise they could not perform their special task.

I do not think Hume would be moved by this argument. The fact that such beliefs are non-inferential indicates, perhaps, that they are among the introspective beliefs about which one is least likely to be mistaken. For they are, presumably, judgments of the circumscribed sort, made with all imaginable caution, that we discussed above. One cannot imagine empirical judgments about which one can be more certain. As such, Hume might say, they can shoulder the quite special burden of being at the very bottom of the structure of empirical beliefs. There is no need for, even if it would be intelligible to seek, a firmer foundation in the form of introspective judgments that cannot, as a matter of logic, be mistaken. Although a foundationalist, then, Hume is not one of the infallibilist variety.

In another connection Hume writes of his 'hope to establish a system or set of opinions, which if not true (for that, perhaps, is too much to be hop'd for) might at least be satisfactory to the human mind, and might stand the test of the most critical examination' (*T* 272). Would he impose stronger conditions on the rock-bottom foundations of empirical belief? With whatever justification, he is prepared to accept no stronger foundations for geometry: 'this is the nature and use of geometry, to run us up to such appearances, as, by reason of their simplicity, cannot lead us into considerable error' (*T* 72; compare *T* 45).

The fact that in the passage we are examining Hume writes of 'exist-

ences' that command our strongest assent may be another source of misgiving about my construal of his foundationalism, and thus of his views
about introspective mistake. Perhaps Hume would introduce a class
of rock-bottom, foundational introspective judgments that we may call
'pure existential judgments'. Such judgments have as their sole constituents demonstrative elements and exercises of the concept of existence (plus, of course, that property of a complex that turns a mere
thought into a judgment). The only concept one exercises in such a
judgment is that of existence. An approximation in speech to a pure
existential judgment *in foro interno* is the austerely construed utterance
'This exists'. Such pure existential judgments, it may be suggested,
Hume neither can nor does admit to be possibly mistaken.

Now there are obvious difficulties in understanding how Hume, or
anyone else, can think of pure existential judgments as foundational
judgments on whose basis one can erect the structure of empirical
beliefs, but I propose to ignore these difficulties. For Hume cannot allow
pure existential judgments to be judgments at all. If this is right he cannot
introduce them to explicate perfect assent. The trouble is, of course, that
Hume requires a judgment to contain an idea, or exercise of a concept,
and also denies that we have a distinct idea of existence. On the standard
reading this rules out the possibility of pure existentials. What of our
alternative reading of Hume on existence, a reading that allows a concept of existence as a second-order concept of a concept's having an
instance? Could Hume in this way admit not-quite-so-pure existential
judgments of the form: Some concept has this as an instance? I can find
no suggestion of such judgments in the text. In any case, they are much
too sophisticated to play a foundational role in Hume's epistemology.
Were he to admit them at all, Hume could allow them to have only some
very different place in his account of the structure of empirical beliefs.
What that place would be I shall not venture to say.

Hume's rock-bottom judgments require the exercise of at least one
first-order concept. When one attempts to further attenuate their content no judgment remains. These minimal judgments, we may assume,
are such as would be expressible by austerely construed utterances such
as 'This is red' or 'This red thing exists'. On my reading of Hume these
circumscribed judgments, when made with all imaginable caution, are
not at all likely to be mistaken. This is all he needs for his foundationalist
purposes; his foundationalism does not require introspective judgments
that are logically insulated from error. And he has compelling intratheoretical reasons for rejecting the possibility of any such introspective
judgments. Without pure and not-quite-so-pure existential judgments
we have a foundationalist, but not an infallibilist, Hume.[13]

5.   At the end of section 2 I constructed three theories of introspective
awareness and judgment, Theories A, B and C, and claimed that each is
a Humean theory. I claimed, too, that Hume must prefer Theory C to

the others. Equipped with a coherent rendering of Hume's views about introspective mishap, let us return to the examination of these theories.

On the matter of mere awareness Hume has only two options that are compatible with the main outline of his philosophy of mind. He cannot analyse mere awareness in terms of some special act or activity directed at the introspected perception and not itself reducible to a perception or some relation between perceptions. Nor can he hold a view, like that once held by Russell, that mere awareness is a matter of an irreducibly mental relation between a perception and some (perhaps momentary) subject, where the subject is neither a perception nor a collection of perceptions.[14] The first of these doctrines falls foul of Hume's reification of perceptions; the second is inconsistent with his bundle theory of the mind. Hume must, then, analyse mere awareness in terms of two perceptions, a first-order and a second-order perception, that stand in some special asymmetrical relation to one another. This option is incorporated in Theory A. Alternatively, he must identify the having of a perception with the having of mere awareness of it, in the manner required by Theories B and C.

Theory A has several merits from a Humean perspective. As we have seen, it countenances the logical possibility of introspective ignorance and mistake. It is also easy enough, within such a theory, to accommodate the notion that introspective ignorance and error are empirically possible in some cases, if not in others. Theory A shares these virtues with the other two theories. Theory A also has the advantage, albeit a double-edged one, of being, in a straightforwardly Humean fashion, an inner sense theory of introspection. It has second-order perceptions, specifically sensations, as constituents of introspective judgments, and first-order perceptions, that is, sensations, feelings or images, as objects of those judgments. The second-order perception P^* may be viewed as a representative of the first-order perception P; in this respect Theory A is isomorphic with Hume's representative realism for the case of ordinary sense perception. Since P and P^* are Humean distinct perceptions mishap is possible at the level of mere awareness; there is, crucially, room for an appearance/reality distinction. This brings in its train the possibility of characteristically perceptual mistakes, that is, of introspective illusion and hallucination. Such introspective mistakes, prompted by features of P^*, would be mistakes not about P^* but about the item it represents, namely P. If Hume is seriously committed to viewing introspection as analogous to sense perception Theory A enables him to fill in some of the details.

There are, however, quite compelling reasons for not attributing Theory A to Hume, despite the fact that, when criticising the theory of substrates, he appears to endorse something like it. For one thing, the duplication of perceptions offends against characteristically Humean canons of parsimony. For another, Hume nowhere mentions second-order sensations of sensations, of emotions, or of ideas. In a less narrowly constrained sense of 'perception' he does, of course, countenance perceptions of perceptions; we saw this when examining his account of personal identity. But Theory A requires second-order perceptions in the narrow sense introduced earlier; it requires determinate mental particulars, specifically sensations, and there are no signs of these in Hume's text. Most importantly, however, Theory A is incompatible with Hume's thesis of the impossibility of mishap at the level of mere awareness. If Theory A is correct, such mishap is possible; if Hume is right, it is not. So, if Hume holds firmly to this thesis about mere awareness, a thesis that seems so centrally embedded in his philosophy of mind as not lightly to be discarded, he must reject Theory A. To do so, of course, is to seriously inhibit the inclination we have assumed him to have towards an inner sense theory of introspection. It is just those features of Theory A that make it a fairly full-blooded inner sense theory that must, upon reflection, prompt Hume to dismiss it. If Hume wishes to insist that introspection is nonetheless analogous to sense perception, this can amount to no more than an insistence that the objects of each, namely perceptions and physical objects, are interestingly analogous.

Incidentally, Theory A, if combined with Hume's claim that one has a perception only if one has mere awareness of it, generates an infinite number of higher-order perceptions for any given first-order perception. If for any perception P of which one is aware one must have another perception P*, then one must also have a perception P** to accommodate awareness of P*, and so on. Hume can block the regress by fiat, of course; but fiats, at least in philosophy, are to be avoided.[15]

If Theories B and C are inner sense theories at all, they are so only in so far as they maintain, in the way just mentioned, a resemblance between perceptions and physical objects. Each has the virtue of being consistent with Hume's complicated views about introspective ignorance and mistake; neither permits a notion of introspective illusion or hallucination or, therefore, a notion of specifically perceptual mistake, for neither permits mishap at the level of mere awareness. By identifying having a perception with having mere awareness each can avoid the vicious regress of higher-order perceptions that is spawned by Theory A. These are virtues common to Theories B and C. It seems clear, however, that Hume must prefer C to B.

Theory B is less economical than Theory C. Theory B requires complete second-order judgments, and hence presumably requires for each judgment at least two exercises of concepts; Theory C, since it does not require complete second-order judgments, can make do with only one. Presumably the conceptual addition to Theory B must be tailored to serve a demonstrative or denoting function; it must tie the judgment to the particular perception that the judgment concerns. Not surprisingly, Hume gives no account of exercises of concepts playing the role of demonstratives; indeed it seems most unHumean to allow the possibility of their doing so. It seems equally unHumean to have no demonstrative constituent at all in the second-order judgment in question. Can Hume eschew such descriptive demonstratives, making do with austerely construed psychological counterparts to the demonstrative pronoun 'this'? If this psychological counterpart is a constituent of the second-order introspective judgment, as any variant of Theory B must require, either Hume is back to Theory A, already rejected, or he must admit into his ontology mental items other than perceptions, in our narrow sense, and exercises of concepts. There are, in Hume's inventory of the mind, no such additional things.

What, then, of Theory C? In addition to the virtues it shares with Theory B it is economical, it can seem to explain the demonstrative character of minimal introspective judgments, and it imports no unwanted and unmentioned items into Hume's ontology. It is just the theory one would expect of a bundle theorist with other reductivist proclivities. At least the embedded theory of mere awareness is just what one would expect of Hume, for it is rather like the theories adopted by later bundle theorists such as James and, at times, Russell.[16] And there is at least one passage in the *Treatise* that, given a contextually legitimate translation from 'external objects' to 'sensations', suggests such a reading of Hume:

> External objects [sensations] are seen, and felt, and become present to the mind; that is, they acquire such a relation to a connected heap of perceptions, as to influence them very considerably in augmenting their number of present reflexions and passions, and in storing the memory with ideas. (*T* 207)

Let us proceed on the hypothesis that Theory C is Hume's preferred theory.

Despite its many virtues for Hume's purposes, Theory C is unacceptable. Let us overlook Hume's failure to explicate the link between perception and exercise of concept, a failure that is merely part of his undeveloped theory of judgment. Let us concentrate on the perceptions in question, perceptions of which one has mere awareness, and that are both object and constituent of the introspective judgments that concern them. We have seen reason for thinking that Hume's view of introspective judgment requires psychological demonstratives in the sense of mental analogues of utterances of 'this' having present mental particulars as their referents. We have taken the thoroughly reliable minimal judgments that provide the basis in Hume's foundationalist epistemology to be, in all likelihood, judgments expressible as 'This is red' or 'This red thing exists'. But of course Hume's foundations are not public utterances but judgments *in foro interno*. So we are left looking for the psychological counterpart to the demonstrative pronoun. Theory A, whatever its defects, can cite the second-order perception P*. Theory B fails, in part because it requires either of two unHumean alternatives: either descriptive demonstratives or non-descriptive ones that are nonetheless not perceptions. Theory C is in no better a position on this matter; indeed it seems to be in a worse one.

Just what, according to Theory C, is the counterpart demonstrative that denotes the perception P ? How are we to understand the demonstrative character of introspective judgments ? Shall we say that the perception P serves the demonstrative role ? This is to have P denoting itself, but the notion of self-referential demonstratives is intolerably paradoxical. Shall we assign the demonstrative task to the whole bundle of perceptions that constitutes the mind (whether we take the bundle to include or not to include P itself) ? I can make no sense of this suggestion. To introduce some second-order perception, however, merely revives Theory A or some less plausible variant.

Shall we construe P as the demonstrative constituent, but interpret its demonstrative role in such a way as to avoid self-referentiality ? Let us suppose P is a sensation of blue. We may say that P presents a particular blue expanse to the perceiver, M, whose sensation P is. Shall we take it, then, that P denotes not itself but the blue expanse that it presents to M ? The manoeuvre cannot serve Hume's purposes. Even if we allow P to be a demonstrative in the sense specified, it does not provide the psychological demonstrative that Hume requires. Although itself a psychological item, namely a perception, it refers not to a perception but to the content or object of one. It provides a way to understand a judgment's ascribing properties to the content or object of a perception, but not to the perception P itself. Such judgments about the content or object of P would not be introspective judgments; so Theory C, construed in this way, would not perform the task for which it was designed.

In any case, one would not expect Hume happily to thus distinguish perception P and its content or object. Although sometimes, especially in some associationist contexts, he appears to make use of this distinction, his official line is to reject it. When doing his serious work about sense perception, for example developing his epistemological idealism and his scepticism with regard to the senses, he treats sensations as substances with qualities, as blue patches, for example, or as rotten-egg smells. Indeed, as we noted much earlier, he tends not to make any distinction between substantival sensations as bearers of qualities and the qualities they bear. In effect, he identifies perceptions with their contents or objects. Presumably he takes the suggested distinction to be empirically empty and hence to be avoided. It is most unlikely, then, that he would adopt this way of treating perceptions as demonstratives even if, contrary to fact, it would provide him with a way of denoting psychological particulars. The reification of perceptions is perhaps the most deeply entrenched element in his philosophy.

If Theory C cannot accommodate the demonstrative character of basic introspective judgments can Hume give up the requirement that such judgments be demonstrative ? It is difficult to imagine a Humean theory without that requirement, for what, then, would be the character of the minimal judgments that must provide the foundational infrastructure for the body of empirical belief? It is useful to note, in this connection, that Russell once took the character of so-called 'emphatic particulars', including 'this' and 'now', to provide the most conclusive refutation of neutral monism as a theory of experience.[17]

It is not to be expected that questions about the demonstrative character of introspective judgments are independent of questions about the nature of mere awareness. Failure with respect to the one notion seems to bring in its train failure to explain the other. Theory C offers an account of mere awareness. Quite clearly, however, that account mangles the admitted distinction between awareness and object of awareness. It is important to recognize that Theory C does concede *some* distinction in this region: the object of awareness is perception P; by contrast, the mere awareness of P is a relational fact having to do with P and its relations to various other perceptions had by mind M. Mere awareness of P is identical not with P but with the ownership of P. It seems plain, however, that this is simply a mistake, and that the distinction between awareness and object of awareness, if it is to have any place at all, must be akin to that between representing item and item represented (as in Theory A) or that between a perception and its content or object (the clearly unHumean view just discussed). What seems plain, however, may merely seem so. Hence there is point to scrutinizing in detail Theory C's analysis of mere awareness. We shall see that this analysis cannot work, given the account of ownership that Hume actually provides. This close scrutiny should also still any lingering doubts about my assessment of the prospects of Theory C.

According to Theory C, some mind M's mere awareness of perception P is strictly a function of P's standing to other perceptions in those relations in virtue of which P and those other perceptions belong to M. No special mental relations are involved; the only relations Hume actually mentions are resemblance and causality. P and the other perceptions are mental entities; merely physical objects do not have mere awareness. Importantly, the fact that P is a mental entity is not sufficient for M's being aware of it; awareness, like ownership, is necessarily a matter of multiple perceptions.

There are intractable intratheoretical obstacles in the way of Hume's relational analysis of mere awareness for both simultaneous perceptions and perceptions that exist at different times. Consider, first, the case of simultaneous perceptions, say P and Q. Causality cannot provide the required relation between simultaneous perceptions P and Q for Humean causes and effects have different temporal locations. Resemblance between simultaneous perceptions seems no more promising a candidate. When analysing ownership, Hume construes resemblance narrowly as a resemblance between recollection and perception recalled. Understood in this way resemblance is no more suited than is causality for the relating of simultaneous perceptions. It is difficult to imagine what non-trivial alternative specification of resemblance Hume can offer. At the one place in the *Treatise* where he comes closest to our present concerns, a single paragraph on the 'simplicity' of the soul at a given time, he refers lamely, and quite unilluminatingly, to an 'object, whose different co-existent parts are bound together by a close relation' (*T* 263).

What relational account can Hume offer for mere awareness of perceptions occurring at different times? If the relation is resemblance, again construed narrowly as a matter of memory, then perhaps Q's occurring at t_2 and suitably resembling P, which occurred at t_1, provides awareness of P. But at best Theory C thus explains awareness of a past perception. Nothing so far said explains either M's awareness of P at the time of P's occurrence, or M's awareness of Q (the recollection of P). By hypothesis, however, if P and Q do resemble in this way, M owns both and is, *pari passu*, aware of both. It is clear something is radically wrong.

When one thinks through the account of non-simultaneous perceptions in terms of causality similar perplexities arise. One need ask only whether M has mere awareness of P *prior to* the occurrence of its effect, namely Q. Any answer made within the confines of Theory C must be unacceptable. To say that M was aware of P prior to the occurrence of Q runs counter to the hypothesis. To say that M becomes aware of P only upon the occurrence of Q, when P, perhaps, no longer exists, entices one into some gratuitous, and surely unHumean, metaphysics. On this account many of one's past perceptions would be perceptions that one neither owned nor had awareness of at the time of their occurrence.

But there is no need to run through the remaining permutations to see the absurdity of this relational analysis of mere awareness. The difficulties of Theory C are not a matter of the specific relations Hume cites; tinkering changes in the theory would not improve matters. For the fundamental idea that generates Theory C, it should now be clear, is quite unintelligible. Ownership and mere awareness of perceptions is alleged to be a product, simply, of the perceptions standing in certain relations to one another. But what sense does it make to say that whereas having and being aware of a single perception is logically impossible the addition of another suitably related perception creates at one shot the ownership and awareness of the two? There may be strength in numbers, but is there magic in numbers as well? Our opening intuition, when tested against the concrete requirements of Theory C, is sound: were he to explicate mere awareness of perceptions Hume must find some theory other than Theory C. Theories A and B having been rejected, however, there is no more promising Humean theory in the offing.

6.   Hume cannot get what he must have or what, apparently, he wants. He cannot get a satisfactory account of introspection with respect to

one's present sensations, feelings and images; he cannot explain one's awareness of the very things that are the building-blocks in his empiricist philosophy of mind. In particular, he cannot devise an inner sense theory for such cases. Of the three alternative theories available to him the first must be rejected given his views about introspective mishap at the level of mere awareness, as well as on other grounds. The second and third theories, in differing ways, fail to capture his presumed commitment to the demonstrative element in introspective judgment. Most crushingly, the third theory, the one that is obviously most consonant with his general philosophical position, turns out, on close inspection, to be unintelligible as a theory of mere awareness. Hume's philosophy of mind requires the existence of determinate mental particulars, that is, Humean perceptions, and the possibility of access to them; these requirements go hand in hand with a doctrine of inner sense. On the showing of the previous section, however, it is a not unreasonable conjecture that there is no such thing as inner sense;[18] one has no access to the desired mental particulars for the very good reason that there exist no such things. This last point, of course, must come as no surprise; we earlier found good reason to reject Hume's reified perceptions. Hume's demonstrated inability to explain awareness of these supposed entities, however, does provide welcome confirmation of their earlier dismissal.

Hume cannot get what he wants; but there is something remarkably like what he wants that, so far as my present arguments go, he can secure with little effort at all. By a simple, if philosophically substantive, emendation of Theory C, Hume acquires the beginnings of an arguable theory of sensory and quasi-sensory awareness and judgment. That there is a promising near-relative of Theory C to be found goes some way, perhaps, towards explaining Hume's adoption of a theory of introspection that is, as I have argued, unintelligible. Also, seeing the contrasts between Theory C and this near-relative can strengthen one's conviction that, whatever must be said of the qualitative features of mental phenomena, one must resist the temptations of inner sense. To highlight its origins, and its similarities to Theory C, let us call this near-relative 'Theory C*'. Although similar to Theory C C* is not a theory of introspection.

Theory C* introduces counterparts to Hume's three kinds of perceptions but refuses to construe these as reified mental particulars. Sensations, feelings and images are not substances that one introspects but states of mere awareness of their own contents or objects. On Theory C, having a perception is identical with having awareness of that perception. On C*, to have a perception is to have awareness of some content or object. To have a sensation of blue is to have mere awareness not of a sensation but of a blue patch. To have an image of blue is likewise to have mere awareness not of some mental entity but of some blue patch. To have a sinking feeling in the pit of one's stomach is to have mere awareness of the content in question. With a hint of Hume's talk of contrasting degrees of vivacity, Theory C* takes the counterparts of Hume's sensations to be states of sensory awareness, and the counterparts to his ideas to be states of quasi-sensory awareness. Capturing one element in his general theory of the passions, C* takes their counterparts to be states of quasi-bodily sensory awareness. Humean passions are, after all, quite like sensations; they differ from them only causally and, in the language of C*, in content.[19]

According to C*, to be in a state of sensory or quasi-sensory awareness is to have mere awareness, albeit not awareness of some mental entity. As with Theory C, no mishap is possible at this non-conceptual level of awareness. By contrast with Theory C, however, the explanation of this fact involves not an identification of ownership and awareness but a refusal to view the relation between a state of sensory or quasi-sensory awareness and its content as a relation between distinct existences.

Items from the level of mere awareness serve, as in Theory C, as constituents of judgments, in this case sensory or quasi-sensory judgments, not introspective ones. The counterpart to a Humean perception plays a demonstrative role, presenting its content or object for the ascription of properties by the judgment in question. The judgment *in foro interno* that might be expressed by the public utterance 'This is blue' is a judgment about the content or object presented by the judgment's sensory or quasi-sensory constituent. Theory C* allows, as does Theory C, the logical possibility of ignorance or error in its basic sensory and quasi-sensory judgments; and it allows, within limits, their empirical possibility as well.

I have mentioned a number of respects in which this non-introspective near-relative of Theory C gives hints of related Humean doctrines. Two further points of contact may usefully be noted. Theory C* permits ascription of colour and shape, texture and felt temperature, to the items of which one has mere awareness. Also, it is compatible with the plain man's view that it is those very things, or at least some of them, that continue to exist when one ceases to have mere awareness of them. Theory C* thus can appropriate the genuine insight in Hume's literally absurd doctrine of the reification of perceptions.

C* denies mishap at the level of mere awareness. Can it nonetheless deny that one must be conscious of the contents or objects of the sensory and quasi-sensory states one has? Perhaps surprisingly, it *can* do so, provided a crucial distinction is made. It can admit the possibility of these sensory and quasi-sensory items being located along a scale in such a way that if they are below a certain threshold their possessor would be unconscious of their content, while if they are at or above that threshold their possessor would be conscious of their content. Position on this scale need not be a matter of the perceiver's conceptual abilities. Nonetheless, there could be a correlation between a sensation's being at or above the threshold of consciousness and the perceiver's being able to judge straight-off that he is faced with an instance of a given concept. A perceiver may have a sensation of a blue patch, say, and be either conscious or unconscious, in the sense here in question, of the blue patch presented to him. If it admits the situation here envisaged, Theory C* would need to distinguish conscious and unconscious instances of mere awareness.[20] In doing so, of course, it would reject any C* variant of Hume's thesis that if one has a perception one is aware of it.

Although a near-relative of Hume's Theory C, Theory C* patently does nothing to relieve Hume's troubles about introspection; it does nothing to salvage the notion of inner observation of mental entities. So it can do nothing to lessen the damage that, as I claimed at the very beginning, Hume's mishandling of introspection must do to other central elements in his philosophy of mind. It is time to make a tally of the damage done.

It should go without saying that Hume's failure with respect to introspection does little, by itself, to raise doubts about his dualist assumptions that sensations, thoughts and the like are items *in foro interno*, and that one's awareness of one's own psychological states is quite different in character from one's awareness of bodies or of the psychological states of others. It does little to intimate some physicalist doctrine. It does, however, eliminate one of the principal supports for his imagist account of thinking. Although one has introspective access to one's thoughts and to what one images, there is nothing that meets the introspective eye; and the items of which one is sensorily or quasi-sensorily aware are simply not candidates for the role of constituents of thoughts.

Rejection of Hume's presumptive views about introspection is, as noted above, intimately bound up with rejection of his reification of perceptions. With the rejection of this doctrine, however, goes the rejection of his epistemological idealism. With his epistemological idealism must go Hume's sceptical arguments regarding the external world, as well as his attempt to show the ineradicably antinomic character of the human understanding on such matters, for each of these contentions has epistemological idealism as an essential premise.

Hume denies that one can observe a Cartesian self. On my reading of his failure with respect to introspection it follows that one cannot observe a Humean bundle of reified perceptions either. The objects of which, in Theory C*, one is sensorily or quasi-sensorily aware cannot fit the bill. If the critical core of the bundle theory is to be salvaged it must be prized free of reification and the notion of inner sense. Of course, if there is no such thing as inner observation in the sense he requires, it is not at all surprising that Hume must fail to execute that part of his empiricist programme concerned with acquisition of the concept of a mind, including the concept of one's self. This is not to say that no empiricist account of mind is possible;[21] but it cannot be an account requiring observation, in one's own case, of instances of the many psychological concepts in question.

Hume's troubles with introspection do no direct damage to that part of his empiricist programme concerned with the conception of physical objects. Indeed it is a striking fact that the whole of his constructive account of the plain man's belief in an external world can be stated within the parameters of Theory C*. As I noted above, C* accepts Hume's characterization of the plain man's attitude towards what he encounters in experience. In any case, as we saw in chapter 1, Hume's epistemological idealism comes on the scene only after he has completed his constructive account of the belief in bodies; there is no essential link between the two.

On at least one point, however, our present results require revision of Hume's constructive views about sense perception. Hume subscribes, if reluctantly, to a representative theory of perception. Epistemological idealism provides part of the motivation for his holding this theory and is a constituent of the theory as he employs it. The direct objects of observation are mental particulars that represent the physical objects to which one has no direct access. Our objections to Hume's account of introspection sink this theory of sense perception as well as their ostensible object. Can Hume be a representative theorist of some description nonetheless? Only, it seems, if one can construe the central notion of representation in such a way that the sensory states of mere awareness introduced by C* count as representatives of the physical objects or events that cause them. Such a non-idealist representative theory would, of course, be a far cry from anything to be found in Hume's text.

If my argument has been sound, much that is most characteristic of Hume's philosophy of mind must be abandoned. Some may feel that nothing that is characteristically Humean emerges unscathed. As I have tried to show at many places, however, what is commonly taken to be characteristic of Hume is very far from the whole of him. Any sound assessment of his position must reckon with this fact.

Notes

CHAPTER ONE. *Scepticism, Perception and Physical Objects*

1. All page references within parentheses in the text are to Hume's *A Treatise of Human Nature* [*T*], ed. L. A. Selby-Bigge; 2nd edition with text revised by P. H. Nidditch (Oxford 1978), or to his *Enquiries Concerning Human Understanding and Concerning the Principles of Morals* [*E*], ed. L. A. Selby-Bigge; 3rd edition with text revised by P. H. Nidditch (Oxford 1975). Unless otherwise noted all italics within the quotations are Hume's.
2. I discuss these arguments in chapter 4.
3. There are, of course, difficulties with the suggestion that impressions appear as internal and perishing existences. See John W. Cook 'Hume's Scepticism with Regard to the Senses' *American Philosophical Quarterly* 5 (1968) 1-17.
4. H. H. Price *Hume's Theory of the External World* (Oxford 1940) 60f.
5. As both Price and Bennett have pointed out, the claim that independence entails continuance is false. However, nothing in Hume's argument hangs on this claim. See Price, 18-19, and Jonathan Bennett *Locke, Berkeley, Hume* (Oxford 1971) 315.
6. See also *Treatise*, 231. As we shall see shortly, the conflict within the imagination mentioned at the end of section 3 is the first stage in Hume's development of this antinomy.
7. I borrow this useful expression from Bennett, especially 31-5. I discuss Hume's reification of perceptions at several places, but see especially chapter 4, sections 4, 6 and 7.
8. This argument concerning secondary qualities is, of course, similar to that against the plain man's naive realism. In order to keep the two distinct we must remember the differences between their targets as well as the gap between the claims that only perceptions are directly perceived and that secondary qualities are properties only of perceptions. We must also recall that curious feature of Hume's language noted a few paragraphs back.
9. Once again, the word 'nothing' must be handled with care.

CHAPTER TWO. *Mind and Body*

1. D. M. Armstrong *A Materialist Theory of the Mind* (London 1968); Donald Davidson 'Mental Events' in Lawrence Foster and J. W. Swanson (eds.) *Experience and Theory* (Amherst 1970) 79-101.
2. The point does not have narrowly to do with thought; Hume here writes interchangeably of 'the causes of our perceptions' (*T* 246), 'the cause of thought or perception' (*T* 247), the causes of 'passion[s] and reflexion[s]' (*T* 248).

3. It may be objected that I have placed too strong a construction on these passages; that Hume obviously does not believe (because it is so obviously false) that we *experience* a constant conjunction of perceptions and physical events. This objection confuses claims about the limited experiential basis on which one normally makes causal judgments with claims about the quite general character of the causal judgments one makes.

4. Some may take Hume's 'account' of the physiological basis of associationism as an intimation of physicalism. I shall give reasons for not doing so later.

5. Confusion may arise here because of Hume's misleadingly restrictive references to the association of *ideas*. However, the relevant principles of association are clearly intended to cover the case of *impressions* causing ideas: 'when we pass from the *impression* of one [object] to the *idea* or belief of another, we are not determin'd by reason, but by custom or a principle of association' (*T* 97, my italics).

6. See Páll S. Árdal *Passion and Value in Hume's Treatise* (Edinburgh 1966) 9; Norman Kemp Smith *The Philosophy of David Hume* (London 1941) 168.

7. On the point about gaps in consciousness see chapter 4, section 5, and chapter 5, section 5; on that concerning dispositional properties see especially chapter 3.

8. By a 'purely mental action' I mean one that does not, as does raising one's arm, involve bodily movement. Working through a mathematical problem in one's head may serve as an example. The volitions involved in 'purely mental actions' may, nonetheless, have physiological effects.

9. Compare: 'The *will* exerts itself, when either the good or the absence of evil may be attain'd by any action of the mind or body' (*T* 439).

10. Donald Davidson, in 'Causal Relations' *The Journal of Philosophy* 64 (1967) 701-2, distinguishes two versions of the nomological claim: a singular causal statement entails that there is a causal law; a singular causal statement entails the truth of a given causal law. Hume appears to adopt the latter version.

11. Keith Campbell *Body and Mind* (Garden City, New York 1970) 52.

12. ibid., 51.

13. ibid., 18. See also Armstrong, 34, 37.

14. See Armstrong and Campbell for the objections of this paragraph.

15. Hilary Putnam 'Psychological Predicates' in W. H. Capitan and D. D. Merrill (eds.) *Art, Mind, and Religion* (Pittsburgh 1967) 37-48. But compare David Lewis 'Review of *Art, Mind, and Religion*' *The Journal of Philosophy* 66 (1969), especially 23-5, and 'Psychophysical and Theoretical Identification' *Australasian Journal of Philosophy* 50 (1972) 255.

16. Davidson 'Mental Events', 89-98.

17. ibid., 97-8.

18. I have pursued some of the issues raised in this and the previous section in two papers that make no mention of Hume: 'The Attribute Theory of Mind' *Australasian Journal of Philosophy* 51 (1973) 226-37; 'Interaction and Physiology' *Mind* 84 (1975) 255-9.

19. A. J. Ayer 'The Concept of a Person' in *The Concept of a Person and Other Essays* (London 1964) 83.

20. William James 'Does "Consciousness" Exist?' in *Essays in Radical Empiricism* (Cambridge, Massachusetts 1976) 8-9.

21. Bertrand Russell 'On Propositions: What They Are and How They Mean' in *Logic and Knowledge*, ed. R. C. Marsh (New York 1956) 299. Russell elaborates his qualified neutral monism in *The Analysis of Mind* (London 1921). For a useful survey of Russell's varying attitudes to the theory see A. M. Quinton 'Russell's Philosophy of Mind' in David Pears (ed.) *Bertrand Russell* (Garden City, New York 1972) 80-109.

22. 'On Propositions: What They Are and How They Mean', 299.

23. Price, 23n.

24. ibid. One should, however, compare what Price says of Hume's purported neutral monism at 105f. Also see John Laird *Hume's Philosophy of Human Nature* (London 1932) 171.

25. I examine Hume's bundle theory in chapter 4, sections 6 and 7, in chapter 5, and elsewhere.

26. On Hume's empiricist programme see especially chapter 5, sections 2 and 3.

27. See chapter 4, section 6.

CHAPTER THREE. *Mental Dispositions*

1. The very important passage in which Hume makes the distinctions I invoke here goes as follows: '[T]would perhaps be more convenient, in order at once to preserve the common signification of words, and mark the several degrees of evidence, to distinguish human reason into three kinds, viz. *that from knowledge, from proofs. and from probabilities.* By knowledge, I mean the assurance arising from the comparison of ideas. By proofs, those arguments, which are deriv'd from the relation of cause and effect, and which are entirely free from doubt and uncertainty. By probability, that evidence, which is still attended with uncertainty' (*T* 124. Compare *E* 56).

2. Gilbert Ryle *The Concept of Mind* (London 1949) 121f.

3. The realist theory of mental dispositions sketched here is similar to that proposed in Armstrong, 85-8, although it differs from Armstrong's on several important points.

4. I shall have much more to say about abstract ideas and general terms in chapter 6, but the brief sketch given here should do for present purposes.

5. For more on some of the issues raised in this paragraph see my paper 'Hume's Conception of Character' *The Southwestern Journal of Philosophy* 5 (1974) 107-13.

6. The story is, of course, much more complicated than I suggest here. For some of the complications see chapter 6.

7. This, it must be said, is not the received view of Hume on causation and explanation, although it is, I am persuaded, the correct one. I say a few things in partial defence of it at scattered places in this study. A full-dress defence, however, would take us a very long way round. So I must simply ask the reader to take the interpretation on faith, or, more respectably, as an exploratory hypothesis that may help shed light on some otherwise very puzzling aspects of Hume's philosophy of mind.

8. Compare Armstrong, 87.

9. The passage continues: 'at least may suppose it such, according to the general opinion, till we can find a more proper occasion to clear up this matter, by examining what objects are or are not susceptible of juxtaposition and conjunction'. In a footnote Hume refers ahead to *Treatise* I iv 5; the reference makes it clear that Hume's hesitation concerns spatial, not temporal, contiguity, for he is concerned to admit causal connections between two non-spatial items, or between spatial and non-spatial items.

10. Compare: 'It is ... plausible to assume that in making an assertion such as "All sugar is water-soluble" we are not just generalizing the observed regularity that things with the secondary qualities of sugar dissolve when immersed in a liquid with the secondary qualities of water, but express our belief that this empirical law admits of theoretical explanation in terms of the microstructures of sugar and water and indirectly confirmable postulates about the interactions of their constituent particles'. Arthur Pap *Introduction to the Philosophy of Science* (London 1963) 283.

11. In contrasting reductionism and realism I have ignored a variant theory that deserves to be mentioned. A reductionist could perhaps argue that, while a statement of form (4) is no part of the analysis of statements of form (3), it is a plausible empirical hypothesis that a statement of form (4) is true whenever a statement of form (3) is true. For an independent discussion of this possibility, see L. Stevenson 'Are Dispositions Causes?' *Analysis* 29 (1968-9) 197-9. It is impossible to decide what Hume might have said about this suggestion; nor, I suspect, would he have found the issue very interesting.

CHAPTER FOUR. *Selves, Substrates and Substances*

1. This way of stating the problems of simplicity and identity, although convenient, is in an important way unfaithful to Hume, since it takes judgments of simplicity to be, in effect, identity judgments. For a more accurate rendering of Hume's views on simplicity and identity see chapter 5, sections 2 and 4.

2. For this contrast see chapter 7, section 2.

3. Bennett, 31-5. Roderick Chisholm discusses reification and Hume's theory of the self in 'On the Observability of the Self' *Philosophy and Phenomenological Research* 30 (1969-70) 7-21.

4. John Locke *An Essay Concerning Human Understanding*, II I 13.

5. The point is Hume's: 'power cannot subsist alone, but is always regarded as an attribute of some being or existence' (T 161). But in terms of what non-dispositional properties is the being to be described? Compare Hume's remark: 'An impossibility of being annihilated cannot exist, and can never be conceived to exist, by itself; but necessarily requires some object or real existence, to which it may belong' (T 230).

6. Having written this paragraph I discovered that H. P. Grice deploys a very similar argument against what he calls the Pure Ego theory. See 'Personal Identity' *Mind* 50 (1941) 338-40.

7. I examine the distinction in chapter 7.

8. The two arguments are examined in sections 3 and 6 of this chapter.

9. Later, in the same section of the *Treatise*, he offers the following as a recapitulation of both Argument and Refutation: 'I have already prov'd, that we have no perfect idea of substance; but that taking it for *something, that can exist by itself*, 'tis evident every perception is a substance, and every distinct part of a perception a distinct substance' (*T* 244. Compare *T* 234).

10. A few paragraphs later he reiterates the 'principle' that 'all our distinct perceptions are distinct existences', glossing this with the statement that 'our perceptions . . . [do not] inhere in something simple and individual' (*T* 636).

11. See *Treatise*, 2, 6, 10, 18, 24-5, 36, 79-80, 86-7, 205, 207, 221, 222, 228, 233, 244-5, 252, 259, 634.

12. But consider the following passage from the 'Appendix': 'We can conceive a thinking being to have either many or few perceptions. Suppose the mind to be reduc'd even below the life of an oyster. Suppose it to have only one perception, as of thirst or hunger. Consider it in that situation. Do you conceive any thing but merely that perception? Have you any notion of *self* or *substance*? If not, the addition of other perceptions can never give you that notion' (*T* 634).

13. For somewhat different accounts of the separability principle and Hume's views about unowned perceptions the reader should consult Bennett, 287-92, 345-9, and Cook, 1-17.

14. See *Treatise*, 207-8.

15. Incidentally, if the substrate theory must be rejected it follows that there is some flaw in the Argument, described in section 6, offered in its support. As I have tried to show, Hume's Refutation does not, indeed could not, reveal this flaw. It seems clear, however, that the flaw must be located not in the Argument's premises but in the transition from its premises to its conclusion. That perceptions and sensible qualities are not logically capable of independent existence does not entail their inhering in substrates.

CHAPTER FIVE. *The Idea of One's Self*

1. W. V. O. Quine 'Identity, Ostension, and Hypostasis' in *From a Logical Point of View* (New York 1963) 65-79.

2. Here, I anticipate a later discussion of Hume's belief in the non-continuousness of minds. And I disregard, as Hume himself does at this point in his argument, the possibility of continuous independent objects other than bodies.

3. See Price, 60f.

4. Despite the use of single letters for momentary objects we are restricting ourselves to compound momentary objects.

5. I simplify matters by bypassing the possibility that the requisite 'non-gappy' pattern may be constructible from overlapping 'gappy' instances even if one has never made a genuinely 'non-gappy' observation.

6. See Bennett, especially 333-40. Bennett proceeds to a stimulating discussion of Hume's efforts to link identity and objectivity, 340-5.

7. A. J. Ayer *The Foundations of Empirical Knowledge* (London 1940) 78.

8. Here I omit consideration of the complications introduced by the fact of other minds. These are, of course, independent of me. Given Hume's

perspective, however, one does not observe them; so the question of their independence is logically later than, and quite different from, that considered here.

9. I here leave open the question whether one must be aware of every perception one has.

10. C. O. Evans *The Subject of Consciousness* (London 1970) 185.

11. Hume suggests that there is a second dimension to memory's discovering role. Because of its connection with our general ability to make causal judgments, we are enabled to 'extend the same chain of causes, and consequently the identity of our persons beyond our memory, and can comprehend times, and circumstances, and actions, which we have entirely forgot, but suppose in general to have existed' (*T* 262). That is to say, memory enables us to infer to past perceptions we can no longer recall!

12. Bernard Williams, quoting Hume's remark about seeing into the breast of another, refers to Hume's 'externalized view of the contents of a man's mind, a view obtainable from no conceivable vantage-point'. Bernard Williams 'Personal Identity and Individuation' *Proceedings of the Aristotelian Society* 57 (1956-7) 245.

13. Interestingly enough, there is one passage in which Hume writes as though thinking of oneself as identical through change involved thinking only of one's *past* perceptions: 'It follows, therefore, that the thought alone finds personal identity, when reflecting on the train of *past* perceptions, that compose a mind, the ideas of them are felt to be connected together, and naturally introduce each other' (*T* 635, my italics). If this were his considered view he would escape my present objection only to run into others. How, for one thing, does my *present* self come into the picture?

14. For a brief examination of two of the many unsuccessful ways in which Hume might be defended against this objection see my paper 'Hume on Self-Identity, Memory and Causality' in *David Hume: Bicentenary Papers,* ed. G. P. Morice (Edinburgh 1977) 171. For a related discussion of Hume on memory and identity see Sydney Shoemaker *Self-Knowledge and Self-Identity* (Ithaca, New York 1963) 152-9. Shoemaker writes (155): '[*H*]ow do I know what it [the past perception in question] was like? I *remember* what it was like. So can I compare what I remember it to have been like with my memory of it, and see that they are similar? But this would be to compare my memory of it with my memory of it, i.e., to compare my memory of it with itself. And surely it makes no sense to speak of comparing something with itself, to see whether there is a resemblance'.

15. Derek Parfit 'Personal Identity' *The Philosophical Review* 80 (1971) 3-27.

16. Parfit, 11. Parfit later (20-1) comes to prefer a relation of 'psychological connectedness' to that of 'psychological continuity'; this move, although important for Parfit's purposes, may be overlooked here.

17. I refer the reader to Parfit's reply (14-16) to the objection that, as a matter of logic, we can remember only our own experiences.

18. See chapter 4, section 5.

19. A. J. Ayer *The Concept of a Person*, 116.

20. ibid.

21. Price, 5-6.
22. ibid., 64.
23. ibid., 23n, 105-6.
24. Hume offers no extended discussion of our knowledge of other minds. In his more or less incidental remarks on the topic he assumes that some form of analogical argument must be employed. See *Treatise*, 151-3, 176-7, 318-20, 324-8, 329, 370, 477, 575-6.
25. René Descartes *Meditations on First Philosophy* VI, in *The Philosophical Works of Descartes*, trans. E. S. Haldane and G. R. T. Ross (Cambridge 1931).
26. This reading of Hume's second thoughts does not require him to become dissatisfied with his thesis that perceptions are distinct existences. For a stimulating discussion of Hume's second thoughts that puts more stress on that issue see David Pears 'Hume's Account of Personal Identity' in *Questions in the Philosophy of Mind* (London 1975) 207-23.

CHAPTER SIX. *Concept, Thought and Judgment*

1. In my thinking about the philosophical issues raised in the present chapter I am especially indebted to the writings of two very different philosophers, Peter Geach and H. H. Price. For Geach see *Mental Acts* (London 1957). For Price see *Thinking and Experience* (London 1969) and *Belief* (London 1969).
2. I borrow this useful expression from Bruce Aune's article 'Thinking' in Paul Edwards (ed.) *The Encyclopedia of Philosophy* (New York 1967).
3. I return to this question in section 4.
4. Price *Thinking and Experience*, 215, expresses an essentially Humean view when he writes: 'The truth seems to be that certain recognizable sounds gradually sort themselves out from the different complex utterances in which they are constituents. And the common feature, e.g. 'cat', in these otherwise unlike utterances is gradually correlated with a common factor in observed environmental situations which are otherwise unlike. Similarly 'black' gradually sorts itself out from another range of utterances which are otherwise unlike, and is correlated with a visible quality experienced in otherwise unlike situations.' Citing this passage Geach (34) uses the expression 'double process of abstraction' that I adopt here.
5. Price *Thinking and Experience*, 115-17, and elsewhere.
6. The further goings-on in question here are not Humean impressions of sensation or impressions of reflection.
7. David Pears 'Hume's Empiricism and Modern Empiricism' in David Pears (ed.) *David Hume: A Symposium* (London 1966) 18, 16.
8. Pears 'Hume's Empiricism', 15.
9. It should be noted that this is an unusual, if convenient, use of 'predication', since it allows predication in existential judgments. It should also be noted that in 'Hume's Empiricism', page 18, Pears states that the idea of existence is a separate idea but *not* a predicate. As I am using 'predication', however, it is equivalent to the inconveniently long expression 'the propositional linking of at least two concepts'.

10. '[T]here seems to have been no good reason why Hume should have extended his over-simplified account of existential thoughts to other thoughts.' Pears 'Hume's Empiricism', 19.

11. Pears 'Hume's Empiricism', 18, 19.

12. Throughout, I freely interchange 'belief' and 'judgment', following Hume's own practice. Humean beliefs are occurrences, not dispositions. But is his use of 'belief' perhaps more restrictive than his use of 'judgment', with the result that one cannot take his explicit theory of belief to provide a general theory of judgment? 'An opinion . . . or belief', he says, 'may be most accurately defin'd, *A lively idea related to or associated with a present impression*' (*T* 96; compare *T* 93); in context, the lively idea mentioned is one that results from causal inference. Whatever one makes of this use of 'define', Hume explicitly allows non-empirical beliefs (*T* 95), memory beliefs (*T* 86) and present-tense sensory beliefs (*T* 86). There are differences, of course, but none that materially affect our present question.

13. We shall shortly have occasion to notice a complication in Hume's account of the purported idea of existence.

14. The view of judgment and predication I have attributed to Hume is very like that expressed by Frege in the *Begriffsschrift*, in 'Function and Concept', and in 'On Sense and Reference'. See Peter Geach and Max Black (eds.) *Translations from the Philosophical Writings of Gottlob Frege* (Oxford 1966) 1-2, 34, 64. The likeness is even greater if what I say below about Hume's view of the non-distinctness of the idea of existence is allowed to stand.

15. Pears 'Hume's Empiricism', 18.

16. Recall that 'predication' is equivalent to 'the propositional linking of at least two concepts'.

17. David Armstrong *Belief, Truth and Knowledge* (Cambridge 1973) 71.

CHAPTER SEVEN. *Introspection and Sensory Awareness*

1. My use of 'exercise of a concept' allows us to by-pass a difficulty Pears raises when he argues, on the basis of Hume's imagist rendering of 'idea', that Humean 'ideas . . . cannot function at all as thoughts that are about contemporaneous sensory impressions' ('Hume's Empiricism', 21). Of course Hume must, for various theoretical purposes, make room for thoughts about one's present perceptions. He seems to explicitly countenance them when he writes of the mind's 'reflect[ing] upon it [an idea], and . . . [being] assur'd of its *present* existence' (*T* 106, my italics) and perhaps also when, sketching his bundle theory of the self, he remarks that sensations 'influence them [the other members of the bundle] very considerably in augmenting their number by *present reflexions*' (*T* 207, my italics).

2. It should be noted that if he distinguishes ideas as images from ideas as concepts Hume can include ideas (as images) among the items on which one performs the operations that give rise to one's possession of ideas (as concepts).

3. Broad remarks that those who 'regard the objective constituents of visual, tactual, and auditory perceptual situations as states of the per-

cipient's mind' are for just that reason prepared to talk, in some contexts, of introspective knowledge of these objective constituents. C. D. Broad *The Mind and Its Place in Nature* (London 1925) 288.

4. Ryle does not subscribe to the distinction in its more-or-less traditional form, but uses it to characterize the doctrines of others. See *The Concept of Mind*, 154-67.

5. For examples of this use see *Treatise*, 18, 24, 25, 69, 104, 133, 141, 147, 172, 181, 186, and *Enquiries*, 50.

6. As Austin has pointed out one may have illusions and hallucinations without thereby being deceived. J. L. Austin *Sense and Sensibilia* (Oxford 1962) 20-32.

7. Earlier, I took 'predication' to be equivalent to 'the propositional linking of at least two concepts'. To accommodate Theory A, as well as Theory C which we shall consider shortly, we must introduce an operation that is akin to predication but that takes a perception and an exercise of a concept as the items to be propositionally linked.

8. Here I by-pass the question whether, at least in Hume's view, an exercise of a concept can occur on its own. Even if he does not think this is possible Hume would presumably insist that the concept-exercise is logically independent of the particular item, whether perception or exercise of a concept, with which it is in fact linked in some complete thought.

9. In formulating the difference between (1) and (2) I have been assisted by Armstrong's related distinction between p's being logically indubitable for S and p's being self-intimating for S. See *A Materialist Theory of the Mind*, 100-2. In distinguishing (3) and (4) from (1) and (2), however, I depart significantly from Armstrong.

10. Typically, Hume classifies perceptions in terms of intrinsic properties. When hard-pressed, he allows classification in terms of a conjunction of intrinsic and causal properties. The clearest instance occurs in his discussion of pity and malice: "tis not the present sensation alone or momentary pain or pleasure, which determines the character of any passion, but the whole bent or tendency of it from the beginning to the end' (T 381; compare T 384-5).

11. I take it that Hume is here not thinking of retinal images.

12. On the significance of this question see Wilfrid Sellars 'Empiricism and the Philosophy of Mind' in *Science, Perception and Reality* (London 1963) especially 127-34.

13. Although it cannot count as an introspective judgment in our present sense, the Cartesian judgment expressible as 'I exist' is particularly interesting in the present connection. What is Hume's view of the claim that such judgments are infallible? Perhaps surprisingly, Hume takes no unequivocal position on the question. In the passages in which he comes closest to the issue his attention appears to be riveted on two closely related but clearly distinct matters: Cartesian accounts of the nature of the self, and Cartesian claims about the use of 'self-evident and convincing' principles (E 150) in inferences designed to undercut the scepticism generated by methodic doubt. In these passages he says nothing that can count as an unequivocal reply to the question that concerns us here. Perhaps he would deny that such judgments are in-

fallible, or would claim that their epistemological status is no more secure than that accorded to the minimal introspective judgments that his foundationalism requires. Perhaps, because of his views about existence or because of difficulties he would have in assigning a judgmental counterpart to the first-personal pronoun, he would deny that the purported judgments are judgments at all. The question of the status of such judgments must, in any event, be a very tangled one within the confines of Hume's philosophy. The reader is invited to consider the bearing, on the status of first-person present-tense existential judgments, of what Hume says at *T* 251 and at *E* 149-50.

14. Bertrand Russell 'On the Nature of Acquaintance' in *Logic and Knowledge*, 127-74. I say this is *like* Russell's view in the paper mentioned. It is also quite *unlike* his view there in that Russell denies that the object of acquaintance, the counterpart to Hume's impression, is a mental entity.

15. Compare the regress that results, as noted in chapter 4, section 4, given the premise that to be aware of some mental item one must be directly aware not of it but of some mental item that represents it.

16. I am thinking of the theories of experience that these two writers propose in the works cited at chapter 2, but only in so far as the specifically neutral monist claims are put to one side.

17. Russell 'On the Nature of Acquaintance', 169.

18. Interest in inner sense is not a parochially empiricist attitude; Kant adopts a notion of inner sense in the first *Critique*.

19. For a discussion of this way of construing Hume's passions or impressions of reflection, see my paper 'Emotion and Thought in Hume's *Treatise*' *Canadian Journal of Philosophy*, Supplementary Volume 1 (1974) 53-7.

20. My discussion of this point has been influenced by Dennett's distinction between awareness$_1$ and awareness$_2$ although it is in several respects incompatible with the intended force of Dennett's distinction. See D. C. Dennett *Content and Consciousness* (London 1969) 114-31. See also Armstrong *A Materialist Theory of the Mind*, 113-15, although Armstrong assumes a theory of inner observation.

21. For some of the difficulties to be faced see, for example, P. F. Strawson *Individuals* (London 1959) chapter 3 ('Persons'); Sydney Shoemaker *Self-Knowledge and Self-Identity* (Ithaca 1963); Bernard Williams *Problems of the Self* (Cambridge 1973); and G. E. M. Anscombe 'The First Person' in S. Guttenplan (ed.) *Mind and Language* (Oxford 1975) 45-65.

Bibliography

Anscombe, G. E. M. 'The First Person' *Mind and Language*. Edited by S. Guttenplan. Oxford University Press 1975.

Árdal, Páll S. *Passion and Value in Hume's Treatise*. Edinburgh University Press 1966.

Armstrong, D. M. *Belief, Truth and Knowledge*. Cambridge University Press 1973.

— *A Materialist Theory of the Mind*. London: Routledge and Kegan Paul 1968.

Aune, Bruce. 'Thinking' *The Encyclopedia of Philosophy*. Edited by Paul Edwards. 8 vols. New York: Macmillan 1967.

Austin, J. L. *Sense and Sensibilia*. Oxford University Press 1962.

Ayer, A. J. 'The Concept of a Person' *The Concept of a Person and Other Essays*. London: Macmillan 1964.

— *The Foundations of Empirical Knowledge*. London: Macmillan 1940.

Bennett, Jonathan. *Locke, Berkeley, Hume*. Oxford University Press 1971.

Bricke, John. 'The Attribute Theory of Mind' *Australasian Journal of Philosophy* 51 (1973) 226-37.

— 'Emotion and Thought in Hume's *Treatise*' *Canadian Journal of Philosophy*, Supplementary Volume 1 (1974) 53-71.

— 'Hume's Conception of Character' *The Southwestern Journal of Philosophy* 5 (1974) 107-13.

— 'Hume's Theories of Dispositional Properties' *American Philosophical Quarterly* 10 (1973) 15-23.

— 'Hume on Self-Identity, Memory and Causality' *David Hume: Bicentenary Papers*. Edited by G. P. Morice. Edinburgh University Press 1977.

— 'Interaction and Physiology' *Mind* 84 (1975) 255-9.

Broad, C. D. *The Mind and Its Place in Nature*. London: Kegan Paul, Trench, Trubner 1925.

Campbell, Keith. *Body and Mind*. Garden City, New York: Doubleday 1970.

Chisholm, Roderick. 'On the Observability of the Self' *Philosophy and Phenomenological Research* 30 (1969-70) 7-21.

Cook, John W. 'Hume's Scepticism with Regard to the Senses' *American Philosophical Quarterly* 5 (1968) 1-17.

Davidson, Donald. 'Causal Relations' *The Journal of Philosophy* 64 (1967) 691-703.

— 'Mental Events' *Experience and Theory*. Edited by Lawrence Foster and J. W. Swanson. Amherst: University of Massachusetts Press 1970.

Dennett, D. C. *Content and Consciousness*. London: Routledge and Kegan Paul 1969.

Descartes, René. *Meditations on First Philosophy*. Vol. 1 of *The Philosophical Works of Descartes*. Translated by E. S. Haldane and G. R. T. Ross. Cambridge University Press 1931.

Evans, C. O. *The Subject of Consciousness*. London: George Allen and Unwin 1970.

Frege, G. *Begriffsschrift* (Chapter 1). *Translations from the Philosophical Writings of Gottlob Frege*. Edited by Peter Geach and Max Black. Oxford: Basil Blackwell 1966.

— 'Function and Concept' *Translations from the Philosophical Writings of Gottlob Frege*. Edited by Peter Geach and Max Black. Oxford: Basil Blackwell 1966.

— 'On Sense and Reference' *Translations from the Philosophical Writings of Gottlob Frege*. Edited by Peter Geach and Max Black. Oxford: Basil Blackwell 1966.

Geach, Peter. *Mental Acts*. London: Routledge and Kegan Paul 1957.

Grice, H. P. 'Personal Identity' *Mind* 50 (1941) 330-50.

Hume, David. *Enquiries Concerning Human Understanding and Concerning the Principles of Morals*. Edited by L. A. Selby-Bigge. 3rd edition with text revised by P. H. Nidditch. Oxford University Press 1975.

— *A Treatise of Human Nature*. Edited by L. A. Selby-Bigge. 2nd edition with text revised by P. H. Nidditch. Oxford University Press 1978.

James, William. 'Does "Consciousness" Exist?' *Essays in Radical Empiricism*. Cambridge, Massachusetts: Harvard University Press 1976.

Kant, Immanuel. *Critique of Pure Reason*. Translated by Norman Kemp Smith. London: Macmillan 1933.

Laird, John. *Hume's Philosophy of Human Nature*. London: Methuen 1932.

Lewis, David. 'Psychophysical and Theoretical Identification' *Australasian Journal of Philosophy* 50 (1972) 249-58.

— 'Review of *Art, Mind, and Religion*' *The Journal of Philosophy* 66 (1969) 22-7.

Locke, John. *An Essay Concerning Human Understanding*. Edited by A. C. Fraser. 2 vols. New York: Dover 1959.

Pap, Arthur. *Introduction to the Philosophy of Science*. London: Eyre and Spottiswoode 1963.

Parfit, Derek. 'Personal Identity' *The Philosophical Review* 80 (1971) 3-27.

Pears, David. 'Hume's Account of Personal Identity' *Questions in the Philosophy of Mind*. London: Duckworth 1975.

— 'Hume's Empiricism and Modern Empiricism' *David Hume: A Symposium*. Edited by David Pears. London: Macmillan 1966.

Price, H. H. *Belief*. London: George Allen and Unwin 1969.

— *Hume's Theory of the External World*. Oxford University Press 1940.

— *Thinking and Experience*. London: Hutchinson 1969.

Putnam, Hilary. 'Psychological Predicates' *Art, Mind, and Religion*. Edited by W. H. Capitan and D. D. Merrill. University of Pittsburgh Press 1967.

Quine, W. V. O. 'Identity, Ostension, and Hypostasis' *From a Logical Point of View*. New York: Harper and Row 1963.

Quinton, A. M. 'Russell's Philosophy of Mind' *Bertrand Russell*. Edited by David Pears. Garden City, New York: Doubleday 1972.

Russell, Bertrand. *The Analysis of Mind*. London: George Allen and Unwin 1921.

— 'On the Nature of Acquaintance' *Logic and Knowledge*. Edited by Robert C. Marsh. New York: Macmillan 1956.

— 'On Propositions: What They Are and How They Mean' *Logic and Knowledge*. Edited by R. C. Marsh. New York: Macmillan 1956.

Ryle, Gilbert. *The Concept of Mind*. London: Hutchinson 1949.

Sellars, Wilfrid. 'Empiricism and the Philosophy of Mind' *Science, Perception and Reality*. London: Routledge and Kegan Paul 1963.

Shoemaker, Sydney. *Self-Knowledge and Self-Identity*. Ithaca: Cornell University Press 1963.

Smith, Norman Kemp. *The Philosophy of David Hume*. London: Macmillan 1941.

Stevenson, Leslie. 'Are Dispositions Causes?' *Analysis* 29 (1968-9) 197-9.

Strawson, P. F. *Individuals*. London: Methuen 1959.

Williams, Bernard. 'Personal Identity and Individuation' *Proceedings of the Aristotelian Society* 57 (1956-7) 229-52.

— *Problems of the Self*. Cambridge University Press 1973.

Index

abstract ideas: as concepts, 106; as images, 106, 107; Hume's account of, 49-50, 100, 102-7; in concept-exercise, 106, 107; role of 'custom', 50, 103, 104-5, 108; used in absence of objects, 108

abstraction: double process of, 102-3, 110; in concept acquisition, 102-3, 106, 110; in formation of general ideas, 106, 108, 111

animal spirits, 28, 29, 31, 39

'antient philosophy', 46, 47, 49, 51, 53, 56

Armstrong, D. M., 25, 121

association: mistakes generated by, 29; physiological basis of, 29-30, 31, 38; psychological laws of, 29, 33, 35, 36, 95

associationist: account of language learning, 103, 104; explanation of idea of mind, 96, 97, 98; explanation of belief in physical objects, 74-5, 95-6, 97

associative conditioning, 103, 106, 108, 110

awareness: conceptualized, 129-30, 131; introspective see introspective awareness; mere see below; of passions, 124, 127; of perceptions, concept-exercise and, 125; of perceptions occurring at different times, 148, 149; of psychological states, 152; of sensations, 124, 127; of simultaneous perceptions, 148-9; perceptual, 126, 128, 129-30, 131; quasi-bodily sensory, 151; quasi-sensory, 150-1; resemblance and causality relating perceptions, and, 148-9; sensory, 150-1, 153

awareness, mere: appearance/reality distinction at level of, 138, 140; causal explanation of, 127; distinguished from introspective judgment, 125, 128, 131-2, 135, 141; having a perception and having, 126-7, 131, 139, 144, 145; introspective mishap at level of, 138-9, 140, 144, 145; multiple perceptions

awareness, mere—*contd.*
and, 148; of perceptions without introspective judgment, 135; ownership of perceptions and, 133, 148, 149; perceptions as states of, 150; propositions concerning level of, 132-3; Russell's view of, 144

Ayer, A. J., 39, 80, 92-3

behaviourism, 25, 38, 46, 112, 123

belief(s): about physical objects, as contrary to reason, 10-11, 16, 19; about physical objects, characterization of, 5-6; about physical objects, Hume's view of, 7-8, 10-12, 17, 22, 153; as mode of conception of ideas, 114, 115, 120, 121; as occurrent judgment, 122; causal properties of, 121-2; constructive explanation of ordinary, 5-6, 9, 74, 153; contrasted with having a thought, 115; degrees of, 121; difference between incredulity and, 118; ersatz, 121; foundational, 141-3; imagination and, 9; introspective, 141-2; joined with conception, 114, 116, 120-2; phenomenological aspect of, 121-2; primitive introspective, 141

Bennett, J., 62

Berkeley, G., 21, 23, 24, 25, 39, 40, 80, 106, 107

body: action of, on mind, 27-31; action of mind on, 31-2; as a physical object, 6, 13; as subject of experience, 67; awareness of own, 6; existence of, 22; Hume's position regarding mind and, 20, 21, 25-45; identity of, 75; knowledge about, 13; mind-body dualism, 25, 38, 44; mind-body interaction, 24, 25, 27-32, 46; not reducible to mind, 93; reduced to neutral stuff, 25; self, personal identity and, 64-7, 91-4

brain, 28, 29, 32, 37, 38

Broad, C. D., 36

bundle theory: accompaniment and ownership in, 70; as alternative to substrate theory, 59, 64-5, 73, 74;

identity, personal: associationist
explanation of, 96, 97, 98; causal contiguity and, 90, 97; consciousness and,
87, 88-9, 92, 97; contiguity and, 85, 92;
Hume's second thoughts about, 74,
95-8; memory and, 86, 89; momentary
objects and, 85, 86, 90-1; Parfit's
theory, 90; past self and, 89; perceptions of perceptions and, 87, 89, 145;
present and past perceptions and, 88,
96-7; problems of Hume's explanation,
88-95; psychological continuity and,
90; regarding passions, 74, 98-9;
resemblance and, 2, 89, 97; thought
finding, 96; use of third person, 85-7,
88
identity, self: judgments of, 84, 86,
87-8; permanent-self objection, 93-4;
resembling perceptions and, 87-8;
substrate-self and, 84; sympathy of
parts, 78, 94
image(s): as external objects, 6; as
introspectively observable, 109; as
objects of reflection, 128; as reified
mental particulars, 124, 125; as representation of external objects, 6, 12-13;
as state of quasi-sensory awareness,
150-1; awareness of, 124; causation of,
110, 127, 128; concept and, 103; conveyed through senses, 12-13, 20-1;
determinateness of, 106, 107; ideas
construed as, 109-10; in concept-
exercise, 107, 109, 109-10; *in foro
interno*, 108, 124; instantiative, 108-9;
introspective access to, 128, 129, 144;
memory and, 85; perceptions as, 14;
present to the mind, 14, 20, 21, 124;
qualities of, 126; resembling objects,
85
imagination: antinomy arising from
activities of, 9-10, 13, 21, 24, 96 152;
causal inference and, 9; concept-
exercise and, 103; constructing a
physical world, 8, 75, 79; disordering
of, 29; impressions and, 8, 75; inference involved in, 8, 9; powers of, 101;
producing belief in continued existence, 8, 9-10; role in identity judgments, 75, 79, 87
imaging: causal settings of, 110, 111,
118, 122; linguistic abilities and, 110;
utterance and, 110-11; with recognition, 109-11
imagism, imagist: account of thinking,
107-8, 112, 152; attraction of, 109;
belief and, 122; explication of com-

imagism, imagist—*contd.*
plete thought, 109, 112; in concept-
exercise, 107-11, 118, 125; instantiative imagery, 108-9; introspection and
Hume's, 124; predication and, 118;
recognition of images, 109-10; theory,
difficulties of, 108-12; thesis on nature
of judgment, 109, 112; view of existence, 119
impression(s): as internal and perishing
existences, 8, 18; as substances, 62;
contrasted with ideas, 51, 135-6;
distinct and continued existence of,
76; extension of, 38; gap-indifference
as quality of, 77; giving rise to ideas,
88; imagination and, 8, 75; in substrate
theory, 62; intrinsic features of, 135-6;
of reflection *see* passions; of sensation
see sensations; original, 28-9; present
to the mind, 21; qualities as impressions in the mind, 18; qualities of, 8,
75, 76; reification of, 62-3; resembling
substrates, 62, 63; role in theory of
experiential awareness, 62-3, 137-8;
variations of, 18-19; with recognition,
109
inference, 48, 114, 141-2
inference tickets, 48
inner sense theory: analogical character of, 126, 129, 130, 131; applied to
images, passions and sensations, 126,
127, 129; contrast between inner and
outer sense, 127-8, 140; Hume's
account of, 126, 136, 140; introspection in, 139, 144, 145, 150, 152;
introspective access, 129; rejection of,
150, 152
intention, 31
interactionism: case for Hume's, 25,
27-32, 40, 81; dualist, 4, 21, 25, 43, 81
introspection: analogical theory of, 126,
129, 130, 144; experiences only objects
of, 61; Hume's views on, 125-31,
152-3; inner sense theory of, 139, 144,
145, 150, 152; likened to perception of
physical objects, 126, 129-30, 144, 145;
outer sense and, 126, 139-40; reflection
and, 128, 134; self revealed by, 64-5
introspective access, 124, 127, 128-9,
136-7, 150, 152
introspective awareness: conceptualized, 131; Hume's views on nature of,
1, 4, 45, 64, 124-30; identity and, 91;
property-ascription in, 131, 133;
theory of mind and, 83; variant
theories of, 126, 130-3, 143-9